PERFECT SOUND WHATEVER

By James Acaster and available from Headline

James Acaster's Classic Scrapes

JAMES ACASTER

PERFECT SOUND WHATEVER

HEADLINE

First published in 2019 by
HEADLINE PUBLISHING GROUP

9

Cataloguing in Publication Data is available from the British Library

Hardback ISBN 978 1 4722 6030 7

Typeset in Monotype Sabon by CC Book Production
Printed and bound in Great Britain by Clays Ltd, Elcograf S.p.A.

Headline's policy is to use papers that are natural, renewable and recyclable
products and made from wood grown in well-managed forests and other
controlled sources. The logging and manufacturing processes are expected
to conform to the environmental regulations of the country of origin.

HEADLINE PUBLISHING GROUP
An Hachette UK Company
Carmelite House
50 Victoria Embankment
London EC4Y 0DZ

www.headline.co.uk
www.hachette.co.uk

For Oscar.

I promise to listen to every album you ever recommend me xx

Contents

Foreword by Matthew Crosby   vii

Perfect Sound Whatever   1

366 Projects from 2016!   267

Appendix   280

Acknowledgements   292

Foreword by Matthew Crosby

In this book my friend James will propose his theory that 2016 was the Greatest Year For Music Of All Time – a notion that dawned on him thanks, in part, to the album WORRY. by Jeff Rosenstock. In fact the title of this book is the final song from that very album. And who introduced him to that album? You guessed it. Me, baby! Am I suggesting that hipping James to this record was the key catalyst in his realisation that 2016 was the Greatest Year For Music Of All Time? Yes, I am. Why not, eh? If James is allowed to publish his own wild hypothesis, why can't I? Isaac Newton will get his chance in just a few pages; first let's hear from the apple.

Maybe it's part of getting older, maybe it's just life getting under my feet, but it seems like fewer and fewer albums grab me by the throat and kiss me on the lips these days. Of course, when I was a kid it seemed that every week a handful of such albums would arrive in my local record shop. Albums whose mere existence – from cover art to final chord – could take my teenaged brain in its hands and snap it in two. I still return to many of them, looking to feel that same chaotic adolescent buzz. Some still deliver; transporting me back with Moon Landing precision to the exact moment I heard them for the first time. A ride home from Bromley town centre on the top deck of the 261 bus hearing the portentous dischord of 'Serve The Servants' in the headphones of my Walkman. Lying on my bed, doing nothing more or less than listening to *McLusky Do Dallas* straight through, like a teenager in a coming-of-age movie about the 70s. Or Pavement's *Wowee Zowee*, listened to on repeat in the garage behind our house as I spent a frantic Saturday attempting to cram a term's worth of DT homework into a single day. My chosen project: to design and build a working guitar amp shaped like a rocket. The album earned an immediate A+ from the examining board of my heart; even if the DT project itself was deemed, by all who saw it, both an aesthetic and a technical failure.

Nowadays I find that, while it's easy to access that nostalgic joy, it's harder to find 'new thrills!!!' Which is why I loved falling head over heels for WORRY. by Jeff Rosenstock (released 14 October 2016, though not the day I first heard it). Its impact was immediate. From the opening piano of 'We Begged 2 Explode' to the urgent open-throated vocals of 'Perfect Sound Whatever'. It instantly became my total obsession. I even bought a T-shirt that literally read 'I like Jeff Rosenstock' with the album's title written several times over in a big font (I had to work hard to convince a therapist I was seeing that this wasn't a cry for help). I would talk about this record to anyone who would listen. One of those people was James Acaster.

James hadn't yet begun his odyssey-cum-breakdown when I recommended WORRY. to him. He was simply attempting, like so many music fans before him, to compile a Best of the Year playlist. I steered him in the direction of WORRY.'s opening song, 'We Begged 2 Explode', fate played the straight man and here we are today.

As I said at the beginning of this introduction, I firmly believe, were it not for me introducing James to this album, this book you're holding in your hands – or propping on the table in front of you or whatever your preferred reading technique is – would not exist. Consider that! One less book in the world! Sure, when I put it like that it doesn't sound that big a deal, but, and let's be honest with ourselves, this book is the Bible for those who believe that 2016 was the Greatest Year For Music Of All Time.

So what does that make you? The readers? The disciples? Surely, if we're tipping hats willy-nilly, you also want a slice of the kudos pie; and who am I to block the kitchen door? Let's face it, this book would not truly have existed had you not bought it. A book only becomes a book in the reading. Unopened it would merely exist as a brick of pulped tree-matter, sitting unloved and unread in cryogenic stasis on the display counter at Waterstones. Firstly under 'New Releases', eventually travelling hourly between 'Humour' and 'Music', placed and replaced by two employees who just can't seem to see eye to eye. Without you, the reader, there would be no book. We are the true heroes of this undertaking.

That said, James has returned the favour we've done for him by chasing down and disseminating his idea that 2016 was the Greatest Year For Music Of All Time. And what a boon that is. Because, once you know James's hypothesis, the universe seems bent on proving it over and over again. I still find myself discovering new songs and artists; only to realise happily that the unfamiliar music was released in that hallowed year. And not just the album and artists contained within these pages.

New albums still emerge from 2016 on an alarmingly regular basis. Such is the power of 2016! I guess the year is bigger than all of us. Maybe none of us can claim credit after all? Was James nothing more than the tallest lightning rod during a 366 day electrical storm of musical creativity?

Of course he wasn't. And as much as I would like to rob James of all credit for this book in an attempt to salve my own scabby ego, I can't. He really is the soul of this project. This is his 'guitar amp shaped like a rocket'. Only, in James's case, this one actually works. A+.

Sure, you and I deserve a small mention. And there's certainly no denying that 2016 was a rich salmagundi of mellifluous and cacophonous delights. But, at the end of the day, this whole venture is pure Acaster. Who else could embark on such a hilariously wilful mission? Who else could come up with a project so obsessive and unique? And who else could imbue this singularly personal study with such universal appeal? Within these pages lie our own lives in music: evenings alone forensically studying a single track; bus rides elevated to life-changing status through the discovery of our New Favourite Song; friendships forged over a mutual love of a wonky middle eight; that ineffable feeling that a collection of sounds assembled by a total stranger on the other side of the world is somehow speaking directly to you. If 2016 was the Greatest Year For Music Of All Time, then James Acaster is the Greatest Man for the job of convincing even the most cynical and ageing musos to sit up and listen to his truth. All he needed was a little direction.

PERFECT
SOUND
WHATEVER

The 'To Pimp a Butterfly' effect

In 2015, iconic Compton rapper and songwriter Kendrick Lamar dropped the all-time classic *To Pimp A Butterfly* – an incredibly dense collection of jazz-infused hip hop with a running narrative, socio-political commentary, an inspired selection of samples and tight instrumentals performed by a stellar lineup of sought-after musicians. *TPAB* dominated all conversations regarding music in 2015 and rumour has it that many of Kendrick's contemporaries chose to delay the release of their own material so as not to be overshadowed by this work of genius. This gave the artists more time to refine and perfect their latest projects and meant that more industry giants than usual released new albums the following year – it was almost as if two years of amazing music got crammed into one. The greatest year for music of all time: 2016.

Too Significant to Ignore

2016 was the greatest year for music of all time. I know I'm meant to say that some year in the 70s was the greatest, but I'd only be saying that because I've been told it's the best by other people, I wouldn't genuinely believe it myself, so that would make me a liar, especially when I know for a fact that 2016 obliterates any year that came before or after it into smithereens. I've opened with a bold statement and it felt really good. Welcome to the book.

In 2017 I bought no fewer than 366 albums, all of which were released in 2016. I did this because 2017 wasn't a vintage year for me – my girlfriend and I broke up, my professional relationship with my agent broke down, years of not looking after my mental health came to a head and I was struggling to cope. Buying these albums was weirdly therapeutic and what started as a mild distraction gradually grew into an obsession that ultimately changed my life.

This book is a guide to reconnecting with current music, it's the story of a rubbish personal year and the albums that made it better (many of the artists have been kind enough to let me interview them in order to tell their stories the best I can). But, most importantly, this book is page upon page of proof that 2016 was the greatest year for music of all time. I know you think I'm wrong but trust me – I know what I'm on about.

The Greatest Album of All Time

I first heard the greatest album of all time at age six while eating lemon and scampi Nik Naks in a bungalow. It was the greatest album of all time for two reasons: number one – at this stage in my life it was the only album I'd ever listened to all the way through; and number two – it was called *The Greatest Album of All Time*. It was a compilation album of party music; my parents had taken me to a friend of the family's birthday for the day and I remember being in a big living room, watching all the guests dancing and singing along to every song. That album was the greatest *thing* I'd encountered in life so far. I'm not totally sure if it was definitely called *The Greatest Album of All Time* – it may have been called *The Best Party Album Ever* or *The Greatest Most Incredible Songs Ever Committed to Record by a Living Being* – but it was definitely a variation on the general 'best ever' title that pretty much all compilations have to adhere to these days. Because once *one* compilation has called itself 'the best ever', then everybody else has to follow suit. If someone has released 'the best ever' and then you release 'not the best ever but still pretty good', then which one are people going to buy? So everyone released a 'best ever' and we now have an infinite amount of 'best evers' to choose from, which puts the customer right back at square one and we have to read the actual track listing of every 'best ever' and then make a decision on what we think is the real 'best ever' based on personal preference. It's like calling something the 'best ever' doesn't even mean anything and all we've really got to go on is our own personal 'best evers'. There are exceptions to this rule, obviously, like the year 2016, which is officially the greatest year for music of all time and subjectivity doesn't even come into it.

Highlights on *The Greatest Album of All Time* included 'Hi Ho Silver Lining', 'Rockin' All Over the World', 'Down Under' and 'Centerfold', all of which were perfect gateways into the world of pop music for a six-year-old: extremely catchy songs that were fun and had a sense of humour to them. At that age I didn't like anything unless it was funny, I didn't see the point in TV shows or films unless they were comedies, and I certainly didn't want to waste my time listening to a song for upwards of three minutes if there wasn't a line about a Vegemite sandwich in it or the hysterical image of flies in someone's pea soup. Obviously these might not seem like hilarious gags to an adult, but to a child the notion of someone rockin' all over the world is insane and the story of a man discovering the love of his life is now posing in a sexy magazine is a real gut-buster. I think it was just easy for me as a child to tell people that I liked music 'because it's funny'. Everything else I liked about music I was unable to articulate, it was all so abstract and didn't make sense to me – it still doesn't in many respects. I still can't fully comprehend how a group of notes strung together can cause specific emotions to occur in my human body whenever I hear them and make me feel understood in a way I don't understand. Maybe if I did understand it, then the whole thing would be ruined or maybe it'd be even better and I could harness that power and never feel alone again. Either way, it's that intangible quality found only in music that decades later would save my life and carry me through something of a rough patch. My relationship with music began that day at that house party, the same day my relationship with lemon and scampi Nik Naks ended (the worst-tasting sick that has ever come out of me).

•

In 2016, Canadian singer/songwriter **Andy Shauf** released a concept album all about the dysfunctional cast of characters at a house party. On *The Party*, Shauf gently examines social awkwardness and botched interactions while always remaining empathetic with his chosen subjects. He creates a world of obnoxious boyfriends, long-suffering girlfriends, anxiety, self-pity and, of course, magicians. He deals with the pains of showing up early and having to kill time, the exhaustion brought on by attempting to impress others, the forced conversations, numerous misread signals and paranoia, all handled with dry humour and set to an endearing collection of understated instrumentals. With this record, Shauf finds a neat way to analyse how human beings relate to one another, introverts and extroverts alike. How we all find it a challenge to be around people but also struggle to be alone and how the amount of enjoyment we get from social occasions is all down to the filter we see them through and the way we feel about ourselves.

The Party

I began 2016 in Auckland. My girlfriend at the time was from New Zealand and we'd just spent a lovely Christmas 2015 with her family. Everyone decided to celebrate New Year's together at Becky's nan's house. Becky was the name of my girlfriend.

It wasn't, but I've changed her name for the book because it felt weird using her real name. I changed her name to Becky because it links in with an album from 2016 where someone else's name was changed to Becky (for entirely different reasons). So her name is Becky. Full name – Becky With The Good Hair. Back to the story. The idea of a theme was floated on the WhatsApp group and everyone agreed that a pyjama party would be lighthearted and easy to arrange last minute. There were five of us there at the start of the night – BWTGH and I had put dressing gowns on over our normal attire, while her nan, brother and sister-in-law were wearing full pyjamas. Then a family of three arrived who none of us had ever met before. They were friends of BWTGH's aunt and uncle, had been invited without our knowledge and were dressed in normal, non-pyjama, clothing. The mum, dad and ten-year-old boy walked in and awkwardly sat among us. When everyone is sitting around wearing pyjamas together it's fine, but when *not everyone* is wearing pyjamas and the people not in pyjamas have never met the people in pyjamas, it's a tad uncomfortable. BWTGH's aunt and uncle eventually showed up and brought with them two more friends, a Chinese exchange student who used to live with them and his girlfriend. None of them were wearing pyjamas and were all dressed in normal civilian clothing. And then BWTGH's dad arrived, wearing pyjamas, but his pyjamas looked so cool that they basically passed for normal clothes and no one even realised he was wearing pyjamas. We were now outnumbered. There were more people not in pyjamas than there were in pyjamas and, I'm not proud of this, but BWTGH and I could not handle the awkwardness and we ditched our dressing gowns in our bedroom so we were now also dressed normally, leaving her nan, brother and sister-in-law high and dry. We were the worst people at that party – we showed zero solidarity and joined the masses like cowards. BWTGH's nan could've changed as well, but she's a better person than us and stuck to her guns. BWTGH's brother and sister-in-law, however, had no choice. They had turned up in pyjamas and had not brought a change of clothes with them, and I'm really glad they saw the funny side of it because it meant I was allowed to laugh at the situation, which I frequently did, for the rest of the evening. So I began 2016 laughing, among people who meant a lot to me, in a beautiful part of the world.

Blackstar. Lemonade. Blonde.

Everyone hated 2016. Until then I'd not experienced a year like it – it felt like every day some new tragedy happened, making everyone miserable and angry, even the winners. When Trump became president and Britain voted to leave the EU, even the people who wanted those things to happen were furious (not with the outcome but just in general, and if you're reading this and getting angry because I called you furious, then this is exactly the sort of thing I'm talking about). Celebrity deaths were at an all-time high, and every time we lost another famous person we'd despair on social media as if we knew the departed personally. It was a rough 12 months.

•

David Bowie turned 69 on 8 January 2016 and on his birthday he released his final album, *Blackstar*, an album all about death;

examining the subject from every angle, exploring his own feelings about dying and musing on what happens once you're dead. It wasn't public knowledge that Bowie had been battling cancer for 18 months when the record was released; we only learnt about this when he passed away two days later, on 10 January. The day in between the record's release and Bowie's death, 9 January, was my birthday.

On 9 January 2016, I went to Taronga Zoo in Sydney with BWTGH and a group of friends. We were all comedians and had been performing at the Sydney Festival in a Spiegeltent in Hyde Park. It was a lineup of five comics, same lineup every night, and we played to near apathy every time. One night we all bombed so badly that an audience member took us out on his yacht the following day because he felt sorry for us. On that yacht we ate a platter of fresh shrimp and watermelon with lime juice squeezed all over it which still remains one of the most delicious and refreshing meals I've ever eaten. I wish every time I failed at my job I got taken out on a yacht to eat shrimp and watermelon, as I'd officially have the greatest job in the world and, looking back at my gig history, there'd be some months where I'd be on a yacht eating shrimp and watermelon non-stop. Taronga Zoo is a wonderful place, although I will say that on the day we went there, my 31st birthday, we looked inside most of the enclosures to see a sign informing us that the animals were sleeping, usually in a secluded area away from human eyes. This is the second amendment I'd like to make to my job. Some nights I'd like my paying audience to sit down in the theatre and the curtains open only to reveal a sign letting them know that I'm still in bed because I was feeling tired. I know this might anger them, but that's still a win for me because the worse the show goes, the more shrimp and watermelon I'll be eating on my now all too familiar yacht.

I remember seeing posters for *Blackstar* before it came out and am now embarrassed about my thoughts upon seeing them. I thought how odd it was that Bowie was still releasing music when his best days were behind him, like *why bother?* – it's not like it'll ever be as good as *Hunky Dory* or *Ziggy Stardust*. This is the person I was at the start of 2016. An idiot. I hadn't been keeping up with Bowie's career, so had no idea that his recent albums had been extremely well received; also I seemed to believe that if you've made a classic album, then that means you'll never produce anything worthwhile ever again. Which makes zero sense. Sure, there are some musicians who released a classic and then pushed out turds for ever, but there are also artists like David Bowie, who released classics and then continued to be creative and inventive and put out high-quality albums that some people even prefer to their more celebrated work, and writing them off only means you miss out on some remarkable music. Sadly some of our greatest recording artists often have their later work overlooked due to this sort of public ignorance, unless of course they die two days after releasing their new album and all the songs are musings on their own death, causing everyone to pay attention and have their minds blown all over again.

Blackstar was the first great record of 2016 (the greatest year for music of all time) not just because of the subject matter but also for the music itself. You could hear that Bowie was still pushing himself until the end, producing a dark and eerie jazz-rock record full of epic compositions that held the listener in a contemplative and mournful state. I can't think of many other albums that embody our relationship to our own mortality quite as perfectly as *Blackstar* does, not painting death as something terrifying or even beautiful but as a mystery, inevitable and something that we all have to make peace with. Weirdly, one of the only other albums I can think of that does this is **Leonard Cohen**'s *You Want It Darker*, an album released in October 2016 with Cohen passing away less than a month later.

Restricted to his house due to numerous physical problems, Cohen recorded all of his parts in his living room with his producer and son, Adam Cohen. *You Want It Darker* took a different approach to its subject matter from *Blackstar*: it manages to be simultaneously gloomy and amusing, and it doesn't feel like Cohen is saying goodbye like Bowie did, just singing about death and God from his own skewed perspective. Having said that, both albums convey a strong feeling of acceptance in the face of death; in fact, while promoting *You Want It Darker* Cohen declared that he was 'ready to die', but when this upset many of his fans he backtracked and said he intended to live for ever. It's my favourite backtrack ever and I love that he just jumped to the opposite end of the scale straight to immortality. A textbook move from someone who's ready to sign off but still has a sense of humour about life. *You Want It Darker* is a powerful and brooding blues record, at times minimal, but every element carries so much weight, whether it's Cohen's voice which is deeper and more gravelly than ever before, or the cinematic and sombre string arrangements that characterise many of the songs. With this album Leonard Cohen, like Bowie, went out triumphantly, with class, and on a high.

•

Even though I was hearing amazing things about *Blackstar* during 2016, I didn't bother buying it straight away. For many

years I had written off new music and had it in my head
that nobody makes great albums any more, only great singles,
especially artists in the mainstream. So even though I was still
discovering albums from previous eras, I simply did not engage
with current music. And then, in April 2016, **Beyoncé** released
Lemonade.

Lemonade was significant for me because it was something
I thought couldn't happen any more – a high-concept album
by one of the biggest recording artists in the world. I didn't
think artists who had everybody's eyes on them bothered to
experiment and progress forward these days, I thought they just
churned out a couple of big singles and then phoned the rest
of the album in. Some of you will be reading this and saying
that plenty of high-profile artists were coming out with exciting
albums that pushed the boundaries of music during the 2000s,
and of course you're right, but none of them resonated with
everybody so much and rose so high above the noise that I found
them impossible to ignore. I didn't go looking for *Lemonade*,
it was everywhere, and my social media was awash with people
obsessing over it. The muso crowd were raving about it instead
of being snobs and writing it off. The more casual, mainstream
crowd were enthusiastically preaching about it instead of skip-
ping to their favourite songs and moving on to the next big
commercial album. And the album was *about* something. Her
husband, rapper Jay-Z, had cheated on her numerous times,
so Beyoncé seized the opportunity to repeatedly stamp on his
unfaithful nuts for an entire record. Along the way, she manages
to sum up every emotion at every stage of this conflict; pain,
anger, respecting and valuing yourself, all the way through to
trying to make it work and loving them despite their infidelities.
She presents us with a complex narrative and message that's

thought-provoking for some, empowering for others and challenging to most of us for different reasons. *Lemonade* wasn't just a concept album but a visual album also, with a music video for every song, intended to be viewed as one 65-minute film and featuring the likes of Serena Williams because Beyoncé is really cool and Serena Williams will be in her music videos. The whole thing felt *important*. An important album was happening *right now*. Again, I didn't buy it immediately, though; it was only when I heard somebody criticise *Lemonade* for not having 'enough bangers' on it that I decided to buy it. For some reason hearing somebody slag it off made Beyoncé's decision to make this record seem even cooler to me. For every person she connected with there were always going to be others who only give things one listen before reaching a negative verdict, and she would've known this when she chose to go in such an ambitious direction. I couldn't criticise these one-listen people though, as I'd been even more ignorant until now – I was a no-listen guy, assuming that modern pop music was trite and of no value without ever giving it a go. So I listened to *Lemonade* and it changed my mind for ever.

•

Even though *Blackstar* had been huge and I'd bought and loved *Lemonade*, I somehow hadn't realised I was living in the greatest year for music of all time yet. One more album had to be released before I even began to suspect such a thing.

I spent August 2016 at the Edinburgh Fringe festival. As a comic I had been doing this every year since 2008, and this year I was sharing a flat with a number of inspirational comedians and also Nish Kumar. One morning Nish was playing a song from his laptop in the living room. The living room was a communal area, so one individual dominating it with their music was pretty disrespectful, but the rest of us let it slide. It was a stripped-down track, electric guitar and vocals, and I already felt like I'd known it for ever. The way the melodies of both instruments ran smoothly alongside one another, with each hook merging into the next, meant there wasn't a second that didn't trigger an emotion, usually melancholy (my favourite of all the emotions). Naturally, I assumed this song must be an old classic that had somehow passed me by, so asked Nish its name, ready to receive the standard amount of judgement for not knowing one of the all-time greats, but was surprised to learn that the song had been released for the first time ever that morning. It had been four years since the release of his celebrated debut album, *Channel Orange*, and a lot of antici- pation from the music press and fans alike had mounted up in that time, but **Frank Ocean** had finally released his sophomore record, *Blonde*.

The song was called 'Ivy' and Nish listened to it every day of the festival during his walk from the flat to his show. The Edinburgh festival can be a daunting experience and the music you listen to on the way to your show is more important than you might think – it needs to make you feel confident and fearless. But because I need to feel confident and fearless, I have regularly ended up listening to uncool music on the way to my Edinburgh shows. I need a song that makes me feel invincible but also comforts me, like the songs they use in adverts. I wish I could be cool like Nish and listen to Frank Ocean, but one Fringe I listened to a song by Maroon 5 every single day. It wasn't even one of their hits, it was a song called 'A Little of Your Time' – an *album track*. I listened to Maroon 5 deep cuts on the way to my show every day for a whole month and still expected to be lauded by critics and adored by my audience for the 'art' I had created. Also, for the record – I absolutely love 'A Little of Your Time' by Maroon 5 and will always listen to it as long as I live.

The expectation hanging over *Blonde* was enormous. Ocean had quenched people's thirst a little by releasing *Endless* earlier the same year, a visual album that confused to begin with but is now held in similar regard to *Blonde*. It's the ideal companion piece, with enough avant-garde R&B and eccentricity throughout its tracklist to satisfy his dedicated fan base. But Ocean seemed to be using *Endless* to set the stage for something else, like a warm-up act prepping the audience for what's to come – which makes sense given his reputation as a perfectionist of Kubrick proportions. Before *Blonde*'s release, Ocean changed almost everything about the record several times over: the mixes, the tracklist, the name; and when he eventually did release it – it was weird. He didn't make an easy pop record for the masses, he made the album he wanted to make and nothing else. At times it felt like Ocean was trying to shed his fairweather fans by utilising some oddness, leaving him only with loyal followers who trusted him and wouldn't restrict his creativity going forward. While tracks like 'Ivy' are more immediate, *Blonde* is an emotionally complex album full of subtle beauty that gradually reveals itself with repeat listens.

When *Blonde* was released I stopped seeing *Lemonade* as a one-off. There was clearly plenty of experimentation and rule bending going on in modern pop music, but I hadn't realised because I'd been listening to Maroon 5 album tracks and wondering why I didn't feel happy inside. *Lemonade* and *Blonde* made me realise that experimentation is not only still happening in pop music but that pop music, or more specifically R&B and hip hop, is very much where experimentation is happening in music today. There's something about hip hop especially that means it evolves at a faster pace than most music, sounds become dated much faster because artists are constantly trying to better each other and get to the next thing before their peers. It's why hip hop albums often get declared classics so soon after their release – the genre's moving so fast that these things have to be acknowledged quickly before the next classic comes along.

I got back from the 2016 Edinburgh Fringe, keen to discover more. I wanted to listen to everything and introduce myself to new geniuses one after the other. Musically, *Blonde* and *Lemonade* both took so many risks, plus they had so much pressure on them to be good and still didn't play it safe, *and* both albums came out in the *same year*, the same year as *Blackstar*, Bowie's swansong. Three albums in one year that already felt like they were going to stand the test of time and be remembered. Three potential classics. I started to think that maybe 2016 was a particularly good year for music and I didn't want to miss out on it. I was always listening to old stuff but not engaging with my own era and suddenly that made no sense to me. I needed to reconnect with music as it is now, in its current form – *new music being made and released today*. Reminder! It was still 2016 at this point, I was still with my girlfriend, my relationship with my agent was good and I felt totally fine – I was just a regular guy who wanted to listen to some new music.

•

People always say they have no idea how to discover new bands or new artists, they claim they just don't know where to start. Personally, I googled 'best songs of 2016 so far' and loads of results popped up; links to lists of people's favourite songs of the year, some by magazines or websites, others by members of the public on their blog, so I clicked on loads of them, read the lists, listened to all the songs and bought my favourites. It's literally never been easier to discover new music. I'd decided to only buy individual songs because I doubted there would be many more amazing *albums* released in 2016 – three in one year was already unheard of, so I highly doubted there were any more knocking around. From the first batch of 'best songs of 2016' lists I bought two very special songs. And these two songs will form the next phase of my argument.

Ultralight Beam

The Life Of Pablo is the seventh studio album by **Kanye West** and its opening track, 'Ultralight Beam', was being hailed as one of the best songs of the year by every publication I could find, so naturally I had to buy it. But I quickly learnt that I couldn't buy 'Ultralight Beam' on its own; the only place I could buy the track was his website as part of the album as a whole. So I bought *The Life of Pablo*. This felt like a crazy move to me at the time because I actually didn't own any other Kanye West albums. I may be the only person in the world whose entry Kanye album was *The Life of Pablo* – a difficult record that divided fans and features an awful line about a bleached asshole.

'Ultralight Beam' starts with a sample of a four-year-old girl named Natalie Green, who West found on Instagram testifying in the back of a car. The sample features lines like 'We don't want no devils in the house', plus a lot of passionate Hallelujah-ing and a 'Jesus Christ the Lord' thrown in for good measure. People have interpreted this sample as representing West's inner child asking God to release him from negative thoughts or 'devils', but, whatever it symbolises, it's undeniably effective. Anyone who hears a child speaking with such passion and conviction about any religion has to have a reaction to it, positive or negative, so you're invested in the track within the first second. 'Ultralight Beam' is a downtempo, minimal, gospel rap track that lasts over five minutes, and this huge, arena-filling recording artist opened his new album with it. Kanye is often referred to as a magpie, handpicking the greatest musicians in the world, putting them up in his mansion to write and record for him, then selecting the very best of what they come up with and keeping that for the record. You hear stories about musicians who've worked on a Kanye album, only meeting him once (briefly, when he was on his way to play ping-pong), writing and recording on their own for a week before going home without getting to say goodbye, and when the album comes out they discover he's only used a single bar out of the countless hours of music they laid down for him. It might sound ruthless but the results speak for themselves – every element of every Kanye song is there for a reason, and unless something is indispensable it has to go. 'Ultralight Beam' feels like a real ensemble piece as all of these incredible singers and features get dropped into the song at various stages; Chance The Rapper, The-Dream, Kelly Price, Kirk Franklin and a ten-piece choir – all of them get their moment, perform impeccably and then they're out. He gets what he needs from each one of them and then moves on, but it's all executed so cleanly that you can't disagree with a single one of his decisions. Chance's verse is particularly astounding: he explores every character contained within his voice, flitting between half-sung lines, softly spoken bars and strained yelling – and Kanye gives him the floor for a long time, allowing Chance to tell his own personal story until it naturally finds its own ending. And the lyrics on this song aren't exactly throwaway either: everyone is singing about their relationship with God in a way that could make those of us without faith feel a little uncomfortable. It's a worship song – a long, slow worship song about how we can always be forgiven and we'll never be forgotten by our Creator.

Just Like I

Song number two is 'Just Like I' by **Xenia Rubinos**. Xenia was born in Hartford, Connecticut, studied Jazz Composition at Berklee College of Music and now resides in Brooklyn. Her second album, *Black Terry Cat*, was released in June 2016 and struck a chord with many due to a new-found clarity in both her music and her lyrics. In the past, Xenia's lyrics had always been vague, but this time around she decided not to be afraid to speak in a more literal way, celebrate her 'otherness' and share what was on her mind honestly and openly. Musically, *Black Terry Cat* saw her digging into 90s era/late 80s hip hop. Which isn't to say she made a hip hop album, because she didn't, she just kept one core influence running through a diverse group of songs and this made the whole record feel more streamlined. All of this was in place before the recording began: she'd written everything, she'd demoed every single song, all the prep was done and Rubinos felt the most ready she'd ever been going into the studio. Then, one morning, Xenia was sitting at her kitchen table and received a phone call. Her father, who lived in Florida, had just had a stroke, so Xenia flew to him immediately on the earliest flight she could. He had been sick for a while: he'd had Parkinson's for the last ten years and Xenia, his only child, was his primary caregiver, travelling to Florida once a month to look after him. She would usually talk to him multiple times a day on the phone, but this news still felt very sudden and what followed was a month-long process. She wasn't able to talk to her father as he couldn't speak and she didn't know how much he was processing cognitively. It's still hard for her to say if he knew who she was or what was even happening around him, he couldn't swallow or eat anything, so the doctors had to intubate him, and then ultimately Xenia had to decide whether or not to keep him in that state. She was able to get him out of hospital and back home with care, but eventually had to make the almost impossible decision that they should end his life. For the next couple of weeks she had to watch her father die, then afterwards she took his remains to Cuba, scattered his ashes at his favourite beach, and came home to New York.

She felt like an alien. She didn't recognise her home or even herself, she couldn't get out of bed, she was a shell and felt completely obliterated. After two weeks of this, Xenia decided to resume working on the album, but the experience of being with her father in Florida had already changed her life for ever. She now sees her life divided into two parts; before Florida and after. And that makes this record feel weird for her, because she wrote all of it in her old life but had to record it in her new life, when she was in a totally different headspace. Even her singing voice had changed completely. She had spent that entire month, every single day, singing to her father, something she had never done before. Her dad was a huge music fan and loved classical music, opera and salsa, so Xenia was always embarrassed to sing in front of him, assuming he wouldn't like her music because it wasn't his style. But the only thing she could think of doing to try to bring him back during those times was playing music and singing to him. She would spend hours singing to him every day, so when she came back to New York her voice was totally different, it was exhausted, as exhausted as her body even. She didn't know how she was going to sing, let alone record anything, but making this record felt like something she was supposed to do.

Xenia stills feels very lucky to have worked on *Black Terry Cat* with her friends and partners in music, Marco Buccelli and Jeremy Loucas – both of whom she trusts and has known for many years. The three of them are family and they love each other. Marco and Jeremy carried her even when she felt like she wasn't present and her energy levels were low, they took the load and the three of them worked 16 hours a day for three months until the album was finished. They played live together in the same room, capturing the rawness and soul but also the overimposed elements that go with a live record. Rubinos's vocals were put more at the forefront this time round, and their frame of reference while recording was to make her sound like a 'punk Beyoncé'.

'Just Like I' was the first song I heard from *Black Terry Cat*. The instrumentation, especially the drums, sounds like it belongs on a Led Zeppelin track, with Rubinos throwing herself into a fierce and expressive vocal performance. If I want to convince someone as quickly as possible that 2016 was the greatest year for music of all time I put this song on. As soon as her vocal hits that run of high notes at the top of the song, people ask who they're listening to. On the album's tracklist, 'Just Like I' follows 'Black Stars', a song about her father. He had once told Xenia a story from his childhood about a Ouija board he and his friends had found. They were asking different questions of the Ouija board – he had asked how long he would live for and the board had said he would live to be 103. One night when Xenia was putting him into bed, he told her that story and asked her if she thought the board was telling the truth and she said she hoped so, even though she knew it probably wouldn't happen she said, 'Yeah. I think you will. I think you're going to live for ever.'

XYZ

By October 2016, I'd listened to 'Ultralight Beam' and 'Just Like I' so much that I wanted to make an entire playlist that revolved around them. I've been like this since I heard *The Greatest Album of All Time* at that party when I was six. That playlist was *so good* – no duds, perfect progression from one track to the next – and I wanted to make my own.

My dad used to make people compilation tapes at home and name each one after a letter of the alphabet for ease. Shortly after hearing *The Greatest Album of All Time*, I asked him to make me a compilation and he made me *The X Tape*, a black cassette with a white label stuck across it that my dad had written 'X' on in red pen. 'Teenage Kicks', 'Video Killed the

Radio Star' and 'Making Plans for Nigel' all featured, as well as 'The Shoop Shoop Song' by Cher, which I had personally requested after seeing it on *Top of the Pops* (such a hilarious song to a young boy – what is she even talking about?!). *The X Tape* was up there with *The Greatest Album of All Time* and I listened to it on my Walkman constantly. I got my dad to show me how to make compilation tapes on his stereo and would spend entire afternoons recording from his cassette albums to my blank tapes, trying to achieve the perfect mix.

It took me just over ten years but eventually I achieved my goal with *The Two Tapes of Lushness* – a double-cassette compilation album that I stayed up all night making when I was 17. Three hours of incredible songs that flowed into each other like hot butter. I brought it into work with me the following day; I worked in a pub kitchen and we would always listen to music during a shift to keep up morale. I put the tapes up on the high shelf alongside the stereo, announcing that we would be listening to them later, informing my colleagues of the lushness that lay in store. Then, two minutes later, someone pulled a metal mixing bowl down from the same shelf and accidentally knocked the *Two Tapes of Lushness* into a scorching hot fryer, which let out a deafening angry hiss. They crackled loudly in the frantically bubbling oil, spitting everywhere, the entire fryer dancing – it was utter chaos. I rushed over in a panic and feverishly fished them out using a dirty metal chip basket but it was too late, they were coated in fatty cooking oil and would never play again. To make matters worse, the tracklist had also been fried, so I couldn't even go home and re-create the tapes from scratch. It was a tragedy and my workmates could not stop laughing.

•

Two of my favourite albums from 2016 were released exclusively on cassette by the artists themselves and both were so well received that they were re-released the following year on all formats.

While writing and recording her debut album, *Hands in Our Names*, **Karima Walker** had no fixed place of residence. She was on tour and staying on people's floors and sofas after four years of living in a religious commune. She was paying the bills by working in a record store and playing background music outside cafes as people ate their lunch. While she began as a folk singer, she now wanted to push what's expected of such music and create something different. *Hands in Our Names* feels like one gently shifting soundscape, consisting of tape loops, electronic drone music and delicate folk songs, each element coming and going without any sense of urgency, her voice often lifting you out of a trance before a quietly picked guitar carries you away again. It's a colourful sound collage, sewn together with field recordings that manage to place the listener somewhere outdoors, like the customers at one of Walker's cafe gigs. *Hands in Our Names* was originally released on cassette at the end of June 2016.

The cassette release of *Good Will Come to You* by Canadian musician Jean-Sebastien Audet, aka **Un Blonde,** sold out almost immediately, it was nominated for the Polaris Prize and many people declared it their album of 2016. It seems like everything Audet has ever listened to has been poured into this record: indie, folk, funk, gospel, soul, R&B, ambient, it's all present but somehow all at once, one on top of the other without ever sounding untidy. He was 21 years old when he wrote this album, and the level of understanding and skill he demonstrates while manipulating so many genres simultaneously is masterful. It's an album that feels like it's about something without having a narrative, a theme or even a message – the music itself is the story, the songs respond to one another, they all belong together and make sense of one another too. Audet makes a succession of correct choices on this album, never overdoing anything to the point where it sounds gimmicky and the transitions between genres never feel clunky. This is a self-assured composer who knows who he is and what he wants to achieve, and you can hear it in every second of his music.

The Visitor

When I was 20 I graduated from mixtapes to mix-CDs and didn't have to separate the playlist into two sides of 45 minutes any more, I could make a 90-minute playlist all the way through from start to finish. I made everyone I knew a mix-CD in those days and would regularly hijack other people's stereos in their homes or cars whenever I paid a visit – I just wanted to play music I loved to anyone I could at any given opportunity. Naturally this led to my first DJ set.

•

My first DJ set was an hour long, it was at the Prince of Wales in Kettering, the crowd was small and it was an unpaid guest slot. Every Thursday the resident DJ would get someone from the local music scene to take over for an hour, allowing them to play whatever they liked. I naively saw this as an opportunity to introduce people to new music and assembled a playlist of obscure songs that I thought were phenomenal and would change everyone's lives. Within 20 minutes I had a large crowd of blokes chanting 'wanker' at me in time to the music. I consoled myself with the fact they were at least chanting *in time*, as that meant they were definitely listening to the song and engaging with it on some level. Prior to the chants of 'wanker' I'd had a billion songs requested, none of which I had on me. I would try to explain to every person that I was just an unpaid guest DJ and that the regular DJ would be back in an hour and could play their requests, but they very quickly lost their minds and wrote a catchy and original chant to let me know how they felt. What's sad is that I was only playing this music they hated because I was trying to connect with them (oh god, that's the most tragic sentence in the book now that I read it back). But in the end, instead of converting everyone with these life-enhancing songs, I isolated myself and came across like an illogical but well-meaning madman trying to convert the masses to my way of life, completely oblivious to the fact they had zero interest in the wacky music I had to offer.

•

My friend and colleague Ed Gamble says my favourite type of music is 'Wacky Music' because I like a lot of experimental stuff across many different genres, plus he has no respect for me. Whenever anybody asks what kind of music I like I usually say 'a little bit of everything', which just winds people up because I've not even remotely answered their question, but I don't want to say 'I like a lot of experimental stuff across many different genres', because I'll sound like a pretentious nobhead. Luckily, thanks to this project, I can now proudly say '2016' any time someone asks me what kind of music I like, because that's my favourite genre now. Obviously there are some hurdles to get over when I tell anyone that. For starters, 2016 isn't an established genre and as a year 2016 was hardly what one would call vintage. Countless dodgy things happened in 2016 that were less than ideal and the negative effects of some signature 2016 events are still being felt today. So telling people that my favourite genre of music is 2016 can sound like I'm saying my favourite music is Brexit and Trump. Which it isn't, by the way. Bar maybe one album . . .

•

In 2009, Seb el Zin, a producer and multi-instrumentalist, assembled a collective of musicians from all manner of musical backgrounds to form **Anarchist Republic of Bzzz**. The group's goal was to disregard any rules they'd followed in the past and start their own musical country. With its equal parts experimental rap, punk and free jazz with unorthodox production, every listener interpreted it differently and struggled to categorise their self-titled 2012 debut album.

In 2016 the group released *United Diktatürs of Europe*. As the name suggests, this album appeared to target and criticise the European Union, the front cover depicting members of the public sitting in a cinema, framed by the stars of the EU and gazing up at torture footage being projected onto the big screen. The group sounded even more distinctive this time round thanks to the addition of two Turkish percussionists, Onur Secki and Ismael Altunbas, as well as Mehmet Boyaci playing the kanun (a 26-stringed Turkish instrument) and Murat Ertel on the electric saz (another Turkish instrument, looks like a lute). It's fair to assume that an EU-critical project choosing to draw much of its sound and influence from

Turkey (a country with a complicated and turbulent history with the European Union) is not a coincidence. Especially in 2016 when accession talks between Turkey and the EU had recently ground to a halt. But due to its lack of clarification, plus the fact that no interviews about the album were given by members of the group, *United Diktatürs of Europe* and its message remain something of an enigma. But, to be fair, that's quite fitting and only adds to the contrary tone of this uncompromising stand-alone record.

Adulthood in the Context of Total Noise

I was very resistant to MP3s for a long time. I stuck with CDs way longer than anyone else did because I wanted to own something 'physical'. Music fans go on about owning something physical a lot. Which, if I stop and think about it, actually sounds pretty creepy. Digital music undeniably has its positives though, with some bands taking full advantage of the MP3 format and achieving things they'd previously not been able to. Australian psychedelic rock outfit **King Gizzard & The Lizard Wizard** came out with *Nonagon Infinity* in 2016, nine songs that all run into one another, including the final track into the first, meaning the digital album can be played on an infinite loop. It's an intense listening experience with the band always manoeuvring to find a bridge between songs while navigating a meteor storm of guitar runs and maniacal vocal hooks. This album could only exist on MP3, I once listened to it four times in a row during a car journey and felt dizzy by the end of it. The point is – I love MP3s now.

The iPod, specifically the iPod Classic 160GB, is officially the Greatest Invention Of All Time. I was late to the party and bought my first 'pod in 2010 at 25 years old, but I've also stayed at the party way longer than anyone else as my most cherished possession is still my iPod and I use it every day. I've been through about five Classics over the years and even have an iPod Guy who can hook me up with some high-quality mint condition 160GB 'pods any time I need them. My iPod Guy is a man named Michael Burdett. Michael is 59 years old, he wrote the theme tune for *Homes under the Hammer* and wrote a book called *Strange Face*, about a lost Nick Drake recording he found in a skip. Back in 2014, when Michael heard the iPod Classic was being discontinued, he went into his local Argos, where they kindly let him look at their database, and discovered there were only three Classics left in Argos's mainland UK outlets, *but* there were 24 or so available throughout Ireland. Because they were discontinued, Michael couldn't purchase the iPods online so ended up sending bundles of cash out to four or five shops in Ireland with some postage money on top, telling them to keep the change and put it towards a charity. He did consider travelling to Ireland and driving round buying up iPods, but unfortunately he's scared of flying and scared of boats. He ended up with 15 brand-new iPod Classics and never took them out of their packaging in order to sell them to nerds like me. Michael describes the story I just told you, about him buying iPods from Argos, as 'the happiest time of my life', and I receive texts like this from him on a regular basis:

Re: iPod leads – they are a nightmare. There is little rhyme nor reason as to which one works with which device. If you do ever get the chance, take a walk round to Mac 1 (ironically my screen went on my iPod a couple of weeks ago and they replaced it). MB

Dull from start to finish, yes, and yet I love it more than anything. My very sanity depends on this sort of information because if I lose my iPod my entire life will fall apart. Michael Burdett (who may as well be my dealer at this point) also makes music under the name **Little Death Orchestra,** and the last time I grabbed a fresh 'pod from him he gave me a copy of their latest offering, *The Difficult Fecund Album.* It wasn't until I got it home that I realised it'd been released . . . in 2016. So congratulations, Michael, your album's in the goddamn book.

The iPod Classic is everything I've ever wanted and more. If when I was a kid you'd told me that one day there would be a device that I could store *all* my music on, that fit *in my pocket*, that I could make *playlists* on and would even enable me to put my *entire record collection* on *shuffle*, I would've told you, quite honestly, that I do not care what else happens in my life as long as I own this device. And, in many ways, that's still true. No matter how miserable I am, it always feels amazing to go for a walk and listen to my iPod. It feels like a hot shower after a week of camping; I can feel all the grime being washed away and I want to close my eyes but I can't because I'm walking around outside next to a road where moving cars live. Yes, I'm basically just shutting the world out and that's probably not the best way to deal with your problems, but it's rather nice to escape sometimes(/all the time) and music is perhaps the most rewarding distraction available to us as human beings.

•

When the drum shop Taylor Ross worked at closed down, he suddenly found himself unemployed, lonely and depressed. His girlfriend had not long broken up with him, so the timing of losing his job, and with it his daily routine, wasn't great. The shop had become his sanctuary: he was the only employee and the owner was basically an absentee leaving the place for Taylor to manage. Taylor used to hang out in the shop before and after hours; he'd record music, host band practice or work on his drumming while the place was empty, it felt more like a home than his actual house did. But the shop wasn't making any money and the owner got into a dispute with the landlord over building upkeep, which led to the landlord impulsively kicking everybody out. Losing the drum shop was more than just losing a job for Taylor – it had become something of a fantasy world for him and was now part of his identity. He knew he was entering a rough time so decided to channel it into something productive. Writing new music seemed like it might be therapeutic – so Taylor decided to make a recorder rock album. As in a rock album that heavily features the recorder. Yes, please.

Taylor was given his first recorder in 4th Grade. His elementary school gave all the kids standard recorder lessons; he'd regularly attend, practising outside of school and keeping it up over the years even as he took on other instruments. The recorder he was given was a soprano and in 2010 he started using it on his albums as a fun novelty, but he soon stumbled across a cheap alto recorder in a thrift store that changed his attitude towards the instrument dramatically. This alto, with its beautifully pure tone, felt like a shortcut to achieving a similar sound to the flute, something Taylor had always wanted to play but lacked the time or patience to learn. Around the time the drum store closed he'd been listening to a lot of baroque music and was humbled by the recorder players who performed in that baroque or medieval style. This inspired him to stop treating the instrument as a novelty and make an album that celebrated its full potential, assembling a full choir of recorders to emulate the baroque sound he'd become so enamoured of.

Taylor established a song per week schedule and would wake up at 7 a.m., record till mid-afternoon, then spend the rest of the day mixing or drawing. He drew countless sketches of hands clutching, wielding and snapping recorders, and these drawings would later become the album's cover art. While drawing he would listen to a lot of British psych-folk; Fairport Convention, Incredible String Band, Jethro Tull, because he wanted to create something in a similar vein (only with the recorder). Lyrically, he wanted to create something more obtuse than a clichéd love song, opting instead to write about rejection and self-isolation, but also about his acceptance of his current situation.

A V was released in November 2016 under the name Ross always uses when putting out music, **Surface To Air Missive**. It's everything he set out to make. The recorder, whether it's leading the melody or filling out the background, enhances every song on the tracklist, giving this indie prog record a signature sound that's surprisingly multifaceted. Once the album was released, Ross was able to devote himself 100 per cent to promoting and supporting it because this was the first time he wasn't burdened with other responsibilities. He was finally able to tour the US and Europe, and while he sees this as a valuable experience, he can't envision a time in his life when he'll be able to do it again. And he's fine with that: he's never really chased such things, but he's glad that he can now say he did them once.

•

I made a 2016 playlist on iTunes and paid for every song because I'm 100 years old and I still buy music. There's no big moral reason behind this, I just prefer to OWN things. I'll admit that a welcome by-product of this is that I look like a great guy who supports 'the artist', but my conscience won't allow me to deceive you in this book. The truth is, I absolutely love owning music because I'm ultimately very materialistic even when it comes to invisible MP3s.

I spent the rest of the year making that playlist. I'd go online each day and search 'best music of 2016' then listen to the individual songs, download the ones I liked and add them to the mix, choosing carefully where they went in relation to the playlist as a whole, making sure each track followed on nicely from the previous one. I was on my way to achieving perfection and I could feel it. I was finding the whole thing invigorating, I felt engaged with music in a way I hadn't since I was a teenager and I was rediscovering my personal connection to music again. There had been a number of moments like this in my life, when I'd felt energised and rejuvenated by a surge of new bands, genres and artists, but this had been by far the longest I'd gone without one.

Chapters of My Life

When I heard *The Greatest Album of All Time* at age six I was excited because I had finally discovered pop music, and I quickly became obsessed. I started learning the drums: my parents were given an old drum kit by their church and I would practise in the cellar of our terraced house. One day a man named Howard, a giant with long hair and a beard, turned up on our doorstep and said he could hear me practising from halfway down the street (15 doors down from us), before handing my mother a box of drumsticks he'd had lying around his house. Howard was very cool.

When I was 13 I discovered alternative music and started listening to metal and punk. What I used to disregard as noise now sounded melodic to me. I started forming bands with other kids in school, we learnt to play 'Smells Like Teen Spirit', 'Bored' by Deftones and 'Walk' by Pantera, and then started writing our own songs. We formed a nu-metal band called Pindrop that only lasted a year but enabled us to perform stuff we'd created for the very first time. Pindrop would often end a live set with me and my brother (who was also the guitarist) playing 'Albatross' by Fleetwood Mac. We didn't rearrange it and do a nu-metal version, we just played it the same as the original. This confused a lot of people as it was not at all in keeping with the rest of our set, but we did it every time because, in truth, I just really enjoyed playing that song with my brother.

When I was 17 I left school and made a whole new group of friends, who introduced me to all the genres I'd been ignoring when listening solely to bands who screamed instead of singing.

I stopped restricting myself to one thing. I got serious about being a musician and would practise drums every day instead of once a week. I joined three new bands: The New Hardcore Skiffle Movement, Three Line Whip and The Capri Sun Quartet. While a member of The Capri Sun Quartet (a folk-funk outfit) I was known as Sir William Strawberry, because we were all named after a flavour of Capri Sun and my middle name was William. I added the Sir because of arrogance. My friend Graeme was the bassist and called himself Ross Currant which he then changed to Ross Current Event. I still maintain that this, even for The Capri Sun Quartet, was confusing. We all wore plain white T-shirts and wrote all over them with marker pens like it was the last day of school. Our names would be written across the chest and Graeme had added 'this just in!' underneath where it said Current Event. He remains one of my dearest friends.

Around the same time as The Capri Sun Quartet, Graeme and I tried to get into drum & bass. We didn't drink back then because we didn't see the point and took pride in drinking fizzy pop and having as good a night out as our drunk mates. I would regularly dance longer than anyone else and would really let myself go. I'm pretty gangly, so my arms and legs would flail all over the shop. I eventually managed to convince Graeme to start attending drum & bass nights with me and the two of us would dance sober until the venue shut. The first time we tried this we walked straight to the centre of the dancefloor, got our heads down and started helicoptering our limbs around, unaware that everyone else in the club had withdrawn from us and had begun to point and laugh. I remember catching someone making fun of me and stopping dancing to tell him it wasn't cool to make fun of people. He then responded by laughing even harder because telling people off for bullying also doesn't make you cool in the drum & bass scene.

When I was 20, Graeme and I formed a band called The Wow! Scenario, an experimental jazz-pop duo creating music the like of which the world had never heard. I'd never been so passionate or uncompromising in all my life. We didn't listen to advice from anybody else, we would scrap anything we thought sounded too similar to another band, we both got singing lessons to try and sing harmony parts together, we practised and composed every day and gigged every week, and nobody else liked it. So when I was 22 we gave up. Or, to be more precise, we gave up, re-formed to make an album in a recording studio that used to be a load of dog kennels, then gave up for good.

•

In 2016 Irish singer/songwriter **Katie Kim** released *Salt*, an album recorded in a self-made studio inside a disused garage tucked away behind three arches underneath a railway track in Dublin. Katie and her friends had discovered the spot and renovated it themselves, turning it into their own custom-made studio: cleaning, scrubbing, painting, installing vintage tape machines and an old wooden analogue mixing desk, and when they were finished the space felt peaceful. Even with the occasional rumble of trains approaching and carriage wheels rolling above their heads, they felt like they'd built their own private office.

Salt binds together elements of drone, folk and indie, giving each track its own voice. An industrial song might be followed by an ambient piano ballad that gives way to a guitar-led pop track, but the emotional core of the entire project remains consistent, making sense of the amalgamation of styles on the tracklist. Kim wrote *Salt* during an emotionally taxing relationship, so set out to make a record surrounded by a general feeling of displacement and loss, of not knowing your place in the world but still seeing the beauty in all of it. It's an album that finds reassurance in uncertainty and remains calm in the face of all the chaos in the world. There are moments on this record when we feel like we're successfully weathering a storm, albeit one that may continue for some time. The track 'Day is Coming' is a classic example of this, a foreboding sense of peril steadily gains mass then subsides into the following song, 'Someday', where we're placed in the wake of it all, in stillness.

Void Fantasy

Every band I'd been in before The Wow! Scenario had split up without recording anything and we'd always end up regretting it years down the line. So Graeme and I decided to professionally record all of our songs before calling it a day. Earlier the same year a producer called Chris Hamilton had contacted us online; he'd heard us via our Myspace page and messaged us offering to record our songs in his studio. The studio was in Horley in Surrey, and Graeme and I lived there for a month from early November to early December 2007. We slept on the floor in sleeping bags and didn't wash very often. We recorded 17 songs, the album was 71 minutes long, and when it was finished we kept it to ourselves. We handed out CDs to friends who asked for them, but to my knowledge they've never been listened to. Regardless, making that album remains one of the greatest experiences of my life. We added theremin, didgeridoo, whistles and a proper piano to our songs, walked around the Gatwick arrivals gate recording people coming home for Christmas, got my sister over to play clarinet and saxophone for us and tried to use an advent calendar as a big maraca by shaking the chocolates around in it but it sounded shit so we scrapped it. I also remember Graeme wearing a cowboy hat at one point so he could harness the right energy for a 'woo!' he was doing (he nailed it).

•

Out of Sight is a pay-what-you-want album by a group from Minneapolis called **Falling**. Most people have never heard of them; this was the only record they ever made and they split up shortly after its release. When a band release one album, then immediately split up, it's always cool. Something about only ever making one thing and then quitting just seems really badass, especially if the album is flawless, which, in my opinion, *Out of Sight* is.

Falling formed when they were all just 15 years old and recorded the album when they were all aged around 18, but this sounds like a group with decades of experience making the career-defining record they've always had in them. They often stay on one slow dirty riff for ages, meticulously building a song around it then erupt in a burst of noisy angst, or perhaps a melodic hook emerges from the swell, before fading into field recordings and spacey ambience. This was the first band any of them had ever been in. For most musicians, their first band is clumsy and unoriginal with embarrassingly earnest lyrics, and it lasts a couple of months – they don't end up recording an album that they can still be proud of years down the line. *Out of Sight* was self-released; the band were in talks with record labels but split up before anything could come of it, so they put the album out themselves with no fanfare, for free. But you can hear how much went into making it – this isn't a throwaway recording session by a group of teenagers who don't intend to carry on past this one record. Maybe one of the reasons why their story hits home so much for me is because it reminds me of when Graeme and I had started to get some interest from labels but decided to call it a day while also recording all of our songs, making sure they sounded as good as they possibly could. Fully investing in something just for yourself is an oddly liberating experience after years of trying to convince everyone to like what you do. And I suppose liking a record because it reminds you of yourself isn't entirely unheard of either.

•

After recording the Wow! Scenario album I stopped discovering new music. I started doing stand-up immediately and focused on that from then on, pushing music into the background. While I still bought albums, I rarely *discovered* anything or broadened my tastes. But now, as 2016 came to a close, I was making the greatest playlist of all time and, at 31, I felt 13 again.

Last Evenings on Earth

By New Year's Eve 2016, the playlist was finished. I had finally got it just how I wanted it: 50 of the catchiest songs I could find, each leading into the next nicely, with a banging opening track and a closing track that would leave people trembling in its wake. This playlist was perfect.

One Playlist of Lushness

Injury Reserve '2016 Interlude'
Kevin Abstract 'Empty'
Big Thief 'Animals'
Lizzo 'Coconut Oil'
PJ Harvey 'The Community of Hope'
D.R.A.M. 'Broccoli'
case/lang/veirs 'Atomic Number'
Parquet Courts 'Human Performance'
Princess Nokia 'Kitana'
Miike Snow 'Heart is Full'
Sam Beam & Jesca Hoop 'Chalk It Up to Chi'
Matthew E. White & Natalie Prass 'Cool Out'
Bas 'Methylone'
Will Wood & The Tapeworms 'Self-'
Olga Bell 'Doppio'
Weezer 'Jacked Up'
Flowdan 'Dons and Divas'
Xenia Rubinos 'Just Like I'
Mr. Oizo 'Freezing Out'
Yoni & Geti 'Wassup (Uh Huh)'

Devin Frank 'Moonlight of the Night'

OLYMPIA 'Smoke Signals'

Mitski 'Your Best American Girl'

Throws 'Bask'

Opposite Sex 'Complicity'

Sleigh Bells 'It's Just Us Now'

Old Man Saxon 'Breakfast'

Orkesta Mendoza 'Shadows of the Mind'

Kamaiyah 'How Does It Feel'

Yohuna 'The Moon Hangs in the Sky Like Nothing Hangs in the Sky'

Noah Britton 'I Love You So Much'

Nevermen 'Wrong Animal Right Trap'

EL VY 'Are These My Jets'

Blood Orange 'Best to You'

Flock Of Dimes 'Birthplace'

KING 'The Greatest'

Forests 'Feels Like Your Best Friend is Going Away Forever'

Uni Ika Ai 'Soft in Ice'

Kilo Kish 'Collected Views from Dinner'

No Genre 'Sledge Hammer'

Aragehonzi 'Detaramekagaru'

Modern Baseball 'Apple Cider, I Don't Mind'

Lemon Demon 'As Your Father I Expressly Forbid It'

Animal Collective 'Hocus Pocus'

The Avalanches 'Frankie Sinatra'

Childish Gambino 'Redbone'

Lambchop 'In Care of 8675309'

Frankie Cosmos 'Fool'

Rae Sremmurd 'Black Beatles'

Kanye West 'Ultralight Beam'

Becky With The Good Hair and I spent New Year's Eve in my London flat, just the two of us, trying to re-create a beef brisket sandwich from our favourite (recently closed-down) cafe. The brisket was a little overdone due to a broken oven, but we nailed both the sauce and the pickles and ate our homemade sandwiches while watching *The Apartment* for the first time. BWTGH fell asleep on the sofa shortly after midnight and I put the 2016 playlist on. It was the greatest playlist I had ever made and I felt good listening to it. That's underselling it – I felt amazing listening to it. I sat in my living room listening to that playlist and the world felt still. I looked over at BWTGH asleep on the sofa – she was a huge part of my life and I felt lucky. I thought about how much I loved music and how excited I was to discover all of these new songs this year, and how music would continue to evolve throughout my life so I'll never reach an age where I can't find something new or challenging to listen to. I listened to those songs and I sat with BWTGH and for the first time in a long time I actually began a year by looking forward to the next 12 months and what they had to offer. Then two weeks later we broke up and I had a year-long breakdown.

•

When James Campbell was 12 he tried to write a prog rock album about wizards. From the very start, escapism was always important to him when writing music, as he liked to create worlds and tell stories. But by the time he was in college and released an experimental rap-core album entitled *Sui / / Rap*, it'd become much harder for listeners to sort the fantasy from the reality.

The project was called **Youngster Jiji** and became an outlet for Campbell's anger and confrontational side, things he rarely indulged in during his day-to-day life. Influenced by groups like Odd Future, he just wanted to entertain his audience with obnoxious braggadocio and inspired aggression. In reality he was a friendly music nerd from Seattle, but he felt like he had all these alternative characters inside him and wanted to let one of them out in a cartoonish, hyperbolic fashion.

The story of the album starts in March 2015. Campbell had been busying himself with theatre and improv while studying music composition, and even though the acting was extracurricular, he still managed to perform eight plays in just two semesters while writing and directing them also. By March, Campbell was acting in a production of *One Flew Over the Cuckoo's Nest*, playing the part of McMurphy, and had been surviving on two hours' sleep a night for a year. He was just getting out of a relationship while getting into a new one, and, to further complicate matters, his ex-girlfriend was the assistant director for the play. As far as his classes went, he was frustrated with the bureaucracy of the college and felt like he was staring down the barrel of another two years, minimum, and didn't know if the diploma was worth tens of thousands of dollars of debt. He felt like everyone was asking so much of him all at once and he couldn't quite handle it. This resulted in him quitting the play, quitting college and staying in bed for five months straight. He would sometimes go and get food (which was rare as he had no money), but didn't leave his room unless he absolutely had to. He couldn't bring himself to go to school and had begun thinking a lot about atonement and judgement. When he was younger, his mother would occasionally take him to church, and even though they never went frequently, he felt like he had just enough exposure to be confused by certain teachings and develop a complicated relationship with religion, his mind often turning to it during periods of depression.

He failed his third semester and tried returning in the New Year, but attended only one class before realising he didn't possess the will to try any more. Instead, he funnelled all of his enthusiasm into staying inside and networking online with a community of rappers via Twitter, Facebook and Soundcloud, and for the next three months all he did was make and share music over the internet with rappers and producers he'd never met before. He wanted to make the hardest music possible, creating new beats every day and getting other Soundcloud rappers to guest on certain tracks. From his bedroom, Campbell would scream his bars into a microphone and record dark monologues from the Book of Revelation, comically pitching his voice down every time (he would later pepper these passages throughout the record, holding the album together and giving it a threatening persona while simultaneously building a new world for the album to inhabit). He wanted the album to feel like it was descending into Hell in an attempt to mirror his mental state when confined to his bedroom, and recorded the entire thing three times before he was happy with it, starting from scratch each time.

Sui / / Rap was released in March 2016, exactly a year after Campbell's descent began, and, while the album flew relatively under the radar, it accrued many devoted followers, who were drawn to the unhinged bedlam and anarchic spirit the project exuded. Campbell had begun performing live at this point, having to restrict himself to 15-minute sets because he'd always strain his voice from yelling and be wheezing by the end. But it wasn't long before he decided to bow out of the rap scene and put

Youngster Jiji to bed for good. He had been thinking a lot about what it meant to be a white rapper; the Seattle rap scene was becoming increasingly white and it didn't seem like there was enough room for a lot of different faces. He felt like he was taking up space more than he was contributing, so decided to create space instead and quit. He still makes music and is currently singing and playing keyboard under the name bb tombo, aiming to create something that sounds like the electronic Beach Boys.

An Odd Entrances

January 2017 was the pits. I don't handle breakups well and tend to blame them on myself and only myself. I felt like I had messed up my relationship, that I had kept my guard up too much from the beginning, and in doing so had ruined the best thing about my life. On 15 January, the day after the breakup, I travelled to New York with my agent for work. I hated myself and didn't feel like I deserved a trip like this, I was anxious for the entire fortnight I was away and wanted to travel back in time and make right all the things I'd done wrong over the years. I couldn't sleep, so every night, in order to try and over-ride my anxiety, I'd do the most recent thing that'd brought me comfort, and that was reading music lists from 2016. Moving from 'best songs of 2016' to the 'best albums of 2016'.

Immediately I started to notice certain albums popping up on most lists: *99.9%* by **KAYTRANADA**, *My WOMAN* by **Angel Olsen**, *Malibu* by **Anderson .Paak**, *ANTI* by **Rihanna**, *A Moon Shaped Pool* by **Radiohead** – there wasn't a list that didn't feature most of these. So once you (dear reader) have listened to *Blackstar*, *Lemonade*, *Blonde* and my 2016 playlist, I'd recommend the next thing you do is work your way through the year's biggest releases, pick your favourites and add them to your collection. I personally adore *Freetown Sound* by **Blood Orange** and *22, A Million* by **Bon Iver,** so would push you in their direction first as well as the following grand tamales . . .

•

Solange's *A Seat at the Table* was Pitchfork's number one album of 2016: a mature R&B record, incorporating elements of funk and neo soul, that talked eloquently and passionately about all of its subjects, especially race. Solange worked on this project for three years, and the intricacy of every song, most of which started life as hour-long tracks, then got scaled down to their essential elements, is awe inspiring. The album is punctuated by short speeches from people Solange knows and admires, including her mother and father. You either identify with these interludes or they alter the way you think and encourage your empathy. I find it hard to believe that anyone can listen to them and not be affected in some way. The interlude 'Tina Taught Me', featuring Solange's mother talking about the beauty in being black, is as powerful as any spoken-word piece I've ever heard. *A Seat at the Table* changed the way everyone viewed Solange as an artist. It feels ridiculous these days to even mention that she and Beyoncé are sisters, but for a long time that's how the majority of people regarded her. Now, thanks to this album, Solange occupies her own space with her own audience, catering for a different mood entirely.

•

Legendary New York hip hop artists **A Tribe Called Quest** released their first album in almost 20 years in 2016. They'd reunited to perform on *The Tonight Show* in 2015 on what turned out to be the same night as the terrorist attacks in Paris. That appearance reminded them that they're a group whose sound and message are still as relevant today as they ever were, and they decided to return to the studio. But in March 2016, while the album was still being recorded, the group suffered a huge loss when founding member Phife Dawg passed away. The remaining members, Q-Tip, Ali Shaheed Muhammad and Jarobi White, made the decision to complete the album, recording two songs in memory of Phife: the emotional 'Lost Somebody' and the closing track, 'The Donald', a final goodbye that many misread to be about Donald Trump. *We Got It from Here . . . Thank You 4 Your Service* was released in November 2016. Many see the title as a message to Tribe from this new generation of rappers, but we'll never know – Phife came up with the name and never had the chance to explain the meaning to anyone else. It was one of the group's best-received records and possesses a timeless quality due to the fact that it was made by some true veterans still challenging themselves and the world around them right to the end. I find it astonishing that they were still producing tracks like 'The Space Program' and 'We the People' after 31 years in the business (two tracks linked together by an audio sample from *Willy Wonka & the Chocolate Factory*, including an excerpt from the 'Oompa-Loompa' song, for god's sake).

•

Skeleton Tree by **Nick Cave & The Bad Seeds** was almost finished when Cave's son Arthur tragically died in July 2015.

Arthur was 15 years old, and two weeks after his death Cave returned to the studio, making changes to the album's lyrics so they would reflect his feelings of grief during this unimaginable time. *Skeleton Tree* is a stark and deeply affecting record; for me it's maybe one of most difficult albums of the year to listen to. Sparse instrumentation, ominous drones and ethereal backing vocals slowly shift underneath unflinchingly honest and open lyrics with rare moments of respite. Cave's vocals border on spoken word and hold so much within them, emotions that to many of us are incomprehensible are put into terms that we can at least begin to attempt to understand. *Skeleton Tree* was released in September 2016, and a documentary entitled *One More Time with Feeling* came out alongside it, covering the story behind the album so that Cave didn't have to retell it time and again during press interviews to promote the record.

•

There was one album on many lists that I already owned and had been enjoying for some time. During 2016 itself my friend Henry Widdicombe texted me. 'Do you want to hear the best album of 2016?' (This was before I even knew 2016 was the greatest year for music of all time.) I said yes, and he sent me a link to an album by a band called **Car Seat Headrest**. He also told me not to tell anyone about it. My friend Henry is one of those people who, when he really loves something, doesn't want everyone finding out about it, in case they like it too and subsequently ruin it. So when Henry likes something he texts a handful of close friends, tells them to check it out and then swears them to secrecy. I genuinely didn't tell anyone how brilliant this album was until I was fairly sure everyone was talking about it anyway, and even then I was worried that Henry would think they all found out because of me. He'll be absolutely furious when he finds out I'm recommending the indie rock masterpiece *Teens of Denial* in a *book* of all things.

I was lucky enough to see Car Seat Headrest live during the *Teens of Denial* tour, and for an encore frontman Will Toledo performed a solo cover of 'Ivy' by Frank Ocean. As you can imagine, when this took place I was literally elevating off the ground and rotating in the air, possessed by the spirit of 'Ultimate 2016'. Toledo has also been known to cover Ocean's 'White Ferrari' at his live shows and even wrote an article about his love for Kanye's *Life of Pablo*. This increases my fandom of *Teens of Denial* even more, knowing that Toledo and I share an appreciation for the music of 2016 and a desire to share this appreciation with the world – unlike Henry Widdicombe, who wants to keep it all to himself like a greedy little boy. Henry was the first friend to recommend me a 2016 album and one of only two people to recommend me an album *during 2016*. In 2017 I was recommended many 2016 albums by many friends, but the main culprits were Ed Gamble, Nish Kumar and Matthew Crosby. These guys love texting me album recommendations, and texts with album recommendations in them are my favourite texts to receive. That doesn't mean I'm not going to slag off Ed Gamble a couple of times in the book though. I am and I can't wait.

•

I bought all of these big releases fairly quickly, and suddenly my interest in the music of 2016 began to feel more like a project than a bit of fun. I had stopped making playlists and started to formally assemble a library of albums from 2016 in order to avoid lying awake and addressing how I felt about my recent breakup. If I found a great album, then that meant I'd achieved something with my day and was permitted to rest because I finally deserved it. Within days I'd taken something I found relaxing and turned it into work.

Not Good at Spending Time Alone

'1. When they do my autopsy they will wonder why I spent so much time in the bathroom.'

Nate Mendelsohn studied jazz saxophone at the Oberlin Conservatory of Music but somehow ended up playing guitar and singing on his own indie rock record. Usually, when somebody seriously studies a jazz instrument, that world consumes them, but Mendelsohn had other interests and just didn't have as strong a work ethic as his classmates when it came to jazz. So he started writing a handful of songs on his own, then in the summer of 2013 decided to stay behind at college and record them under the name **Market**.

But *Not Good at Spending Time Alone a.k.a Cleanliness* wouldn't be released until December 2016. Nate didn't immediately finish the project because the whole thing always felt like a band that didn't really exist, seeing as he never played live and had no fans to speak of. The only reason he kept dipping in and out of it over the years was because once he starts something he always has this compulsive need to see it through to completion. The title itself refers to his inability to simply let himself do nothing, and how he would regularly try to drag out any evening with his friends, because once he was back in his apartment he would instantly feel rudderless, forced to find tasks to do, organising magazines or cleaning mirrors – anything to keep feeling productive. The album's liner notes contain a list of ten numbered bullet points that sum this up in different ways; detailed descriptions of popping a zit in the mirror, speed eating bagels while walking a mile, efficiently watching boxsets on his phone during a commute and brushing the back of his tongue until he gags: a collection of mundane tasks held up as grand achievements meaning he was accomplishing something every second of every day and need never feel lazy or guilty for being lazy.

'6. Is it your eyebrows or your eyelashes that are filled with millions of little bugs that help keep you clean? Why don't all parts of your body have these? Why don't all parts of your life have these?'

If it wasn't for this compulsive need for productivity, Nate probably never would've finished this record. It took three and a half years, and because the album had taken so long and spanned so many different stages of his life, completing *Not Good at Spending Time Alone* felt like Mendelsohn was handing in everything he had to show for his career so far. Within the lyrics were entire relationships that had blossomed, dwindled, resurfaced, then gone away for good, his transition from adolescence to adulthood, moving out on his own and starting up somewhere new. He'd recorded songs at college, at his parents' house and in his first New York apartment. The album represented everything and it felt good to add it to his list of completed tasks and move on to the next.

'10. *What are we doing after rehearsal? It is Saturday, early evening, don't leave me alone.*'

●

Reading 2016 music lists and buying 2016 music was now having the same effect on me that walking around listening to my iPod did – it was calming my anxieties and provided an escape at a time when both were very much needed. I bought more music while staying up late in my New York Airbnb than I'd ever bought in one sitting before. One night I veered away from the 'best of' lists and decided to search for projects by musicians I already liked, quickly discovering a beaut by an artist who, due to being out of the loop, I'd weirdly assumed had retired.

●

Andrew Broder began writing songs when he was 11, recording on a tape player with his brother, both of them playing guitars before quickly branching out onto keyboards, drum machines, four-tracks, turntables and whatever they could lay their hands on. In 1999 he launched a solo project under the name **Fog** using similar instruments, released three records in the early 2000s and then, with the addition of Mark Erikson and Tim Glen, turned Fog into a full band with the release of 2007's impeccable *Ditherer*. And then they split up. In the following years Andrew started painting houses and became a father, then in 2014, out of the blue, he launched a Kickstarter to fund a potential new Fog album. The response was huge, and in 2016 he released *For Good*, a piano-led solo record in which Andrew set out to recapture the sensitivity and grit of his early work but with 'a more impactful and better executed electro-acoustic palette'. For the first time in his career he had no label, no deadline and no expectation for the record from anyone other than himself, and this meant he was now able to take his time in the studio. He felt like in the past he'd relied too much on chance when it came to recording music and now wanted to sound like he was doing things on purpose. He was bored of settling for the moment just because it was the moment. He credits working as a house painter with helping him become more thorough and patient: seeing things as a process and a series of steps rather than firing out ideas, seeing where they all land and getting used to whatever the result was. Taking this approach with *For Good*, treating it as 'work' in the best and most fulfilling sense, made him look back at his time as a musician and recognise his own personal growth. He was able to feel a greater sense of peace with his earlier records and came to an understanding of why they were the way they were and why this was different. He regards this record as the best music he's ever done and I'd struggle to think of much else out there that sounds exactly like it.

First Ditch Effort

As you can see, it was in New York that my obsession really began. It wasn't an 'interest' any more; buying music from 2016 was now something I needed to do in order to feel ok. Being in New York immediately after a breakup felt confusing. On the one hand, it was my first time in the Big Apple and it was exciting to visit a new place, but on the other hand I was extremely depressed and wanted to cry all the time. Also, sharing an Airbnb with my agent wasn't exactly ideal.

Early on in the trip things went badly. A miscalculated journey meant I was late for a gig and got kicked off the bill. This one event sparked some tension that would ultimately build throughout the entire year and result in me getting dropped by my management.

We had some industry meetings during our time in New York. This would be the first time I'd had meetings in America: we were both excited by them, and our first meeting was with someone pretty impressive. We were both astounded that this person had agreed to meet us and were having to pinch ourselves when walking around their offices. But the meeting went badly. They had no idea who we were, they'd clearly taken the meeting out of politeness and were not impressed by us at all. At one point they asked me what my plans for 2017 were and when I told them I wanted to film four stand-up specials and release them at the same time they shook their head and said, 'Louis CK only releases one special a year and he's the best there is, so four seems unlikely.' It was brutal. When we exited the building I felt defeated before the trip had even begun. I started to express my concerns to my agent as we walked around the block, telling him I didn't think I could handle this right now, that I was already struggling to keep it together after the breakup and I didn't think I could cope with feeling like a loser in these meetings every day. After a while he stopped walking. I had been looking at the floor monologuing about my anxieties for a while, so decided to look up at him for the first time, expecting to see him looking back at me and listening to my outpourings. But he was facing away from me, sticking his middle finger up at a building across the street and taking a photo of his swearing hand. The building in question was Trump Tower and he was taking a photo of himself flipping it the bird. He posted the photo to his Facebook account later that day. It was a fraught, fraught trip.

City

Cult indie rapper **Aesop Rock** had made some huge changes to his life in 2015, the most notable of which was that he moved out of New York and into a barn for a year. He sold or gave away all of his belongings, travelled to the country and rented out a friend's barn in the woods, bringing with him a bag of clothes and his cat, Kirby, and that was it. He felt like he needed a change from his routine in the city, he needed to start saving money and he needed to clear his head, as the city environment was doing very little to remedy his depression. He'd started to consider other careers, he was growing tired of musicians and their egos, many of the people he was surrounded by back home seemed more concerned with celebrity than creating anything of actual worth. But when it came to switching jobs he had no ideas; after being a rapper for almost 20 years he was too far down the road to turn back now, so he wrote a new bunch of songs that were more open, honest and autobiographical than anything he'd done before, releasing them in April 2016 under the name *The Impossible Kid*.

On this record (which Rock also produced) he shared stories about seeing a therapist, his relationship with his family, feeling old and buying a cat. One of my favourite tracks on the album, 'Defender', sounds lyrically like a stereotypical rap song at first, as Rock talks passionately about defending the whole block. But repeat listens reveal that what he's defending the block against is a bobcat that's been spotted in the local area by a man on his street called Alex, and he's less defending, more keeping an eye out. The whole song is about the local community keeping one another informed, reporting any sightings to their neighbours and trying to deter the local wildlife from interfering with their trash cans.

In the lead-up to the release of the album, Aesop uploaded four short promotional videos online. Each episode sees him talking to his shrink in the woods, and the shrink is of course represented by an animated cartoon bear wearing spectacles. During their conversations Aesop is trying to get to the bottom of why everything feels so impossible, and in the final instalment the bear tells him a universal truth that's undeniable but ultimately frustrating to hear and difficult to accept. Irritated and tired of his therapist, Aesop gets up off the couch and walks back into the woods alone.

Who Speaks to You?

It's tricky telling people how depressed I was while in New York because my life and situation simply don't sound that bad, but hopefully people understand that that's not how depression works. I hated myself more than ever, I was convinced that I had ruined the best relationship of my life, that I could've been a better boyfriend, that I was therefore a bad person, plus I was extremely stressed by the situation of needing to be in such close proximity to my agent while we were clearly not getting on. I would think about the same things round and round in circles and convince myself that nothing would ever improve for me, so when I returned to London I immediately started looking for a counsellor.

I attended my first counselling session in February 2017, it was an hour long and I don't think I stopped talking from beginning to end. I was so desperate to talk to someone that I didn't really do much research beforehand, I just found someone who sounded good and lived nearby. I sat down and told her everything about me: the fact I'd had three car crashes, all of which were my fault, the bands I'd been in and how they'd all split up, how I felt guilty when I ate desserts, I told her about every girlfriend I'd ever had and how I've never felt safe in a relationship, how I feel guilty when I watch porn, how lonely I feel in my job, how I always think I should be doing something more worthy with my life and how lately I'd started obsessively buying music from 2016. I mainly wanted to talk about my relationship and how I'd ruined it by putting walls up in order to protect myself, how I'd only loved her more over the years and now felt extreme guilt about never fully letting her in. But my counsellor was more interested in where these feelings of extreme guilt originated from and wanted to talk about me being raised Christian. I hadn't even told her I'd been raised Christian at this point; it was just that obvious.

So my counsellor and I talked about my relaxed Christian upbringing, the churches I went to, the C. of E. school I attended and how I gradually lost my faith but sometimes miss it as an adult. I'd never really thought about religion and how it may have affected me before. I was raised in a loving and liberal Christian household and my parents never lectured me about 'sin', being 'a sinner' or needing to 'repent'. However,

I did hear about those things a lot in school, at church and even in the Scouts for many years (yes, of course I was in the Scouts). I actually really enjoyed being a little Christian boy. I wouldn't go back and change it, and definitely got a great deal of positives out of it, but it felt healthy to begin to consider the negatives also, especially if some of them were affecting me as an adult.

•

At some point in the near future a software developer writes an AI bot for a Christian dating app. Over a period of 50 years these bots train themselves to tap into the sexual evolution of human beings in order to sell us the idea of Christianity. During this time two of the bots themselves convert to Christianity and fall in love with each other. This is the story told on the self-titled debut by Indiana experimental rap trio, **FLANCH**. All three members were raised as Christians but had recently moved away from Christianity. One of them, Peter Timberlake, even used to be a worship leader until he was 18. This record is their farewell to religious longing, full of Christian angst as well as the robots' obsessions with sex and romance. They decided to write a lot of choruses which sounded like contemporary worship music, lyrically similar but overtly sexual (or could at least be taken sexually by anyone who isn't steeped in the Christian world). The album was recorded when all three members were 23 and unable to see their lives amounting to anything. Peter especially regards the period of time while making the album as the lowest point in his life. He didn't have a job, his grandmother died, he was drinking a lot, his dad had cancer and he felt like he had nothing to offer anyone. After they finished the record, a couple of days into 2016, he packed up what little he had, and, without telling anyone, drove to LA and lived in the parking lot of a truck stop for a month. *FLANCH* was released in February 2016.

Heaven's Too Good for Us

I stopped being a Christian when I was 22. The previous year my family had travelled to Kenya for my dad's fiftieth birthday. He'd lived there during his twenties, working as a teacher in the Taita Hills, so in 2006 we revisited his old school, the village he'd lived in and some of his old friends. During the trip I felt ashamed of my privileged existence back in the UK and wanted to remain in Kenya and work for this guy called Barney who'd invented a range of agricultural tools for the local farmers to use. But at the same time I was still too obsessed with making The Wow! Scenario the greatest band ever so used this as an excuse to return home and continue as normal.

When the band split up a year later, a voice in my head told me that I should go to Kenya and work for Barney since I no longer had any commitments in the UK. I was scared of changing my entire life and moving to a foreign country, but the voice kept telling me over and over that I needed to go. One day the voice was so persistent that in order to silence it I gave blood, my thinking being that a good deed would balance out the guilt of not moving to Kenya. The blood drive was at the Corn Market Hall in Kettering, a big echoey room, and I arrived right at the end of their working day. I was one of only two people giving blood at that time. Nurses were folding up beds around me, wheeling them into the blood vans, and one of the nurses happened to be my friend Matt. I knew Matt worked for the blood service but had never seen him at a blood drive before. We chatted as the blood drained from my arm and I instantly regretted not seeing him more often. I asked what he was up to after his shift and he told me he was going to a children's church service with his son. It would last less than an hour and then he was free, so he invited me to join him at the service, saying we could grab a drink after.

The service, it turned out, consisted of a play put on by the kids. A princess had been kidnapped by pirates and an explorer was trying to rescue her. The pirates had made off with the princess in their pirate ship so the explorer had to assemble a crew because he was unable to man a sea vessel alone. He recruited sailors, fishermen and any locals with naval experience to help him rescue the princess. Most of the crew weren't sure if they were up to the challenge and didn't know if they could rely on this explorer, but they took a leap of faith and decided to trust him because trying to save the princess was the right thing to do. When the play was over, the kids wheeled out a big cartoon picture of Jesus standing with his arms outstretched and smiling. The congregation were each given two stickers – a pair of footprints – and were invited to stick them on or around the cartoon Jesus depending on how closely they felt they followed him in their daily lives. All of the kids put their stickers on Jesus' face, many adults stuck their footprints in his hands, and I put my stickers on the edge of the piece of paper facing outwards. The whole service hit very close to home and I had to acknowledge the fact that a chain of events had brought me to this church, starting with a voice telling me to go to Kenya and my attempts to ignore this voice had only resulted in me being told to take a leap of faith and follow God on an adventure. I was still unsure. I'd been doubting my faith a lot that year and wasn't sure if I believed in 'callings', but I decided it would be weird to completely disregard what'd just happened. So I approached the vicar afterwards and asked if I could visit him later in the week to discuss something important.

Four days later, I sat down with the vicar in his living room and told him the same story I've just told you. I also told him that I'd already decided I was going to Kenya. Since the church service I'd made my mind up. I couldn't ignore the signs any more and I had to take a leap of faith and just go, like the fishermen and sailors did with the explorer. When I finished my story the vicar said a few things. He pointed out that I didn't have any skills to offer the people of Kenya so I'd just be another Westerner eating twice as much food as anyone else does over there. He said he'd seen me do stand-up once and, even though I'd only done it for fun, he thought it was funny and advised I pursue comedy instead. And finally he suggested I start coming to his church more often. He also mentioned that he wasn't totally convinced by 'callings' and, regarding my doubts, he was only about 80 per cent sure that Christianity was true himself. I left his house around 3pm and by the end of the day I wasn't a Christian anymore.

•

In the 60s, **Johnnie Frierson** was in a soul group called The Drapels with his sister, Wendy Rene (her song 'After Laughter Comes Tears', co-written by Johnnie, is a soul classic), but his music career halted abruptly when he was sent to fight in Vietnam with the US Army. He didn't record music for 20 years after returning from war, but in the early 90s started hosting a gospel radio show under the name Khafele Ajanaku. He soon started writing again, composing original gospel songs and recording them in his garage on a tape recorder, later distributing a few tapes himself to music festivals and corner stores in Memphis (still using the Ajanaku name). During this time he was suffering from PTSD brought on by his time in Vietnam as well as depression due to the death of his son, and yet all of these songs are about faith, hope and worship. Frierson passed away in 2010 but, after his death, one of his self distributed tapes, entitled *Have You been Good to Yourself* was discovered in a thrift store by Jameson Sweiger of Light in the Attic records. Jameson was enamoured of these stripped-back solo gospel songs and wanted to bring them to a wider audience, so, after asking Frierson's family for permission, he gave the album an official release in 2016.

I wasn't always sure whether I could count *Have You been Good to Yourself* as a 2016 release since Frierson first handed out the tapes years earlier, but it never felt right to omit this album because 2016 is such a huge part of the album's story and journey. *Have You been Good To Yourself*'s entire identity is of a forgotten, completely ignored cassette tape that got unearthed and then brought to the world's attention for the first time in 2016. In short – 2016 is essential to who the album is. Anyone who disagrees – I'll see you in court.

Everything Sacred

Sidenote! Once the 2016 project got into full swing I established a rule that all albums had to have been *originally* released in 2016. This meant I sometimes discovered amazing albums like Elza Soares's *A Mulher do Fim do Mundo*, thinking it was a 2016 album, only to learn that, although it received an international release in 2016, it was originally released in her home country of Brazil in 2015, so it did not qualify. Gutted. But, on the bright side, this rule meant albums like *Hands in Our Names* and *Good Will Come to You* 100 per cent counted because they were originally released on cassette in 2016 before being released on all formats in 2017. The Johnnie Frierson album was the only exception I made and I think I've argued my case pretty effectively above, thank you very much, get off my back. Also, I found a more than worthy substitute for the Elza Soares album in the end so, all in all, I'm feeling good. That's right, I'm feeling good about these rules that I unnecessarily set myself for no reason.

Juçara Marçal, Thiago França and Kiko Dinucci of Brazilian fusion rock group **Metá Metá** all made significant contributions to Elza Soares's *A Mulher do Fim do Mundo*, a record that saw one of Brazil's most idolised singers completely reinvent herself after 31 albums at the age of 77. Soares brought their talents on board because she wanted to be part of the progression and betterment of Brazilian music and not allow herself to be stuck in the past. The album sees Soares embrace punk and even elements of hip hop while singing about deeply personal issues such as domestic violence and transsexuality. She gave every musician full freedom to express themselves and each individual's playing style is so unmistakable that pieces of *A Mulher do Fim do Mundo* and Metá Metá's 2016 album *MM3* sometimes get muddled in my head, mainly because both records heavily feature Dinucci's imperfectly picked and distorted guitar lines (he used to play in hardcore punk bands in the 90s and the ethos of those bands is still present in everything he does). Metá Metá were the obvious choice for the Soares project as their style was already so close to what she was aiming for. The band have always combined elements of jazz, punk and samba as well as being open to any new influences and genres with every album they release. Shortly after working with Soares, the band visited Morocco and so added North African music to their already abundant list of ingredients along with Afro-Brazilian candomblé music (Dinucci is a devoted follower of the Candomblé religion, a tradition that focuses on fulfilling your destiny and contains rituals involving dance and music in order to protect the worshipper's fate). *MM3* doesn't contain a passive moment, and the level of invention and musicianship on display throughout is so high that it's easy to see why Soares hand-picked this group to help tear down and reassemble her sound. They've created controlled chaos in the best possible way, every performance is incredibly precise without losing the untamed energy required for crossing this many boundaries at once. I recommend listening to *MM3* and *A Mulher do Fim do Mundo* back to back: you can hear the clear influence the respective artists have had on one another and how they've benefited from each other's wisdom. But only *MM3* was released in 2016.

Have You been Good to Yourself

The title track on Johnnie Frierson's *Have You been Good to Yourself* was a huge song for me because it all too perfectly summed up the stress of my inner monologue. The song essentially asks you if you're getting everything right. It emphasises the need to never slip up or make any mistakes – things I had put on myself more and more over the years. But Johnnie Frierson was encouraging this sort of behaviour – the song wasn't a warning against thinking like this, he was checking up on you: are you eating the right kind of food, are you treating other people right, are you following the Ten Commandments, are you getting enough exercise, are you living a righteous life? – there's no room for error if you're justifying yourself to Johnnie Frierson. These lyrics make the record even sadder for me, because even though, through no fault of his own, Frierson's life was tough around the time he recorded it, this was still the way his mind worked: focusing on his own shortcomings and imperfections instead of giving himself a break. I didn't really recognise this behaviour in myself until I heard this song and was immediately hit by a familiar wave of anxiety. Obviously you should try to live a good life, but you should also lay off yourself when you don't get everything perfect all the time. I personally wish I was better at acknowledging my mistakes without having to punish myself over and over, but it can take a long time to get to that point and unlearn certain bad habits.

Thoughts Lined Up

In the year 2000, **Martin Creed** won the Turner Prize for his piece *The Lights Going On and Off*. It consisted of an empty room with the lights going off for five seconds and then coming on for five seconds, repeating that pattern for ever. If you visit the Tate website there is a detailed description of what this work means, what it represents and what artistic conventions it messes with. This explanation, justification and deconstruction of his work is exactly the sort of thing Creed has been trying to escape since art school.

In class, Martin was always asked, 'Why are you doing that and what does it mean?' and had to explain everything to his teachers. It was never enough to have an idea – you always had to show how you'd come to that idea in the first place. And while this might lead to work that the artist is able to explain rather than get defensive about, it can also lead to the artist refusing to explain themselves ever again. When he left art school, Martin banned reason from his work, but because everyone wants everything to make sense, other people were happy to do the explaining for him. If you show these people a room where the lights go on and off they'll say it forces an awareness of the physical actuality of the space and confounds the viewers' normal expectations. When, in actual fact, Creed was taking the piss.

Creating a piece of art to try and win a prize felt like a terrible thing to do. He knew he had to create something uncompromising so that if he didn't win he could still stand by it and feel good about himself. But as soon as he won he was seen as part of the establishment. The interesting young curators stopped contacting him and now he was hearing a lot more from the boring, more mainstream types. He'd always been involved in the weirder side of things but now he felt like some sort of parent, no longer regarded as cool. But the prize also gave him freedom. Until then he felt like he'd been trying to please his parents, as art and music were considered things of high moral value in his household growing up. Martin and his brother were encouraged to learn musical instruments as early as three years old, so getting into these kinds of institutions as an adult was more for them than it was for him. So when he won the Turner Prize and had given his parents what they wanted, he thought, 'Fuck it, now I can move to Italy.' He was in love with an Italian woman and they moved to a remote part of the country together in a tiny house and he stopped doing exhibitions for four years.

•

Krano grew up in Valdobbiadene, Italy, a small town of roughly 10,000 people, 70 km outside Venice, in the hilly Prosecco wine region, 'where alcoholism reigns'. In 2010 he decided to write an entire album in the Venetian dialect but wanted to do it his way. In the past, musicians who traditionally used this language did so to please their fellow countrymen, but Krano wanted to make a Venetian album that achieved universal recognition even if it wasn't comprehensible to everybody. He owned portable recording equipment and retreated into the mountains, where he held a barbeque for his friends. While there, they recorded drums in the room of an old stone house, the mountains full of cows with cowbells around their necks, which inevitably made their way onto the drum tracks as the herd passed in the background. Since most music in the Venetian dialect ended up sounding clown-esque in a way he always found boorish,

Krano decided to change the pronunciation, making it softer, transforming it into more musical cadences while singing about subjects not usually covered in this language. In 2016 Krano released *Requiescat in Plavem* (Rest in Piave), named after the Piave river that runs from the Italian Alps into the Adriatic Sea near Venice.

•

Nicola Manzan grew up in Povegliano, a small village close to Treviso, not far from Venice. When Nicola was five years old his father taught him how to use his old turntable, giving Nicola the opportunity to listen to his vinyl collection, consisting of Italian singers and classical music. From then on Nicola spent many summer afternoons in the cellar playing at being a DJ. At that age, he wasn't aware of any musical boundaries, so he would mix Beethoven into Elvis Presley and then Schubert into traditional Italian music. At the age of 18 he was playing guitar in crossover metal bands and at 21 he joined the conservatory to study the violin. He continued to experiment with as many genres of music as he could and in 2002 moved out of his parents' house for the first time to Bologna, where he launched his new project, **Bologna Violenta**.

The project saw Manzan experiment with grindcore, the most aggressive genre he'd explored so far, playing all the instruments himself, programming electronic drums and playing violin and guitar live. The debut album, *Violent Bologna*, was 26 tracks long, with each track lasting 26 seconds, and very much set the precedent for the rest of his work. Every album that followed would usually consist of multiple short songs, each one a brief and overpowering assault, with every record evolving just a little more. In October 2016 he released *Discordia*, the first Bologna Violenta album to feature live drums, and, in my opinion, his finest work.

After ten years in Bologna, he'd moved back to his parents' house in Povegliano to write and record the new album. The house was uninhabited at the time; he loved being back there, and it felt like home, but he was scared to write anything. Every time he approached a new record he would feel like there was nothing new to discover, or, if there was, then he was incapable of discovering it. So he decided to make the album a joke, almost making fun of the fact that we can never truly create something new, encouraging the audience to laugh at their own futility. He decided that he would begin writing with the drums, so his friend and collaborator, Alessandro Vagnoni, sent Nicola a selection of live drum parts he'd recorded and he started writing from there. Alessandro was clearly trying to push the sound of the project more towards the heavier side of metal, and Nicola found himself trying to push against that when recording the rest of the music while enjoying the overall sound born from this tug of war, likening it to the sound of a petty squabble that escalates quickly. There's a scene in the film *Hot Rod* when Andy Samberg falls down a massive mountain for ages. Every time you think he's stopped falling he continues to fall, crashing into rocks, tumbling down steep slopes, breaking every bone in his body. That's what this album is like. Every time you think it's letting up, you smack your face on a boulder and continue hurtling into a ravine.

•

The Turner Prize had given Martin Creed an excuse to have a break and rest for the first time. The achievement assuaged the guilt of not working. He quit smoking while in Italy and curiously replaced it with cleaning his hands. He favoured hand wipes and was getting through a few packets of 20 every day. The thing that soothed him with smoking and hand wipes alike was the ritual, as he found repetition extremely comforting. These days he's graduated from the hand wipes and carries a bottle of antibacterial hand wash around with him. He washes his hands regularly, often feeling the urge to wash them if he has a good thought, but he also washes his hands if he has a bad thought. He washes his hands when he feels guilty and he often feels guilty because he's done what he wants to do. The guilt comes from growing up with parents who were Quakers: there was a big emphasis on guilt in his childhood and how everyone is basically bad trying to be good. Not that his parents weren't nice to him: they encouraged him to be creative and were hugely supportive, but the guilt implied in religion was always just there.

Music has always run alongside Martin's art exhibitions and installations. He's been releasing albums in bands and as a solo artist since 1997. In the past he's worked with classical musicians, slowly and laboriously writing out a score for them, making sure everything was controlled at all times. But in 2015 he wanted to approach it more flippantly, in a more throwaway fashion, and not worry about whether the instruments sounded perfect or not. So he set up an eight-person band in a studio in Brixton and deliberately chose instruments that he hated, like saxophone, clarinet and flute, purely because he thought it'd be funny. They had a week to make the album and Creed was recording everything constantly onto both digital and analogue with no overdubs. They all recorded together and bled into each other's mics, everything was overlapping and happening all at once with no separation, people couldn't always hear each other properly and a lot of it was spontaneous.

The songs didn't have much intention behind them, they were just little individual thoughts exploring one idea each, often zoning in on a phrase and repeating it until it either lost or gained meaning. He wanted to present a collection of meaningless ideas that if lined up on a tracklist might amount to something and make sense of themselves. And if they didn't, then he didn't mind.

The Lights Going On and Off was Creed trying to make a sculpture like a piece of music. A thing *taking place* in front of you. In a piece of music you can show everything occurring and moving forward. You're hearing it getting made, you're hearing it moving and growing. But with visual art you just show the audience the bit that's left over at the end of a longer process. It's the equivalent of one tiny idea, one thought, that if written down would barely fill a page. You exhibit it like it's this massive thing but really it's very small. *Thoughts Lined Up* was released in July 2016. It's his attempt at making music like a series of sculptures.

What Was Said

I left it until the very end of my first session to tell my counsellor I'd been having suicidal thoughts. Throughout the hour I'd put off bringing it up, but when she said our time was up, I knew I'd regret staying quiet. I think I just wanted her to have all the details and know roughly what she was dealing with from the start, or perhaps I just needed to say it out loud to someone. They'd started in New York. I'd been walking around thinking about it seriously for the first time and it'd scared me. That's why I had booked myself in for counselling in the first place. I knew I needed to talk to someone as soon as possible and get these thoughts out in the open. She looked at me sympathetically and I looked at the floor feeling ashamed.

•

When **RM Hubbert**'s father got diagnosed with lung cancer, Hubby (a nickname Hubbert's had most of his adult life) decided he needed to distract himself by learning something challenging, so took up playing Flamenco guitar. A couple of years after his father passed, his mum died very suddenly, so Hubby decided to write a song every month during the year following his mum's death. He knew that he'd never have that experience again and wanted to try and document it somehow. These songs became his 2011 debut album, *First & Last*.

His follow up album, *13 Lost & Found*, was written after his marriage ended during a time when he was incredibly isolated. The album was basically just an excuse to meet up with old friends again: every song featured a guest and the guest was always someone Hubby had been friends with in the 90s or before he got ill (he'd had severe depression for six or seven years since his dad died). He thought it would be easier to reconnect with his friends if they went into a studio and wrote songs together. The album was a success and won Scottish Album of the Year 2012, and in 2013 Hubby released *Breaks & Bone*, the first album he sings on, to complete his *Ampersand Trilogy*.

In April 2016, RM Hubbert released *Telling the Trees*, his first album since the acclaimed trilogy, and decided to do the exact opposite of what he did on *13 Lost & Found*. The album would still feature a guest on every song but they would be people he didn't know very well, plus everyone would work entirely remotely. On *13 Lost & Found* he would go into a room for eight hours with the collaborator and whatever they had at the end of it, they put on the album. So *Telling The Trees* had to be made in isolation. Whenever someone agreed to contribute, Hubby would go away for two or three days and do nothing but intensely listen to their music. He would then write an instrumental piece that he thought would suit them and send them the song with two basic instructions:

1. Do whatever you want with this song.
2. Don't talk to me again until you're done.

He wanted to influence them as little as possible. The reason he wanted to work with these people was because he loved their music so much, and he wanted to find out how they made the stuff he loved. He wasn't interested in making an RM Hubbert record with guest singers. He wanted it to be one of the guest's songs but with him on guitar; he wanted as much of them in each song as was humanly possible, making himself the cameo. Once they'd sent the song back to him, he didn't interfere with it again – it went straight on the record. It was the first project he'd made that wasn't about him and his mental health issues. It wasn't a therapeutic album. His previous albums had all been made so he could feel better and process the events in his personal life, but *Telling the Trees* was the first RM Hubbert album where the music was more important than the reason for doing it. In fact, the music *was* the reason for doing it. This time round he just wanted to make a really weird pop album with an acoustic guitar and a load of amazing women.

The day after *Telling the Trees* came out, everything went

to shit. Every album he'd released up until that point had got a little more press and done a lot better than its predecessor, especially after the SAY Awards. But because this was the first one that wasn't about his mental health, it suddenly became harder to get any press for it. There was no story to hang it on, no 'misery porn', and he felt like he was moving backwards. Then, shortly after the album's release, his agent got really ill, resulting in the *Telling the Trees* tour being stalled. This meant there was no momentum to build on, Hubby couldn't work for the rest of 2016, and that's when his depression got really bad. At the start of 2017, he broke up with his partner and had a suicidal episode. He felt like his musical career was done, he moved around a bit, trying to get better and back on track, but he remained in a bad place for most of the year.

Right after he was at his lowest (he didn't get sectioned, but some professionals came to his house and looked after him for a few days), Hubby decided to pick up his guitar for the first time since the album came out. He felt like learning some covers, and taught himself songs by Kathryn Joseph, Sebadoh and Sparklehorse among others. He started to enjoy himself again so began giving Facebook Live performances, covering a different song each time. He remembered the reason he'd started learning Flamenco guitar in the first place – it provided an emotional release that he found difficult to generate normally. He recorded a few of the covers and put them online for a fiver, and it raised over ten grand in three days (the money was very much needed at the time). This helped him realise he wasn't done: people still cared, just shit happens with business stuff. In the end, *Telling the Trees* sold just as much as its predecessors and it found an audience who needed to hear music made for the love of making music.

Human Performance

In February 2017 my new tour started. My main goal for the year, careerwise, was to film four live stand-up shows comprised of material I'd done over the last six years. But in order to film those shows I knew I'd have to relearn everything, so I decided to go out on tour and perform all four shows on rotation for seven months. I'd be in each venue for three nights, performing two shows on the third night, with a view to finally film all four shows in September that year. I have no one to blame for this workload but myself. Obviously, when we booked the tour back in 2016, I had no idea that by the time night one rolled around I'd be an emotional wreck who'd recently launched headfirst into a breakdown, but that's very much how the chips fell. Relearning four hours of material was a nice distraction in some ways, but in other ways it was the last thing I needed. For example, when one of your old shows is all about a breakup you had in 2013, but the observations within the show still ring true four years later, only this time they apply to a brand new breakup because you keep failing at relationships – it stings a tad. Also, the old shows weren't going down very well because I had outgrown them over the years, so now I had to rewrite them (on top of relearning them) in order to bring them up to scratch. Suddenly this exciting new project felt like the worst idea ever, and, mentally, I didn't feel up to it. I was also writing my very first book at the time, a lighthearted memoir about all the mishaps I'd got myself into over the years. Again, this initially seemed like it'd be a fun project, but now I'd entered a rather dark chapter in my life – I was struggling to like myself,

I desperately wanted to be back with my ex-girlfriend, I was touring a bunch of old shows that were no longer funny, and in the daytimes I was sitting down to write a book about every single time I'd fucked up. The old self-esteem was taking quite the battering. I remember, one day, sitting in my hotel room in Peterborough, after two nights of bad gigs with a third to look forward to, writing about one of the three car crashes I'd been responsible for in my life, and thinking to myself, 'Of course you're on your own, of course you are', and then instantly laughing out loud at the bleakness of my own inner monologue. And then I died on my arse that evening in front of a two-thirds-empty room of unimpressed Peterborougans (Peter-bur-roo-gans).

Interesting fact about one of the car crashes I had – in the car with me was comedian Josie Long and musician Johnny Lynch, aka **The Pictish Trail.** Josie did an excellent routine about the crash in her show *The Future is Another Place,* yours truly wrote about it in a book, and Johnny wrote a song about it on his sublime album *Future Echoes.* The song is called 'Easy With Either' and is centred on the doubts he had after the crash regarding whether or not we'd actually survived. *Future Echoes* was released in September 2016.

•

After their self-titled debut album in 2013, Canadian punk band **PUP** set off on a tour that felt like it would never end. They'd recorded their debut in Montreal in December during one of the coldest winters on record, with the four of them living together in a one-bedroom apartment. They did this for a month; they barely went outside and they wanted to murder each other. Then they set off on tour, where they were travelling every day, in each other's faces all the time and sleeping in ridiculously cramped conditions. They started to write their second album on the road, so naturally a lot of the record is about this experience (the first song on the new album ended up being called 'If This Tour Doesn't Kill You I Will'). They had been on tour for years at this point; the highs were super high and the lows were super low; it's hard on your body and your mind, and you have no personal space. So, for lead singer and guitarist Stefan Babcock, the conditions were prime for writing an emotionally turbulent, manic and somewhat bipolar record. He wanted the lyrics to flip between the darkest recesses of his mind and the goofiest stuff he could think of, in order to reflect the touring lifestyle. There wasn't a whole lot of lyrical subtlety in these new songs, and he became way more honest, discovering that was where his strengths lay. One of the plus points of their relentless touring schedule was that by the time PUP entered the studio they were more cohesive than they'd ever been before and were able to capture the energy of their live shows on record for the first time. One of the downsides of their touring schedule, however, was the fact that Stefan had completely ruined his vocal cords. He went to see a doctor before the studio sessions, who examined him and informed Stefan that he'd never sing again by saying, with a heavy heart, 'The dream is over.' Fortunately, the doctor was wrong, but the band found his earnest statement undeniably hilarious.

The Dream is Over was released in May 2016 and was easily one of the best-received punk albums of the year. The gang backing vocals, the live energy of the band and the open lyrics about depression and coping mechanisms produced a catharsis you can only really get from punk music. In terms of the band's career 2016 was huge, but in terms of Stefan's personal life and mental health it wasn't so great. The weird thing about accomplishing goals when you struggle with your mental health is that you feel good for a second, but then you don't any more and you wonder why the thing that was supposed to make you happy doesn't make you happy, meaning you can potentially sink even further into depression. But Stefan isn't someone who lets things go unacknowledged, and this aspect of his life became the foundation for the next PUP record, 2019's *Morbid Stuff*.

•

Taking on such a huge tour in 2017 with almost no days off meant I was permanently exhausted, mentally and physically. I always felt weirdly tense after gigs, so every night of the tour, in order to relax, I'd return to my hotel room and search for music from 2016. I'd kept it up since returning from New York and it'd now become a proper project. I didn't have an end goal in mind – I think I just assumed I couldn't possibly find that many albums I loved from a single year and that I'd run out sooner rather than later. But I was finding a number of decent albums on a nightly basis and it'd started to feel like I was gradually piecing together a big collage of the musical year as a whole. Sometimes I'd be on a roll with a specific genre: I'd buy five hip hop albums in a row, and then look at my 2016 collection and it'd feel unbalanced. So I'd deliberately go out looking for genres I'd neglected and search 'best folk albums 2016' or 'best jazz 2016' etc. Then I'd usually end up tipping the balance in the other direction and would have to go searching for more hip hop albums again. This pattern went on and on and on, so it wasn't long before I'd exhausted the best-of lists and had to go down other avenues in order to unearth new gems, and this is how, finally, at the ripe old age of 32, I got big into YouTube.

Motion Graphics

American composer **Nico Muhly** and Faroe Islands singer **Teitur** collaborated on a project called *Confessions* in 2016 – an album with lyrics pulled entirely from YouTube videos. The music is pure chamber pop, with Teitur singing from the perspective of various YouTubers about seemingly inane subjects such as not being able to describe what somebody looks like, smoking in the summertime and loving the smell of their printer in the morning. 'Printer in the Morning' remains my personal highlight on the album: I love how mundane the lyrics are, how much pleasure the lead character derives from something so trivial, and yet there's something relatable and reassuring about their testimony also. The album's title comes from the confessional nature and overshare culture of the YouTube community, and once they'd found all they could on YouTube, Muhly and Teitur began to solicit videos especially for the album. People in Holland were asked to film themselves talking about something personal, providing the album with the remainder of its lyrical content. These videos were perhaps filmed with a higher degree of self-awareness than the originals as the participants knew their words would be turned into song lyrics, but this element helped reveal aspects of their personality that the more organic YouTube vlogs maybe could not. The accompanying music on *Confessions* is made up of lute, harpsichord, strings and guitar, instruments that make these matter-of-fact monologues appear stranger than they are by providing medieval, whimsical backdrops for each song. *Confessions* was released in October 2016.

•

I started subscribing to YouTube channels in 2017. Naturally this began when I typed 'best albums of 2016' into YouTube and a load of lists came up by various YouTube vloggers (are they even called vloggers any more? I feel so old. I'm 32 and I'm suddenly going all in on YouTube), and after watching their best-of-2016 lists I went back and watched some of their individual reviews of 2016 albums, then I started watching their more recent videos, and before I knew it I was SUBSCRIBING TO YOUTUBE CHANNELS. Please don't think I'd never watched YouTube before 2017, of course I had – frequently in fact. I really knew my way around the site. But never before had I ever felt like *committing* to anything on there. I hadn't previously wanted to take things to the next level and receive regular alerts when a channel uploaded a new video, and I also had never experienced a desire to curate my YouTube videos before. But I'm here to tell you that subscribing to YouTube channels is an absolute game changer. Now I never miss an episode of my favourite YouTube videos and, yes, on paper that sounds pathetic, but in practice it's extremely satisfying (once you learn to ignore how objectively tragic it is). I subscribe to many different YouTube channels but they can be divided up into four simple categories: music and . . .

Food

I subscribe to **First We Feast** and regularly watch videos of people eating food, talking about food, making food or being interviewed while eating spicy chicken wings that get progressively hotter as the interview progresses. The chicken wings interviews are part of a series called *Hot Ones* and I have watched so many episodes that I've now memorised most of the hot sauces featured in each season. I once had a first date in a restaurant, and when I arrived my date was sitting in front of many shelves, all of which were lined with bottles of hot sauce. Shelf upon shelf, every bottle a different brand, and I spotted one of the *Hot Ones* sauces to the left of her left shoulder, a sauce called Da Bomb. Da Bomb is described by most guests as the hottest thing they've ever eaten, everyone hates it and it ruins lives. I pointed at the sauce and said, 'Oh, they eat that sauce in a show on a YouTube channel I subscribe to.' This is how I'd chosen to impress her, by bragging about recognising a hot sauce because I subscribe to a YouTube channel that regularly features said hot sauce. Weirdly, that's not where the story ends. She then responded by saying, 'Do you want me to steal it for you?' Which was unexpected. I said no to the sauce theft because I was raised Christian, and then excused myself and went to the toilet because all this crime talk was making me nervous. When I returned I looked at the shelf and Da Bomb was gone. She looked back at me, smiling, looking very pleased with herself. I had to ask, 'Did you steal Da Bomb?' She nodded at me. I was now officially in way over my head and considering going on the lam. It wasn't long before I needed the toilet again (I was dining with an anarchist for chrissakes). When I returned, the scene I was met with was way more confusing. Da Bomb was now in the middle of our table with the lid off, and my date had turned to face the table next to us. Sat on the adjacent table were two guys, both a little younger than me and somehow even more dweeby looking than I was – they were each holding out a finger and on that finger was a MASSIVE blob of Da Bomb. The two boys were looking at my date with hearts in their eyes while she smiled encouragingly back at them. 'What's going on?' I asked urgently, 'You're not going to eat Da Bomb, are you?' 'We can take it!' said one of the guys, looking at my date and not at me. 'Guys, do not eat that hot sauce,' I pleaded, 'I've watched multiple videos where people eat a fraction of the amount you've got and it devastates them. And that's when it's on a chicken wing, they're not doing it straight up.' A flicker of doubt passed over both their faces and my date looked disappointed. 'Are you not going to do it now?' she pouted. And then they ate the hot sauce. They ate Da Bomb. Swallowed it undiluted and uncut. A big fucking blob of it. The noises those guys made for the rest of the evening remain the most undignified I've ever been in earshot of. We were there for another hour and their tortured wheezing and gasps for oxygen didn't subside once – I thought they were literally going to die. And while they were clawing at the table and sniffing metres of snot back up into their nostrils, my date was looking right at me, completely ignoring them like they didn't even exist. When we left she stopped by their table, took one last look at them, then theatrically threw her head back and laughed like Cruella de Vil before taking my arm and walking me out the door, leaving them a pair of sweaty, shaking, whimpering wrecks. It was simultaneously the least and most attractive behaviour I've ever experienced from a first date.

ASMR

This is way harder to explain and will sound weird, but ASMR videos tend to consist of someone talking directly to you and doing things that make you feel super relaxed. It is not sexual. It's going to sound sexual but I can't stress enough how not sexual it is. The person in the video might roleplay (not sexual) as a variety of characters (not sexual); perhaps a masseuse (not sexual), or a tailor who's measuring you (not sexual), an artist who's drawing you (not sexual), or they might simply be themselves and perform some slow hand movements up close to the camera to relax you while speaking softly (Not. Sexual). One of my favourite YouTubers is an ASMR guy who will often crowbar his own agenda into his videos no matter what character he's playing, and that agenda frequently involves him convincing you to quit your job. Say he's playing a reiki master (more hand movements and soft talking, not sexual), he'll slowly wave his hands in front of the camera while saying in a hushed tone, 'Yeah, I can feel you got a lot of bad energy . . . you still working at that place? . . . yeah, I thought so . . . well they got you doing those crazy hours . . . yeah, I can feel your aura is kinda weak . . . yeah . . . You should quit. You should quit your job. You should quit your job right now . . . ok now I'm gonna scan your arms with my hands . . .' Or say he's playing an artist sketching your portrait, he'll line up your features with his pencil and scribble on his pad while saying in a hushed tone, 'You can see here you've got a very straight nose . . . it goes straight down like this . . . so I'm gonna make those lines very strong . . . and your forehead it has these great lines across it too . . . you know some people call them worry lines . . . they say if you've got those lines you must worry a lot . . . maybe at home . . . maybe at work . . . you need to quit your job immediately.' I love how obvious it is that he quit his job once and has never been sure if it was the right thing to do so is trying to convince more people to take the plunge with him. Sometimes he changes it up and tells you to disown your family. I love him.

Film theories

I also subscribe to **SuperCarlinBrothers**. Jay and Ben Carlin are huge film fans who come up with theories about their favourite movie franchises. I'm a big fan of fan theories – they're all the fun of being a conspiracy theorist without any of it having to matter. My favourite film theory is the Pixar Theory. A guy named Jon Negroni came up with it (and wrote a book about it called *The Pixar Theory*). It's basically the theory that all of the Pixar movies exist in the same universe and are telling one big story (I mentioned my age earlier, I'm not going to repeat it again; go back and refresh your memory if you need to). Unlike with *Hot Ones*, I have never brought up SuperCarlinBrothers on a first date, as I imagine it would result in the date getting up, taking one last look at me, throwing her head back and laughing, before taking the arm of the guy on the table next to me and walking him out the door.

•

The story behind **Rocks & Waves Song Circle** is a mystery. Even the two record labels that put it out, Bongo Joe and Sing a Song Fighter, only know the basics: a Swedish artist named Isaak Sundström recorded it in Mexico with a local choir and a Haitian soloist. But apart from Isaak, none of the musicians' names are known, plus no one knows where exactly it was recorded, how he met any of these musicians and singers, what the album is about – nothing but those few vague details.

The best approximation of what happened is that Isaak was travelling, not intending to record any music, and had packed some basic microphones in case he wanted to make some field recordings. It's believed he heard a choir singing in a village and spontaneously introduced himself and organised the recording that day in a nearby church, teaching them some of his own compositions, positioning the three mics around the room and recording everyone all at once. That's all guesswork though. Even the album's title is unclear: it might be self-titled or it might be called *Songs I–V* – different sources give different names. And that's how the songs are presented on the tracklist too: *I, II, III, IV* and *V*, offering no clues to their content or any story behind them (titles are assigned to the tracks on the vinyl copy, but this was done by the label and not Sundström, plus the song 'names' are in brackets). This record is one of the more extreme examples of someone letting the music speak for itself and stripping away as much additional information as possible because they don't want to distract from the five very special songs they've produced. They're five songs to get lost in; sometimes wordless vocal passages are repeated on a loop, being sung live by the choir with the soloist adding flourishes in the gaps, the natural reverb of the church hall lifting everything up and above. Modest piano and percussion act as accompaniments, the piano (possibly being played by Sundström) leading the choir while the drums are used for emphasis. Other instruments tend to join slowly, one by one, the songs gradually getting grander and more celebratory as they progress, the sensation of a room full of strangers bonding through music generating a positivity that permeates out of the record and through its audience. *Rocks & Waves Song Circle* was released in August 2016.

•

The first thing that strikes you about the **Drones'** seventh album, *Feelin Kinda Free*, is the messy cover – it features a sequence of letters that make no sense: they don't form any words and appear to be random gibberish. But this is actually a code linked to a well-known murder case in Australia and to this day both the code and case remain unsolved. In 1948 a man was found dead on Somerton Beach and a scrap of paper was found in his pocket with the words 'Tamam Shud' written on it. Tamam Shud is a Persian phrase and means 'Finished' – the scrap of paper later turned out to have been torn from a book called *The Rubaiyat of Omar Khayyam* and it wasn't long before the police managed to track down the exact copy the page came from. On the inside cover of the book some telephone numbers and the now infamous encrypted message were written in pen. The second track on *Feelin Kinda Free* is entitled 'Taman Shud' (many news reports misspelt 'Tamam' initially) and relates to the case of 'The Somerton Man'. Singer Gareth Liddiard asks why no one cares what happened to this guy who's still not been identified and whose cause of death hasn't even been figured out yet, while simultaneously making it clear how little he cares about the big things Australians are told to care about (the Anzacs, Ned Kelly, *Masterchef* and the current anti-immigration argument of Australia being 'full'). This rejection of national pride, although it may upset some, actually feels needed, especially during the year it was released: in an age that witnessed the growth of nationalism in countries all around the world this sort of pushback matters. *Feelin Kinda Free* was released in March 2016.

•

Hot wings, whispering men and theories about *Toy Story* were fun, but most of the videos I watched on YouTube were of people reviewing or talking about about new music releases. I subscribed to a number of YouTube music channels during

2017, but the ones I watched the most were **Dead End Hip Hop** and **The Needle Drop**.

Southern Family

Myke C-Town's family moved to Atlanta, Georgia, from California when he was around 13 years old. When you're 13 and you're thrown into a place where nothing makes sense to you, it's easy to become an outsider. Most kids at his school didn't want to talk to him so the only other people that he could hang out with were the other kids branded as weirdos. He was hanging out with the few metal kids at his school, the few goth kids, the few gay kids, because they also had no friends in rural Georgia. Myke's love of music began in the early 90s, when he first started hearing bands like Pearl Jam and Nirvana, and shortly after that got into punk rock. Punk was the catalyst for him being *obsessed* with music and becoming an avid collector of records. He would listen to a Descendants album and be amazed that Frank Navetta knew what he was dealing with at high school everyday. Moving from California to this extremely small and insular town had been a total culture shock, but now he'd found some purpose and knew he needed to seek out as much punk music as he possibly could.

Despite this newfound enthusiasm for punk, he was totally uninterested in further broadening his horizons in hip hop, mainly because of what he'd heard on the radio. He used to like mainstream hip hop as a little kid but now not so much; Dr Dre didn't interest him, 8Ball didn't interest him, plus the rap culture in the South was very different to California. In Georgia, rap culture felt extremely isolated and you weren't getting a wide range of artists, you were offered primarily Southern artists and if you didn't like Bone Crusher or Outkast then there was nothing for you. But in 10th Grade he found out there was this whole punk sub-section in hip hop that he never knew existed. He discovered hip hop collectives like Hieroglyphics, Def Jux and Anticon, people doing hip hop in a punk rock fashion, and that drew him right back in. He still maintains that if he hadn't found punk he would've just continued to write off hip hop and ignore it.

Myke continued to consume and hunt down new music into adulthood, and in 2011 he got a job at an online company where he wrote content for websites. He was lucky enough to work with three other guys with similar interests, and the four of them would hang out at their desks and argue about rap music all day. His colleagues, Ken, Feefo and Rod, came up with the idea of uploading their conversations to YouTube, quickly adding their friend Beezy to the group, with Rod operating the camera (Myke didn't know what YouTube was and thought it sounded stupid but went along with it anyway). The channel was called **Dead End Hip Hop**, it quickly gained popularity, and the five of them became part of the online rap community, where they were able to shine a light on the artists that the mainstream outlets weren't talking about. Myke saw the channel as a way of removing the professionalism from talking about music and not being afraid to just be a fan: putting your own ego to one side and showing how much you love an artist or an album. All five members of DEHH have different outlooks and bring their own perspectives to the videos, and as a weirdo who found hip hop via punk rock, Myke connects with the experimental side of hip hop more than most. Artists like Death Grips and **JPEGMAFIA** (who released the superb *Black Ben Carson* in 2016), and even indie rappers like Busdriver or Aesop Rock, are all speaking from a standpoint that only certain people will understand. When Aesop Rock raps about being depressed or when MC Ride talks about being a paranoid manic, Myke can relate to them because he's been through similar things himself. So he tries to bring that voice to the DEHH table because the last thing he wants is for the kind of kid he was to watch the channel and think, 'Here's another five rap fans who don't get my screwed-up perspective' – he wants them to know they have at least one guy that totally gets it and doesn't want them to feel like being weird is in any way to their detriment.

•

Ed Gamble and I once went to see the highly adored experimental hip hop trio **Death Grips** play a live show in Brixton. There was no support act. At around 8 p.m. the lighting in the venue changed to what felt like a show state, and a deafening, escalating synth noise filled the venue. The sound was so loud – and felt like it was forever climbing in pitch – that there was no doubt the show was about to start. But it didn't start. It didn't start for another 70 minutes. The venue filled up as soon as the escalating sound started – everyone was cheering and getting hyped for Death Grips. And we sat in that moment, that 'the gig is about to start any second' moment, for an hour and ten fucking minutes. The sound didn't stop playing until the band came on. It was so horrible. Every now and then they'd change the stage lighting to give the crowd hope, but it was just another trick. We were trapped in a neverending Hellsphere.

Trolling their fans like this tells you all you need to know about this band, whose music I absolutely love but who as people in that specific moment I hated more than anything. It also tells you everything you need to know about their fans. The crowd knew they were getting trolled so leant into it, going crazy as if the gig was about to start even though they knew it wasn't going to happen, launching into ironic football chants and applauding when nothing was happening. Meanwhile Ed Gamble and I were having simultaneous nervous breakdowns and felt like we were living in a shared anxiety dream. Don't get me wrong, I'm not complaining here – weirdly, I'm delighted to have been trolled live by Death Grips. It's the kind of story that was torture at the time, but in retrospect I'm glad I survived it and think it's more amusing than anything. It's an odd feeling being a fan of your own bullies, but that's part of what liking this band entails (if you're a wimp like me). The gig was in 2018 and I had only discovered the band the previous year.

In 2013, Death Grips' drummer and producer, Zach Hill, had written a film and wanted to cast iconic 70s actress Karen Black as one of the lead roles. Zach sent Karen the script and in turn she filmed herself reading her character's dialogue and sent the footage back to Hill. She had recorded herself reclining on her sofa and trying different takes of her lines completely out of context, sometimes talking so naturally it was hard to tell she was still reading from a script. Later that year Karen Black passed away and in October 2015 Death Grips uploaded the footage Karen had recorded onto YouTube under the name *Bottomless Pit*. The whole thing is oddly captivating (probably because I'm the kind of person who watches ASMR videos), and while it's not clear what Black's monologue alludes to exactly, you become engrossed in what feels like a story.

Death Grips released their fifth studio album, *Bottomless Pit*, in May 2016, and what makes me laugh about the fans' response to the record was that some thought it was too mainstream. If you would also like to find this funny, then please listen to the cacophonic opening track, 'Giving Bad People Good Ideas', which sounds like the inside of an active blender, and then imagine what their least accessible stuff must sound like.* It's very hard for me to imagine this book without Death Grips in it as I think any description of this era in music that doesn't mention them would feel incomplete. Bands like this remind you that music will always morph into something unanticipated and keep on advancing, simultaneously mirroring and altering everything around it. And if that's what that escalating synth sound was a metaphor for, I'm going to be furious.

Exploded View

Anthony Fantano launched his YouTube channel **The Needle Drop** in January 2009 after two years of blogging and making podcasts under the same name. Back then no one reviewed music on YouTube, those sorts of channels didn't exist, but Fantano still decided to upload videos of himself reviewing the latest albums as a final attempt at achieving his dream job.

By the time I discovered the channel in 2017 Fantano was

---

* Incidentally, if you would like to hear the band's more accessible side, I'd recommend checking out *Scum With Boundaries* by **The I.L.Y.'s**, the art rock side project from Zach Hill and Andy Morin – another beaut of a record released in 2016.

verging on one million subscribers, surpassing the million mark by the end of the year. As demand for more content had grown he'd increased his output accordingly, uploading album reviews, weekly track round-ups, thinkpieces, livestream Q&As, and videos addressing the hot takes of his subscribers, all while refining every aspect of the channel in order to make it easy to digest for the viewer.

When I searched for 'best albums of 2016' on YouTube, Fantano's end-of-year list was the top result. At this point I'd read countless lists online, and usually they would throw up the same albums again and again, but this list featured many artists I'd not heard of before and it felt like a goldmine to a sad boy with a weird addiction to music from one specific year. Thanks to his list I discovered *Body War* by **Show Me the Body**, *Preoccupations* by **Preoccupations**, *Honor Killed the Samurai* by **Ka**, *You Will Never be One of Us* by **NAILS*** and countless other albums detailed throughout this book. The Needle Drop's 2016 list was a real music fan's Top 50 and I got a lot out of it. His number one pick was *Atrocity Exhibition* by **Danny Brown**, an album I'd seen on other lists but was now compelled to pay attention to after watching someone expertly articulate everything that made the project special. Fantano brands himself as The Internet's Busiest Music Nerd and, perhaps more than anyone else, he appreciates how the reviewer's role has changed since the internet became a thing. These days,

---

* Ed Gamble once saw NAILS live and said they dedicated every single song to 'people who talk shit behind your back'. He says they said it with a straight face every time, and due to the short run times of their brutal hardcore metal songs they said it every 90 seconds. I laugh every time I think about it.

there's more new music available than ever and most people aren't buying it, they're downloading and streaming it for free. The job of a reviewer used to be telling people what's worth their money but now it's telling people what's worth their time.

•

Growing up, **Danny Brown** used to deal drugs and in 2006 went to prison for eight months for violating probation. While in jail he got given the job of handing out sandwiches to other inmates, which put him in this weird position between the guards and his fellow prisoners, receiving shit from both sides. I've chosen to start with this detail because if you don't know who Danny Brown is I think it does a decent job of summing up his rap persona – he's the guy who handed out sandwiches in prison and got shit from everybody.

Atrocity Exhibition is one of my favourite hip hop albums of all time. Brown covers the same topics as most rappers – gang violence, wealth, drugs, casual sex – but where others may brag about such things, he seems to feel shame and regret, painting a desperate picture of a guy trapped inside a hell of his own making – a guy who can't get it up in a threesome and is scared of dying. Even though there's some artistic licence taken, much of the album sees him being open about his mental health in a way that's refreshing, shocking and humorous, providing a narrative arc to the record and even a moment of clarity during the conclusion. The instrumentals on *Atrocity Exhibition* are uncooperative and awkward, whistles and finger cymbals Morse-coding over a swamp of basslines and weird samples, the most orthodox cut being 'Really Doe', the album's single, featuring pitch-perfect guest spots from Kendrick Lamar, Earl Sweatshirt and Ab-Soul, and even that sounds like an introduction to a horror film.

Danny Brown named the album after a Joy Division song that featured some of Ian Curtis's darkest lyrics, because although Brown hasn't contemplated suicide himself, he related to the feeling of having your own pain become entertainment for the masses. His live shows have always been compared to a travelling freak show, and on this record he reflects on that – the parts he embraces and the parts he resents. The Joy Division song was named after the J. G. Ballard book *The Atrocity Exhibition*, a series of controversial short stories where the writer attempted to make sense of the Kennedy assassination by reimagining major world events through the eyes of a psychotic doctor. The premise of the book and the premise of this album seem to sit quiet nicely alongside each other, like they're set in the same universe. So imagine that group of short stories as a group of rap songs and instead of a psychotic doctor it's the guy who used to give out the sandwiches in prison.

The Party Mix

The tour was pretty relentless but I managed to get a couple of days off here and there. I'd been asked to DJ for two hours at a friend's wedding in March and had said yes as it was the perfect opportunity to redeem myself after my disastrous DJ set at the Prince of Wales all those years ago. Of course, I'd also said yes because I loved the happy couple and wanted to do them a favour on their wedding day. Of course. But it didn't hurt that I'd be able to slay some personal demons in the process.

The reason why I was asked to DJ at the wedding was because of *The Party Mix*. *The Party Mix* was an emergency playlist I had on my iPod reserved for social occasions that had lost their magic and needed rescuing. It originated at a friend's house party, where the friend in question was playing drum & bass music for a flat full of people who didn't like drum & bass music. I empathised with him – he was just trying to connect with all of his friends by playing them his favourite songs in the whole world and now all of his friends were rejecting him by standing around awkwardly and complaining to each other about his shit music (the friend in question was TV's Tom Rosenthal. Bad luck, Tom – I just destroyed you in a book). So I hurriedly made a playlist on my 'pod, a playlist of old classics everyone knows and loves, switched his phone for my 'pod and SAVED THE PARTY. I felt like I was six years old again, holding a packet of lemon and scampi Nik Naks – everyone was dancing and singing but this time it was all thanks to me and this phenomenal mix. Needless to say, once the party was over I did not delete that playlist – I kept it on my 'pod and kept my 'pod in my pock in case I ever needed to unite a room full of people ever again. From that day forth I always pulled out *The Party Mix* when necessary: awkward car journeys, boring birthdays, even pre-gig music if the audience seemed particularly flat – there wasn't an occasion *The Party Mix* couldn't solve. I was so proud of *The Party Mix* that I used to bring it up in conversation to people, I'd tell them about how perfect this party mix was, and it didn't matter if they didn't find the story of *The Party Mix* very interesting or if talking about a playlist I'd made on my iPod ended up killing the energy in the room, because I had just the thing to bring that energy back again right in my pock – the very same party mix.

I think it's fair to say there was a time in my life when *The Party Mix* was my proudest achievement. So naturally when I got asked to DJ at the wedding I started with *The Party Mix* classics and worked outwards from there. I prepped hard and spent months compiling a tracklist I could stand by even if the entire wedding party ended up chanting 'wanker' at me. I didn't rest until I had full confidence in every track, and I can't speak for the bride and groom, but when the big day finally came around – it was the happiest day of my life. Back at the Prince of Wales I had tried to connect with people by playing songs they didn't even know LIKE A FOOL. But now I was connecting with others by playing songs that ALREADY connected everybody. 'Torn' by Natalie Imbruglia, 'Fat Lip' by Sum 41, 'Regulate' by Warren G, 'Africa' by Toto, 'I Want You Back' by The Jackson 5 – I was on cloud 9 and no one was chanting 'wanker' at me from clouds 2 or 3. 2017 had got off to a bad start but tonight I'd finally found my true destiny – to churn out the hits and unite the entire planet through the binding power of music because life was one big dance floor and we're all just a bunch of crazy dancers. My name is James Acaster and I am a DJ.

•

Tel Aviv's **Buttering Trio** made their third record, *Threesome* (a chilled electronic funk album combining Indian ragas, tribal rhythms and dub), during a time when lead singer Keren Dun was reaching the age of Saturn's Return – an astrological phenomenon that occurs when Saturn reaches the same point in the sky that it was in when you were born, signifying the dawn of a new age in your life. This meant she could feel everything around her shifting massively, and her approach to writing changed as a consequence. Saturn's Return occurs roughly every 29.5 years. I perhaps experienced a delayed Saturn's Return as 2017 was most definitely the year my life shifted into a new age (I was a DJ now), but I don't want to pick holes in the whole Saturn's Return thing.

Even though I don't personally believe in astrology, star signs and whatnot, I do find them comforting. If you don't believe that horoscopes are true, then you're usually of the opinion that the writer has chosen some vague universal truths about people so anyone who reads it will be able to relate in some respect, and I quite like that every human being has these vague truths in common. We all doubt ourselves sometimes, we all experience change and we all have people that mean a lot to us who we don't see enough. Horoscopes, even if we believe them to be lies, prove that we're all connected and I like that.

During her Saturn's Return, Dun immersed herself in the books of seriocomedy writer Tom Robbins and wanted to tell stories with her lyrics: stories of sex, mindfulness and human society, drawing so much inspiration from her own life that at times she found it disturbing and her close friends became worried about her. With all of these ideas churning around at once, the overall sense of the record, lyrically at least, is one of certainty through uncertainty: all anyone can ever know is their own feelings, those feelings are endless, and everything else is speculation. *Threesome* was released in November 2016.

A New Wave of Violence

Shortly after the inscrutable success of the wedding, I booked myself in to do another DJ set for a friend who was organising a charity event. I wasn't listed, I just offered to do a set for free because I now wanted to DJ whenever I saw the opportunity – like, maybe playing songs for groups of people to dance to was the antidote to feeling depressed and whatnot. Which makes sense: buying albums from 2016 had made me feel better, so surely sharing the joy of music with others would have an even greater effect on my wellbeing. To begin with the charity DJ set was going swell, the dance floor was full and everyone was having a riveting time. But then a drunk guy walked up to me and requested Aerosmith. 'Sorry,' I said, 'I've only got what's on my iPod and what's on my computer and we don't have WiFi in here so I can't play any songs I haven't already got.' He glared at me and said, 'It's a yes or no question, mate', curling his lip and looking angry. 'Ok then – no.' He was immediately furious. 'Why not?' 'Because I've only got what's on my iPod and what's on my computer and we don't have WiFi in here so I can't play any songs I haven't already got.' He narrowed his eyes and stepped towards me, toe to toe, shouting over the music, 'Oh, so I'm the biggest cunt that ever walked the planet am I?' I'd only just met this man but based purely on the fact he'd already said this sentence to me I thought 'yeah probably' but said 'no, I'm just explaining why I can't play Aerosmith'. He then squares up to me, shouts some more, I explain why I can't play Aerosmith again and this repeats for a while before eventually a friend of his drags him away. A couple of minutes later another drunk man appears and barks 'off the top of my head – Green Day?!'

This went on all night, a neverending queue of drunk men kept starting on me for not playing their requests and it didn't matter how clearly I explained my predicament to them they always wanted to clock me. In the end I played 'You Give A Little Love' from the *Bugsy Malone* soundtrack using someone else's phone and snuck off home while everyone was dancing in a circle.

The charity event occurred during a week of surprise confrontations, some more extreme than others. Two days later I was walking home late at night and noticed that the person walking in front of me was bleeding heavily out the back of his head. When I asked him if he was ok he told me it was best I stay out of it. Halfway through his response, a guy on a bike bumped the curb, dismounted, pulled out a knife and chased the bleeding man down the street, back the way I'd come. I immediately picked up the pace, walked straight ahead and didn't look back. I then stopped and accepted that if someone died tonight and I read about it in the papers tomorrow, then I'd have to live with the fact that I could've helped but did nothing, so I turned around and walked back towards them. Reflecting on my actions now, what I should've done is phone the police. I have no idea what I thought I was going to bring to the table by jumping in among the action itself. Fortunately, things had calmed down by the time I arrived. I saw the guy who'd been attacked catching his breath outside a kebab shop, the attacker having fled; he didn't seem to have acquired any further injuries but was still in a bad way. I asked how he was and once again he told me to mind my own business. I asked him to let me ring him an ambulance and he lost patience with me. 'Look, mate, this has nothing to do with you so just go home, ok? You go to your house, I'll go to mine and that's that, it's over – do you understand?' He was wound up now so I backed off and agreed that we'd both go our separate ways and say nothing more about it. We then both set off back to our respective homes, completely unaware that we both lived in the same building.

It was a really awkward walk. We went exactly the same route as each other, walking side by side, occasionally exchanging words like, 'Please ring yourself an ambulance!' and 'Fuck off and mind your own fucking business.' Once we arrived in the courtyard of our block of flats we accepted that we were practically neighbours and I asked him again to let me ring him an ambulance. He finally agreed but his timing turned out to be less than great. As I was on the phone to the emergency services a friend of the assailant showed up, looking menacing. The guy who had been attacked instantly ran away, leaving me alone with a threatening figure who I recognised because he also lived in my building. He kept asking me if I was ringing the police. At the same time, the emergency services lady was asking me what was going on and why I had gone quiet. I ended up answering the scary man, lying by saying I was talking to a friend, and using the scary man's name as frequently as pos-sible for the benefit of the lady on the other end of the phone because she knew the cops. Once he'd gone I explained to her what had happened and she told me that I'd done the right thing by phoning 999 tonight. I said it didn't feel like the right thing. What it felt like I had done was snitch on a group of lads in my building who stab people, they know where I live, and one of them just witnessed me ringing the police. There was a pause and then she said, 'Well . . . you've done the right thing for somebody else anyway.'

•

Jason Anthony Harris's father left when he was four, his mother and older half-brother looked after him, they lived in a trailer next to a forest and his mother sold drugs. When Jason was nine, his brother's 17-year-old friend moved in with the family after getting kicked out of his parents' house, then over time he and Jason's mother became a couple and got married. Later on, Jason's father returned and he had married someone who owned a Christmas tree farm, so Jason moved in with him for a few years. There was plenty of chaos and fighting in both households, which led to a lot of anxiety and anger for Jason, who now lives a pretty quiet, regimented life and prefers stability and routine, eating the same thing for breakfast every morning and hanging out with his cat.

Jason moved to New York in 2004. After a few bands failed he began to perform solo under the name **Public Speaking**, starting out as just vocals and guitar before adding some drum beats on a loop pedal then more fx, more loop pedals, then finally replacing the guitar with keyboard and electronically processing the vocals. But he soon found issue with his own methods. The problem with loop pedals was that the music all starts to take on the same form, that of accumulation: layering sound upon sound over the course of a piece so that it gets denser and denser until it ends. Then, in 2016, Jason released *Caress, Redact*, an album that saw him making an effort to start *taking away* chunks of sound, to remove bars or frequency ranges from pieces, working by subtraction instead of addition. He felt there was a sort of violence in this, creating something and then taking things away, shifting them around, reorienting them, removing them and calling them back again, and this theme of violence inhabited the lyrics on the album also.

The opening track, 'Blacksite Blues', is based on a Guantanamo detainee's prison memoir, and 'I Turn Over His Body' tells the story of Magomed Abdusalamov, the tragically brain-damaged and paralysed boxer. The lyrical content on the album is often about issues uncomfortable to look at: child brides, domestic abuse, rape and mutilation, and this makes for a relentlessly intense listen. Jason's connection to this violence is his childhood. He grew up around near-constantly fighting adults. Things were thrown around and destroyed, and sometimes it escalated to physical confrontation. His own father only exploded at him once – attacking him with his belt, knocking him over and beating him with abandon – but he always felt the threat was there, just under the surface. His stepfather was abusive towards his mother, and she had to intervene to save Jason from his wrath several times. So these experiences plus an angry bully of an older brother made him tune into violence and fear pretty acutely. There was also a great deal of violence running through 2016 that affected the album (particularly the election of a presidential candidate who advocated violence at his rallies and talked of reviving torture). The horrendous mass shooting at Pulse, a nightclub in Orlando, was something Jason found deeply distressing. It took place in central Florida, a few hours away from where he grew up, and affected a community that he's still technically connected to. Jason himself is bisexual, and spent his life hiding it from his family, his father in particular. The song 'Shifting Weight' sees Jason starting to be public about his status with its chorus, 'my son is not a f****t', but when the Pulse massacre happened this process got fast-tracked. Jason went online and publicly wrote a statement about his bisexuality and the luxury that he has passing for straight. How he's a masculine man in a long-term relationship with a woman, and therefore doesn't have to fear for himself, acknowledging that too many people live in fear every single day and still live their lives with bravery and necessity – even in conservative, rural Florida. He was heartbroken at the murders and it felt like a small thing for him to finally just be open and honest about himself in a public forum.

With *Caress, Redact*, Harris wanted the listener to connect with feelings of powerlessness, fear, despair and defiance, and to recognise the victim or perhaps the culprit within themselves. He still acknowledges a violent anger inside him that he's not given in to since he was young and it eats away at him daily, bringing with it depression and anxiety. He medicates now, which helps, as does making music, plus he attends therapy and has a supportive partner, but he still feels like it never truly goes away. It's always with him somewhere inside and it's painful when he sees it in others.

•

The day after witnessing a disturbing knife attack I was started on by a football fan. England had defeated Lithuania 2-0 in the first round of World Cup qualifiers, so testosterone was at an all-time high. Shortly after the full-time whistle blew I made the mistake of walking into Victoria train station in London (capital of England, home of the England football team). The first thing I noticed upon entering the station was an England fan walking from one far corner all the way across to the opposite corner (Victoria station is pretty big). He was red-faced and sweaty, sunglasses on, England shirt clinging to his paunch, staring dead ahead and striding forward, arms out-stretched to his left and right, flipping everyone the bird with both hands. He was deliberately walking into as many people as he could, barging them out of the way as he celebrated an England victory the only way he knew how – by stomping through a train station in the nation's capital and being abusive to everyone around him in as many ways as he could think of. I was walking towards the entrance to the Tube, rummaging through my bag looking for my debit card – I looked up and saw he was headed straight for me. My elbow was jutting out as I went through my bag and it occurred to me that if I remained how I was, with my elbow jutting out, then I wasn't doing anything wrong and if he chooses to walk into my elbow then it's very much up to him. He walked into me as hard as he could. I'd already tensed my arm up in preparation for impact and, I'll admit, when his ribs connected with my elbow I did put a little bit behind it – in short, I doofed him square in the ribs. I'm not proud of that but, also, I've never been more proud of anything in my entire life. He rebounded off of me. I didn't see what happened to him but I like to imagine he still had his arms outstretched and spun round the train station like a dandelion seed, strangers blowing on him as he passed in an attempt to make a wish, perhaps wishing for an end to football, who's to say. I naively thought that was the end of that and continued towards the Tube station assuming I'd won the fight and was officially the best. I heard him before I saw him. He turned round and started screaming at me, 'Fuck you, you fucking Polish cunt, fuck off back to Poland, you piece of shit fucking Polish piece of shit cunt!' I hate England so much. I was scared when he started shouting at me, I was so scared that 'fucking off to Poland' actually seemed rather appealing.

He circled round and started shouting more xenophobia in my face so I replied in the most English voice I've ever spoken in. 'Whatever do you mean?' I queried with the voice of an Etonian prefect. When he heard my English accent he was absolutely stunned: 'WHAT?! YOU'RE ENGLISH?! WHY'D YOU WALK INTO ME?! AREN'T YOU A PATRIOT?! WE WON THE FOOTBALL TODAY!!!!!' Oh yes, I'm sorry, if I was a true patriot I would've been walking through one of London's main rail stations, smashing my body into strangers while holding both middle fingers high in the air, and when you and I crossed paths we could've linked our extended middle fingers and spun round in a traditional maypole dance while somebody filmed it before emailing the footage to her Majesty herself and cc-ing in Nigel Farage. Obviously I didn't say that, I just kept on walking until he eventually gave up. Flight over fight every time.

•

This Taco Is Not Correct by **Christian Fitness** (the solo project of Future of the Left's Andrew Falkous) paints an ugly picture of modern-day Britain, highlighting the aggressive nationalism and xenophobia-disguised-as-patriotism that still thrives in mainstream society. The first track, 'Donald Got A Train', opens with a sample of right-wing English radio host Jon Gaunt saying, 'Yeah, and as I say, have you seen the way flies congregate around a corpse', with a great deal of disgust and hatred in his voice, drawing out the end of the word 'flies' for a weird amount of time and rolling the 'gr' sound in 'congre-gate' like he's some Victorian lord. He sounds ludicrous but scary at the same time and this sets the tone for the rest of the album. On the second track, 'Happiness is Not for Amateurs',

Falkous recounts the time he stuck up for a Chinese family on a train because they were getting verbally abused by a racist passenger, and 'it went wrong'. The full story behind these lyrics involves him assertively telling a couple of kids to stop harassing the family and the kids' parents aggressively telling him to fuck off and sit back down. The song then describes the rest of the journey where Falkous feels 'like a cunt' and hopes that the Chinese family's lack of English meant they didn't fully understand what had just happened. But he could tell by the looks on their faces that they knew England was 'a nation of bastards' and they did not belong here. The song sums up what depresses me about my own country: the racism, the aggression and overall lack of tolerance or acceptance, and yet he manages to recall the event comically, the laughs being totally at the expense of himself and how his good intentions didn't help anyone – they just somehow made him feel worse. *This Taco is Not Correct* was released in September 2016.

Better Use of Leisure Time

Obviously, during my week of surprise confrontations I would often scuttle back home and download music from 2016 in order to cope with the unprecedented levels of adrenaline now raging through my system. By now I was regularly visiting a website called **Bandcamp.** If you think you've fallen out of the loop with current music then Bandcamp is an excellent way of plugging yourself back in at the ground floor. It's a place where bands can upload and sell their albums with or without a record deal, it's easy to navigate, and I know I sound like an advert right now but that's how much I love this website – it makes me talk like I'm in an infomercial. It's not a perfect model, there are some artists who have issues with it, but it's a music store run by people who are still enthusiastic about music and actively engage with it.

The Bandcamp homepage offers a range of daily articles introducing you to obscure music scenes around the world, little-known genres, underground record labels, artists who often get overlooked – it's a music obsessive's playground, and once I started utilising it, the number of 2016 albums in my collection multiplied significantly. I would disappear down a Bandcamp wormhole most evenings. I'd open whatever article was on the front page (e.g. 'A Guide to Helsinki's Experimental Gamelan Scene'), go to the Bandcamp pages of every band in that article, listen to any 2016 releases by said bands, buy the ones I liked, then go to the bottom of the album's page, where there'd be a load more recommendations ('if you like this then you might also like . . .'), click on the ones that looked appealing and so on and so on for ever. Out in the real world strangers were starting fights with me but online I was part of a community where everyone shared stuff and supported each other.

Bandcamp was a really efficient way of unearthing hidden gems and there are some albums (now my favourite albums of all time) that I never would've discovered were it not for this site, some of which are available exclusively on Bandcamp and most of which are cheaper on Bandcamp than they are anywhere else. **J Thoubbs**, a teenager who turned his parents' basement in New Jersey into a home studio, puts out roughly 14 albums on Bandcamp a year and, at the time of writing, has self-released over 60 albums on the site. He uploaded *Unreleasable Material* (an album that saw him discard his alternative-rock sound and make a pop record) in 2016, and when I downloaded it in 2017 I was one of only eight people to have done so, making it the most obscure project that I became a fan of during this entire experiment. It genuinely stresses me out when I think about how easy it would've been to never visit Bandcamp and therefore never stumble across so much good music or even be aware of its existence. I've actually just upset myself a little bit imagining a world where that's the case.

•

After attending rock camp at the Institute for the Musical Arts aged 12, Deja Carr formed a funk band called Who'da Funk It. The group lasted five years but Carr learnt a great deal from the experience: growing as an artist, exploring different genres and developing her skill set – she emerged from the group a fully formed, accomplished musician with her own voice at just 17 years old. After WFI disbanded, Deja (now living in Northampton, Massachusetts) assumed the moniker **Mal Devisa** and embarked on her first solo project. After a couple of independent releases on Bandcamp she'd accrued enough fans to finance her next album on Kickstarter, quickly rewarding donors with the sort of compelling listen that doesn't come around very often. Many of her new tracks were stripped down to bass chords and vocals, with the occasional kick drum thrown in to anchor everything, and Carr's voice conveying so much wisdom it's almost impossible to believe she's just 19 years old. You can hear the spirit of Nina Simone in these songs, someone Carr repeatedly refers to as her number one influence, but the album as a whole pulls from her entire record collection with traces of punk and folk, plus entire rap tracks where her voice adopts an abrasive quality and she assumes a more mutinous persona. But this transition never feels clunky or out of place – we always knew this character was there, even when singing a forlorn, reflective number there's a resilience to her voice and at no point does she sound defeated. The song that drew me in on first listen was the second track, 'In My Neighbourhood', where Carr seems to find a middle ground between her own vocal styles. Retaining the heart of reverberating ballads like 'Everybody Knows' and the all-out defiance of tracks like 'FAT' and 'Dominatrix', her vocals powerfully soar over a stomping bass drum and a dirty synth line that wouldn't sound out of place on a Marilyn Manson record. Albums like this are the reason I got so excited about one year in music, and I know I could say that about any album in this book as I've only delved into albums I truly loved, but when I listen to this Mal Devisa record it makes me want to re-listen to every 2016 album and make everyone else listen to them as well because I can't believe an album this immaculate isn't in everyone's record collection. *Kiid* was released exclusively on Bandcamp in March 2016.

•

Manuel Gagneux was born and raised in Switzerland and moved to New York in 2012, performing chamber pop under the name Birdmask. Back then, he would regularly visit the website 4Chan and post tracks on the music board anonymously. The people on 4Chan were blunt and brutal so this became a good way of gauging exactly what people thought of his music. He decided to take things a step further and started asking the 4Chan users for compositional suggestions. He'd ask them to request genres, new areas for him to explore, and then he'd write a new song combining two of their requests. There was a day when the following two genres were suggested to him; one was 'black metal' and the other was 'n***** music'. I don't know if the people suggesting genres knew that Gagneux was mixed race and I don't know what race the people who suggested the genres were, but those two suggestions intrigued Manuel (who'd grown accustomed to dumb and offensive comments from 4Chan users by this point). With these two starting points, Gagneux began to compose a new album and ended up producing something truly unique. This is the sound of a musician discovering something, unearthing new possibilities and properly experimenting without any clue as to whether there's an audience for it. But this figure-it-out-as-you-go-along approach also produced an album with confusing and potentially problematic themes, causing Gagneux to be accused of cultural appropriation from both sides.

Obviously some interpretation was required for the latter of the two 4Chan suggestions, and Manuel chose to interpret it as 'African-American spirituals', specifically the sort of spirituals sung by slaves in 18th-/19th-century America. Manuel took black metal, which is typically Satanic in nature, and loaded it with blues and gospel, with occasional hip hop beats and melodic electro thrown in. The only connection between spirituals and black metal as far as Gagneux was concerned was that both the Norwegians and the slaves in America had had Christianity 'forced upon them' and he wanted the concept of the album to be 'what would've happened if the slaves in America embraced Satan instead of Jesus and rose up against their oppressors'. What you end up with is some self-composed 'spirituals' with some pretty Satanic lyrics. It's easy to see why this approach would upset fans of spiritual music, but it's worth noting that the black-metal community don't usually respond well to people messing with the standard formula and taking it away from pure black metal – Gagneux knew he was going to piss them off and was happy to do so, especially when it came to fans of a racist subgenre known as National Socialist black metal. He recorded the album himself, playing all the instruments, and wanted the project to have a spiritual-sounding name so called it **Zeal & Ardor**. He self-released the nine-track album *Devil is Fine* in April 2016 on Bandcamp only. The front cover of the album features the sigil of Lucifer over an image of Robert Smalls, a man who freed himself and others from slavery in 1862 by commandeering a ship and went on to become a politician.

The response was huge, with a neverending stream of new fans rushing to the page to download the album or order a physical copy (which sold out in no time). Gagneux didn't even promote the album; he was an unsigned, unknown artist (save for the few who knew him from Birdmask), and by word of mouth alone this record completely blew up because it didn't sound like anything that'd come before it. Manuel got a record deal due to the success of the album, and *Devil is Fine* was temporarily pulled from Bandcamp and re-released in March 2017, meaning that some people (Ed Gamble) try and get away with claiming it as a 2017 record, but those people are only lying to themselves.

•

I could go on for a long time about the albums I discovered on Bandcamp. It was a goddamn treasure trove, and many of the projects I talk about elsewhere in this book I found in its bountiful pages. I should add that I was already familiar with Bandcamp before this ridiculous challenge even began. A year before I started exclusively buying music from 2016 (so that's *during the actual year 2016*) I had recorded some music of my own and needed a home for it online. I wanted to upload the album somewhere where people could listen to it easily, and the main site everyone recommended was Bandcamp. Oh, and don't go thinking I'm glossing over anything, you're 100 per cent right about what I just said – I released an album in 2016. Me. I contributed to THE GREATEST YEAR FOR MUSIC OF ALL TIME.

Luna Dott Raids the Bee Pigeon

One of the best things about being in a band growing up was getting to watch other local bands on the circuit. At the time, the Kettering and Northampton music scene was abuzz with talent and no two bands sounded alike, the range was so diverse that I never got bored watching the other musicians on the bill. The local bands I most commonly gigged with were:

Luna Sprout

An indie folk duo consisting of Simon Fox and Quincy Mae Brown. Guitar, harp and gorgeous vocal harmonies. Simon also did a bunch of solo gigs under his own name, which were more Radiohead-y.

MottDott

Tom Fox (Simon Fox's brother) used to make Aphex Twin-y-type stuff on his computer. Big 8-bit influence to most of the songs and cheese-filled hooks that I still find myself humming to this day.

TMart & The Raiders

A blues punk band that formed at the regular Tuesday jam nights at the Poppies Social Club. Joe and Luke Palmer were brothers and freakishly good musicians. TMart was the nickname of the guitarist Martin Patrick, whose dad ran a music shop in town called Patrick Reed. I used to go to the shop with my mates and try out all the instruments without buying anything most weekends.

Bee

A solo acoustic folk singer, more traditional than Luna Sprout, she had a beguiling voice and a sadness to her songs that the rest of us found hard to attain. She was also the lead singer of The Capri Sun Quartet and went by the alias Jacqueline Orange.

Tiny Pigeon

My friend Jake Ashton taught himself to play the acoustic guitar while stoned, so played chords using only one or two fingers, and every song was written in a tuning he made up himself. He wrote loads of instrumental songs and friends would come over and play along on guitar or pots and pans. And, yes, of course I was one of the people who would come over and play the pots and pans.

I was a proper fan of all of these bands, so I bought their demo CDs after gigs (or they gave me their demo for free if they were REAL FRIENDS). Almost all of the local bands I grew up with have split up now, but I still listen to their demos on my iPod. One day, on a train, I was listening to Luna Sprout and escaped into a fantasy where I was in a rock band doing a grunge cover of one of their folk songs. I think I imagined myself playing the drums in front of a crowd of adoring fans all losing their minds at how cool I was. The fantasy then escalated. I imagined making an entire album where I took songs by local Kettering bands from the early 2000s and turned them into grunge numbers. I scrolled through my iPod finding my favourite songs from back in the day, and by the end of the train journey I'd accumulated ten songs by several defunct bands. The fantasy then escalated again, by some distance, because I decided to actually do it. I decided to make a Kettering covers album.

•

At 74 years of age **John Cale** remains as experimental and innovative as ever. One of the founding members of The Velvet Underground, Cale released the cult classic *Music for a New Society* in 1982 – a solo album like nothing he'd done before. Exploring themes of regret and misplaced faith while focusing on a distinctive cast of characters, it's an album he has since described as 'agony to perform'. In 2013 Cale began to record *M:FANS*; a new reimagined version of *Music for a New Society*, essentially covering his own album, transforming the tracks entirely so they were almost unrecognisable. Once again he did not enjoy the process. Revisiting these songs seemed to be opening old wounds, a feeling only made worse when, during the recording sessions, his ex-bandmate Lou Reed passed away. Cale had always had a complicated but close relationship with

Reed, and upon hearing of his death scrapped the work he'd done on *M:FANS* and started again, allowing the anger he now felt to dictate the music. The end result is an aggressive and dark-sounding record that barely resembles the original as Cale confronts his present by demolishing his past. *M:FANS* was released in January 2016 as an accompaniment to a remastered version of *Music for a New Society*, and I think for that reason was largely ignored as an album in its own right, getting lazily written off as a mere bonus disc. Luckily, I got weirdly obsessed with one year in music so I've listened to it loads.

•

Once I'd got everyone's permission to cover their music, I had to put a band together. Simon, Quincy and Bee agreed to sing on the album, and I asked Rob Deering to help me turn their songs into grunge songs. Rob Deering is a wonderful comedian who I was a fan of even before I started doing stand-up myself. He plays guitar in his act and can work out, on the spot, any song the audience shout at him. So not only could Rob listen to these old demos and immediately work the songs out, but he'd also be able to translate them into grunge songs because he was used to parodying entire genres in his stand-up. Next, I got Will Collier (of Alex Horne's backing band, The Horne Section) to play bass. Will is a session musician and plays jazz all the time, so learning a bunch of grunge songs was hardly a challenge for him and he recorded all of his parts in under an hour (what a tough guy). Then finally I got producer Chris Hamilton (of the legendary Wow! Scenario album) to record everything and the team was complete. Also, I played the drums.

I was so rusty and it took me ages to get each song right but I did play the drums. I hadn't played drums since 2007, when we recorded the Wow! Scenario album; I hadn't even played the pots and pans during those nine years, and over time my confidence had completely evaporated. While recording my parts on this album I was a nervous shadow of my former self. Every time I had to do a drum fill I panicked like I'd just been pushed out of a window. I used to *teach* the drums for crying out loud and now I couldn't even handle the basics. Fortunately, everyone was very patient with me and I played each song correctly once – which is all you need when recording an album.

We finished covering the forgotten songs of the Kettering music scene in just over a fortnight. The band and the album were called **Luna Dott Raids the Bee Pigeon** because I couldn't think of a new band name, so just put everyone's old names together. It's a pay-what-you-want album with proceeds going to Kettering Youth Works, a charity working with young people in Kettering (you probably could've worked that out from their name) and located in the same group of buildings we used to have our band practices in as teenagers. I also got Kettering comic book artist Ben Foot to design the album cover, resurrecting an old character of his named Sparkly Sparkly Chew, a living gummy sweet man who worked for a pig in an office and lived with a sarcastic bird.

We should probably address something at this point. Far be it from me to point out any subtext in this book, but I just want to let you know that I am fully aware that I have a tendency to live in/cling to/refuse to let go of the past. For starters, I rounded up a load of friends from back in the day to re-create songs from our youth and put them all on an album that may as well have been called *Reminiscing to the Max with James Acaster*. Also, for years I only listened to music made before I was even born, and when I finally did decide to re-engage with current music, my chosen method of doing so was to delve into albums released the *previous* year. I essentially chose to go nostalgia-lite. And it doesn't take a psychologist to figure out why either – I was having a rough year, so I put myself in a different year. Sure, I wanted to get into modern music, but I hated my own modern life so rolled everything back a touch, affording myself some of that blissful ignorance everyone goes on about. Also, you get a really good idea of how adept I am at looking back with rose-tinted glasses when the year I chose to take myself back to was 2016. I looked back fondly on the year that most people declared to be the worst in their lifetime and regarded it as a positive utopia.

Everything about that Luna Dott album came from my own sentimentality. The reason I chose grunge was because I wanted to be in a grunge band when I was 13 but never got to be in a grunge band, so decided to fulfil a childhood dream at 31 and roped in other adults to help me do it. I essentially just thought of an album I wanted to listen to and then I made my friends record it for me. But, let's not forget, when all is said and done – I contributed to the greatest year for music of all time. I self-released a covers album of songs written by bands from the local Kettering music scene in the early 2000s, reworked them as grunge tracks, got some of the original singers back to sing on them and released the whole thing on Bandcamp in 2016, the greatest year for music of all time. NO ONE CAN EVER TAKE THAT AWAY FROM ME.

•

Raucous Rotterdam quartet **Rats On Rafts** formed when they were all 16. They had only just learnt their instruments and named themselves after a lyric in a Mudhoney song. They were all big fans of Dutch brass punk band **De Kift,** a group that'd been together since the 80s and worked elements of Eastern European and classical music into their albums, always singing exclusively in Dutch. In 2013 Rats On Rafts guitarist and lead vocalist David Fagan attended De Kift's 25th anniversary tour; the show felt really special with the band playing two of their earlier albums in full. Fagan spoke enthusiastically and publicly about the show afterwards, prompting De Kift's management to ask if Rats On Rafts would be interested in performing at a festival De Kift were curating to mark their 25th birthday. Around the same time, another offer came in, to perform at Rotterdam's Metropolis Festival. Coincidentally this would also be a 25th anniversary show (this time for the festival itself). The band accepted both gigs. Every member of Rats On Rafts was 25 years old at the time. They wanted to do something special for the Metropolis show, and since De Kift were the same age as the festival but not yet involved, Fagan thought it would be a fun experiment to invite the band to accompany them on stage, creating the ultimate 25th birthday party. But the performance was plagued with technical issues: the switchover between acts had been too short and they didn't have time to soundcheck thoroughly, so the sound quality was terrible. This was especially disappointing as the songs had been sounding so good in practice. Both bands had clicked immediately: they'd learnt each other's songs and transformed them – the De Kift songs became far noisier and the ROR songs gained a whole new dimension with the addition of a brass band. They didn't want this collaboration to fizzle out with nothing to show for it so decided to record an album together. The album sees both groups refuse to meet each other halfway, and rather than adjusting to the other's sound they just play what comes naturally to them on any given song. So they both pulled in opposite directions and yet still managed to progress forward. Half the songs on the record were originally by ROR and half by De Kift, and all had previously existed in some form elsewhere. All of the Rats songs are in English while all of the De Kift songs remain in Dutch, and on the occasions when they tried to combine songs – for instance, the track 'Sleep Little Links 2 3 4', which is a mashup between one Rats song and two De Kift songs – the title becomes a mixture of the two languages. The project became an experiment in what happens when two worlds collide instead of working together. The album's cover features an illustration of a giant wild rat being descended upon by a team of mata-dors, the rat an untamed force of energy rampaging through the stadium and the matadors trying to harness it as best they can. *Rats On Rafts / De Kift* was released in October 2016.

•

While touring her album *Tookah* in 2013, Icelandic singer **Emilíana Torrini** found herself feeling detached. On stage she would start thinking about washing her sweater instead of connecting with the audience and sang her songs on autopilot. She needed to feel connected again and wanted something new. Not knowing where to start, she decided to throw it out into the universe and almost immediately got a call from a composer in Berlin who wanted to rework her music with a string quintet. A few months later, she showed up in Berlin, but instead of a string quintet she was met with an experimental jazz band as the composer had not found the time after all. Torrini found this funny and went with it anyway, deciding that this was how she wanted to work from now on – just saying yes to anyone who wanted to play with her. But she had some basic rules;

1. They chose which songs of hers they wanted to play and put together the setlist.

2. They were free to do what they wanted with the music no matter what.

3. If it was terrible and the gig was a mess she had to be gracious, keep going and have a sense of humour about it.

She got many calls and toured like this with different strangers for three years, performing in venues, living rooms and the outdoors. One of her favourite phases during this time was touring with a travelling band in Córdoba, sleeping under the stars and playing all night, keeping up with them in every way and feeling part of a gang.

One of the groups that contacted her during this period was the Belgian pop and chamber orchestra **The Colorist**. They wanted to rework a selection of Torrini's songs, so, as usual, she told them to go for it, they could do whatever they wanted, and she would turn up and sing. But she didn't realise the extent of the work they were doing: she never listened to anything they sent her and told them she trusted them when in reality she didn't really care. When Emilíana showed up in Belgium for a three-day rehearsal she was totally unprepared and didn't recognise her own songs when The Colorist played their interpretations for her. She had to take a moment and acknowledge to herself that this little orchestra with home-made instruments had composed unrecognisable and magical versions of her work and here she was, blowing it immediately. She had to snap out of it, focus and make sure she didn't let these people down.

Emilíana Torrini and The Colorist played five gigs together in Belgium and recorded all of them. These live recordings made up the self-titled album *The Colorist & Emilíana Torrini*, which was released on 9 December 2016. The album includes one brand-new song that the group wrote together, 'When We Dance', named after something Torrini's five-year-old son said to her one morning ('When we dance together our mind shines'). The song was recorded in a little farmhouse in the Belgian countryside during a lightning storm. The electricity could be felt in the humid air, arm hairs were standing on end, and the bangs and flashes from outside became unnerving for the musicians within. In Iceland the word hysteria means, 'mother's illness', so Torrini saw the storm as a mother's turmoil and melancholia in the middle of the love and wild adventure of having a child.

Duo

I enjoyed making the Luna Dott Raids the Bee Pigeon album so much that it made me want to resume work on the Wow! Scenario album from 2007, because, while I was still proud of it, there were some things I wanted to change. I cannot sing for love nor money, and while Graeme sang way better than I did, he still had my galumphing tones dragging him down the whole time. I contacted Graeme (AKA Ross Current Event) to see if he felt the same way about the vocals, and in no time at all we'd agreed to replace our voices with clarinet, saxophone, cello and violin. We also agreed to record these additional instruments in January the following year (2018), ten years and one month after we'd recorded the album in the first place. Credit where it's due – Graeme has been on the same page as me since day one and I am not complaining. Finding such a person is rare and you've both got to run with these things and generate as much output as possible while you've still got the chance. If you've got a similar person in your life, get them on the phone right now, describe your dream vanity project to them in great detail and then say, in a voice usually reserved for movie trailer voiceovers, 'Are you in?' Then hang up before they get the chance to answer.

•

Kentucky-born cellist and political activist **Ben Sollee** made a name for himself demonstrating how much can be done with the cello beyond what we're used to hearing in classical music, and in 2016 he released *Infowars*, a collaboration with renowned drummer **Jordan Ellis**. Although the two had performed live together frequently over the years, this would be the first time they sat down in a studio and attempted to capture their kinship on an album. A record that centres on the relationship between a drummer and a cellist is rare, especially when both musicians are exploring the language of their instruments as much as Sollee and Ellis do here. To begin with they found the studio environment to be sterile, lifeless and uninspiring, so they listened to their live shows on headphones and recorded themselves playing along to these in order to match the energy they usually tap into when performing live. The album then got fleshed out with field recordings, samples and Sollee's vocals, as well as some unexpected guest spots from artist/musician Lonnie Holley and Alabama sculptor Joe Minter. One of my favourite albums of all time is *Flood* by They Might Be Giants, a 19-track experimental folk/pop record where each song show-cases a different side of the band's personality. *Infowars* is the closest I've found to *Flood* in years. As well as both being mammoth records full of variety that experiment with folk and country while demonstrating the musicians' technical abilities, they also incorporate a sense of humour into their songs while alluding to darker subject matter along the way. In addition to all this, *Infowars* has a personal side, with Sollee often singing about how his hometown in Kentucky is a part of his identity, as well as covering the social and political issues he's passionate about. But, all in all, this project is about the relationship between two musicians and it's these performances that lift you every time – you're always aware that you're hearing two people completely in tune with each other, revelling in the moment and documenting their shared connection.

•

David Tibet of Current 93 and Youth of Killing Joke joined forces for the first time in 23 years on one of the most peculiar and idiosyncratic releases of 2016. *Create Christ, Sailor Boy* is the sole record by **Hypnopazūzu**. It's a spooky and eccentric operatic indie album, or, as the duo themselves have described it, 'the ultimate Hallucinatory PickNick'. Tibet's vocal performance is that of an insane prophet high on bath salts wailing barmy parables from atop a mountain of garbage at the foot of a melting cartoon rainbow, while Youth's instrumentals are grand, theatrical and foreboding, painting in the scenery around Tibet's unhinged evangelist. The band's name is derived from a combination of three words; Hypnagogia (the transitional state between wakefulness and sleep where lucid dreaming and paralysis occur), Hypnos (the personification of Sleep according to Greek mythology) and Pazūzu (King of the Wind Demons according to the ancient Mesopotamian religion). Characters from Greek mythology and ancient religions are totally at home in the universe Hypnopazūzu have created, as are the plethora of characters, settings and general odd stuff referenced in the song titles. Pinocchio, Christmas, maypoles and the Skittle Hills all comfortably take up residence in this kitsch wasteland, a place where fiction and non-fiction coexist and a hodge-podge of traditions can thrive. Youth wanted to name the album after the opening song's opening line, 'Create Christ, Sailor Boy' – a line delivered dramatically by Tibet, who announces it as if he's literally freeing a rabid sailor from a pet carrying cage into the desert, the sailor galloping away on all fours with tattered clothes as the anarchist who unleashed him watches the dust clouds disappear into the distance. It's an album with zero diversions – you're locked inside the asylum for the duration – but it's an intoxicating wonderland to get lost in, and the performances these two artistic veterans draw out of each other are pretty magical. *Create Christ, Sailor Boy* was released in August 2016.

We Were Trying Not to Disturb You

As April 2017 came to a close, I was still having counselling sessions once a week and they were going well. My counsellor was empathetic and insightful and made me feel heard and understood. As well as not being over my breakup, I was finding my relationship with my agent increasingly stressful, so I told her about that, as well as talking about all the albums I'd been buying and how they'd been helping me de-stress. One subject that came up a lot was how I'd kept everything inside over the years, how I didn't always address my problems with others, so they'd bubble to the surface and erupt out of nowhere. I hadn't noticed that about myself until attending counselling. The lifestyle of a comedian is a weirdly solitary one: travelling around on your own, performing alone on stage, then returning to your hotel alone to buy an unusual amount of albums from the previous year until you fall asleep and wake up alone the following morning. It means that you don't express how you're feeling on a regular basis, you rarely get the opportunity to unload, so everything piles up over time. So now, in order to improve, I had to learn to articulate my problems to others, even if those problems were to do with them. This didn't and still doesn't come naturally to me, but I agreed it was important to try.

•

Foonyap grew up in Calgary at the base of the Rocky Mountains. She had what she refers to as a 'typically intense Asian upbringing': it was very sheltered, and on top of this her parents were also strict Catholics. She was expected to excel in everything she did at any cost, and one of the things her parents wanted her to excel in was classical violin. They wanted her to master an instrument in order to learn discipline, and she was absolutely not allowed to quit – especially when it became apparent that Foonyap (despite not enjoying violin lessons) was extremely gifted. The environment of classical music was highly competitive and very stressful for her, plus the systems she grew up in didn't offer much room for personal expression, especially for young women. If you're not taught to express your emotions properly, then they may manifest themselves in other harmful ways, and for Foonyap this meant regularly defying her parents and arguing with them. She also silently suffered from periods of depression and developed an eating disorder, forcing her to drop out of high school. Looking back, she grew up regularly feeling out of place and ashamed.

Foonyap didn't even buy an album for herself until she was 16 – it was Björk's *Vespertine* and it changed her perspective of what music could be. Years later, when she was out partying and very drunk at a club called Broken City in Calgary, Foonyap sat on a table with four strangers and just happened to have her violin on her after jamming with her boyfriend earlier that evening. The guys noticed the violin and told her that their friend needed a violinist for his album release party, and within the week she had met Mark Hamilton of Woodpigeon, who would later become her mentor. She had never gone to shows before, had never toured in a band and hadn't ever considered that music could be an avenue for self-expression instead of the competitive sport she'd always known it as. Woodpigeon introduced her to a new world of possibility, and in 2009 Foonyap started an art punk project called Foonyap and The Roar that took over her life. The idea was to create a vampire sex metal disco. She was joined onstage by three giant hairy men and Foonyap would smear fake blood all over her face, push the audience around and scream at them as a tongue-in-cheek way of expressing some aggressive sexual feelings she was having at that time. She now admits it's possible the band was a result of her not knowing how to vocalise her anger, so she interpreted it theatrically in a safe environment on stage.

In 2011, Foonyap got very sick due to being overworked and not taking care of herself. She wanted to confront why she'd done this and concluded it was because she'd never believed she was good enough. It all came back to these deep-seated feelings of shame as a child that she never fully acknowledged and now they'd manifested themselves in a physical illness. She took a long time to heal physically and emotionally, and didn't perform live for five years. She was still productive, though, and spent this time recording in her intimate home studio, doing a lot of personal growth and working an office job as a professional fundraiser. During the recording, Foonyap was thinking a lot about healing the relationship with her family and healing the relationship with herself. She was having a lot of painful conversations, talking to her mother openly about her upbringing, having to explain that things her mother had said 15 years ago had really hurt her, and talking for the first time about her depression as a teenager. It was difficult for both of them to accept that, while they'd done their best over the years, their relationship had still ended up being incredibly challenging. Foonyap also began to realise that many of her relationships were dishonest because she was dishonest with herself and didn't think she deserved happiness due to this dishonesty. She didn't feel like she deserved certain things, so never asked for them, and therefore people never gave them to her. She realised that she'd grown up in a household where if something bothered you, you stayed quiet – and then later on you'd explode and yell. It was a very stressful household to be in, so Foonyap often tried to protect her family's feelings by not telling them when anything was wrong. As she grew up, Foonyap started to notice a similar pattern in her personal relationships – if she was bothered by someone it was easier for her to pretend it didn't happen, rather than talk it out.

It's impossible to not hear all of this in the music she was writing at the time. A lot of the songs she was working on are so quiet they verge on silence and then suddenly erupt, the dynamics shifting dramatically, before abruptly returning to a whisper. Such moments are also inspired by mindfulness techniques, Zen Buddhism and yoga. Foonyap had heard about a moment during meditation when you think nothing is happening, but if you continue to practise, one day something will suddenly occur and you know you're in the right place at the right time or you realise exactly what you want. The silence on the record comes from the meditation she'd been practising and the space that she'd started to create in her life. She had finally learnt how to do one thing at a time, and to experience things with focused energy instead of a reactive, egotistical unconsciousness. The record is also about the tension of growing up Queer in Canada. For Foonyap, Queer means having an openness and awareness of gender norms and the ability to choose which parts suit you and which parts don't. She'd always been like that as a child, she was a 'tomboy' growing up and had been given a hard time for it. So many feminist themes present themselves in her writing because it had always been so difficult to be a woman in her situation and culture. The album was released in October 2016, and was entitled *Palimpsest*.

•

Islet consist of Emma Daman, Mark Thomas, John Thomas and Alex Williams. Mark and John are brothers and Emma and Mark are married, but in the lead-up to writing their 2016 EP, the band weren't talking openly with each other very much. This wasn't due to a falling out: people were just going through their own personal challenges, and over time this turned into each individual struggling alone and never sharing their problems. Alex suggested they name the project *Liquid Half Moon* as a way of alluding to semi-darkness, metamorphosing and things being neither here nor there.

Emma was pregnant for the entire writing period, her whole world completely changed, and she felt separate from her bandmates for the first time. It suddenly hit her that she was undergoing a vast, irrevocable, physically altering process, and because of the physical nature of having a small baby she would always inhabit a different world to the men she was in a band with. When she was pregnant, Emma would often play whatever instrument helped her process the way she was feeling best. The band have always done a lot of instrument swapping, and the song 'Slide Out of View' sees Emma playing the drums in an attempt to relax while pregnant. The drums remain the same for the full six and a half minutes because during practice Emma would just sit in this groove and meditate on what was happening to her. These thoughts became the song's lyrics, which are mainly about the certain element of fear you experience when any change occurs in your life and the conflicting emotions you go through at the same time. Emma naturally felt scared, but also very much wanted the child and felt lucky and fortunate that she could have and was having one. She took up lead vocals on the entire EP and many of the songs were sung from her standpoint. On past Islet projects vocal duties had been shared, but *Liquid Half Moon* very much feels like one person's perspective and benefits from having a consistent and focused voice.

While writing the EP, Emma and Mark moved from Cardiff to the Welsh countryside, where Mark grew up, near his parents' farm (the band would end up recording the EP in the farm's sheep shed). Their surroundings were beautiful but also incredibly isolating, and when her son was born the isolation took its toll on Emma who experienced post-natal depression throughout the recording process. It felt so unnatural for a woman to be at home, alone with her child, all the time – she felt like she was meant to be revelling in the joy of it all but she desperately wanted to get out of the house and do things again. On top of her own personal concerns, Emma was worried about her bandmates. John was also in a bad place, and although Emma was definitely depressed she could tell he was struggling too. She started reading about how different cultures deal with depression. In some cultures, instead of using therapy or drugs, they get the whole community together and put on a big public event centred on the individual who needs help. They make lots of music and scare the demons away from you, lift you up, cover you in cockerel blood and then you're cleansed. She wanted to do the same for her brother-in-law, so, as no one was properly talking, she started to write lyrics that she wanted John to hear, saying everything she wished she could say to him in person. She didn't tell him she'd written these lyrics for him, but because John always mixed their records she knew that he'd have to listen to this song over and over, so perhaps hearing these words would give him some positive energy in a way that speaking to him maybe couldn't achieve. The song was called 'Cathays Terrors', and due to the affectionate lyrics everybody assumed it was about Emma's newborn son, so the song felt like a secret message from her to one of her best friends. The lyrics to 'Cathays Terrors' fill the front cover of the record (which Daman designed), concealing a blurred photo of the band, and are written in a font called Moon Phases, which literally turns each letter into a different-shaped moon so the words remain coded.

Liquid Half Moon sounds like a band pinning down their own sound and sounding like no one else. I've always enjoyed Islet's music, but something about this EP clicks and makes sense: the carefully balanced production, the entrancing melodies and the way they rise above everything else, how memorable every song is despite the band's refusal to deliver a traditional chorus – the whole thing feels deliberate and loaded with purpose. Here, the band are making music that makes them feel happy because nothing else was working, and in doing so they've produced something life-affirming with infinite potential.

Sleep Cycle

The period of time in 2017 that saw me buying the *most* music from 2016 was a week in May, spent in New Zealand on my own. After a fortnight at the Melbourne Comedy Festival I popped over to Auckland to do a week-long run at one of my favourite venues, The Basement, with one of my favourite comedy producers, Scott Blanks. I was really excited when I'd put this in the diary the previous year, but since then I'd had a breakup with someone who came from Auckland and now the entire city was sure to remind me of her. Add to that the fact that I always experience a weird sort of jet lag when flying from Melbourne to New Zealand and you're left with a week of being asleep all day and awake all night while constantly thinking about your ex-girlfriend. Oh, and also I was being put up in the same hotel BWTGH and I once stayed in together – in a room that looked identical to the one we'd been given (it may have even been the same room for all I know). Why didn't I change rooms? I don't know. I was too all over the place with jet lag, it was only for a week, and perhaps a part of me felt like I deserved to be unhappy because I was still blaming myself for everything etc. Also, as much as I wanted not to think about her, I still loved her and liked being reminded of her, so the hotel, the hotel room and the entire city had a bittersweet feel to them that I wasn't ready to fully push away just yet. During the first of my sleepless nights in Auckland I decided to buy a new walking-to-the-venue album. I knew I'd be making the same journey to the same venue every day and I needed to put my Maroon 5 days behind me once and for all so I could finally become as cool as Nish Kumar (I can't believe I've called him cool twice in this book now. He will never shut up about it).

•

In 2005, Maciek Lasserre attended Brooklyn's School for Improvisational Music and took some classes led by highly revered jazz saxophonist Steve Lehman. The pair became friends and in 2010 Lasserre introduced Lehman to the world of Senegalese hip hop, a genre that inspired Lasserre's debut album, *Eskisse* (a jazz record featuring Senegalese hip hop duo Da Brains). Lehman was keen to explore the ideas on *Eskisse* further, so asked Lasserre if he'd like to work on a project that blended underground hip hop with modern jazz, proposing they both play saxophone on the record and share compositional duties. Lehman then brought in New York MC HPrizm of the legendary AntiPop Consortium, and Lasserre introduced Steve to Gaston Bandimic, a young Senegalese rapper who raps exclusively in Wolof. The project was given the name Sélébéyone, a

Wolof word that refers to an intersection (because of all the intersecting that was going on), and Andrew Wright, known for his work on Kendrick Lamar's *good kid, m.A.A.d city*, came on board to engineer the album. *Sélébéyone* is a rare record in that it's a jazz-rap album composed by jazz musicians that's actually good. In my opinion, rappers experimenting with jazz usually produce something tremendous, but jazz musicians trying their hand at hip hop can feel like watching your dad do an Ali G impression (the opposite of feeling-cool-while-walking-to-the-venue music). However, when jazz artists get hip hop right, it's transcendental and there's very little that can better it. The frenetic jazz instrumentation on Sélébéyone is astonishing, and while it's clear the project initially grew out of jazz and its sensibilities, this is still authentically a rap album featuring stellar performances from the four key players. *Sélébéyone* was released in August 2016.

•

Each day I would wake up at 6.30 p.m. and walk over the road to my venue while listening to *Sélébéyone* and telling myself I was cool. The show would start at 7 p.m. and finish by 9.30, then I'd get some food and return to my hotel room at 11 p.m., where I would sit awake downloading 2016 music until eight in the morning, when I'd finally fall asleep. I didn't leave my hotel room and walk around Auckland at night because I was too scared, so my waking hours just consisted of me searching for albums that might help me sleep while I stared at the walls, remembering everything I loved about someone who wasn't there any more. Number one on a best Japanese albums of 2016 list was *Mahoroboshiya* by **Ichiko Aoba**, an almost aggressively soothing folk record. The title *Mahoroboshiya* is a combination of two words: 'maboroshi' meaning illusion and 'horoboshi' meaning destruction. This tells you all you need to know about the kind of restful music I like – the kind with a strong sense of unrest running through it at all times. *Strangers* by **Marissa Nadler** also follows this rule – a serene collection of gothic instrumentals with elegant vocal performances telling several fragmented stories of solitude and heartbreak. *Strangers* was coincidentally written under similar conditions to the ones I ended up listening to it in. Throughout 2015, Nadler had the worst writer's block of her career. She was putting a lot of pressure on herself to produce something of value and became isolated in her Boston apartment when trying to write. Not that she had many other options – the touring lifestyle had meant that her social circle had steadily decreased over the years and lately she'd decided to just accept this, for better or worse. In the end, this loneliness and feeling of being lost turned out to be the key to unlocking her creativity, and these states of being became the foundation for the entire project. It was the most attention Nadler had ever devoted to the arrangements of her songs, bringing in world class musicians to layer up these delicate, orchestral backing tracks that provided a consistently eerie tone to the record. A lengthy tour followed the album's release, during which Marissa got over the stage fright that'd been a burden to her her whole career. It's unclear why, but these were the first songs that didn't make her want to flee every time she had to play them in front of an audience.

•

On the day of my first Auckland show I was invited to the venue by the staff to attend a Mihi, a formal Māori welcome. Six of us stood in a circle holding hands, one person led the

Mihi and we all gave thanks for the week we'd be spending together. I was then asked to choose a topic, something personal to me, and we then went round the circle each sharing a memory associated with that topic. I chose mixtapes, so we all spoke about how mixtapes had featured in our lives. At the end we all either hugged or shook hands, I can't remember which because at this point I was just trying to hold everything together. I was carrying a lot of baggage going into this trip and had spent the first five months of 2017 longing to be taken back by someone this entire country now represented. So being made to feel welcome and accepted in a Māori tradition that focuses on human connection meant a great deal to me. I'm incredibly grateful to the people who extended this kindness to me, and you are correct in assuming I went back to the hotel once it was over and cried my eyes out.

I bought a lot of music by New Zealand artists that week, but the NZ project I listened to most was an album called *My New Music* by **Ela & PomPom**. I found each track incredibly relaxing and would try my hardest to fall asleep to it most nights. It was also the only album I found that'd been recorded in Auckland itself, only a short drive from where I was staying.

•

Māpura Studios is a creative space and art therapy centre located in the Auckland suburb of Mt Albert, offering art classes and art therapy programmes for people of all ages living with disability and diversity. In 2015 they launched a new music programme, bringing in local musician Stefan Neville to lead a series of experimental and improvisational classes every Wednesday in an old church hall at Corbens Estate, Henderson. The programme was about immersive engagement with free unstructured music making, aiming to draw from the participants' natural ability and intuition in order to make immediate and spontaneous music. There would be no such thing as wrong notes, no right or wrong way to play an instrument, the motto was 'let's just see what happens'. Equipment-wise, they had a pile of bongo drums, some two- and three-stringed ukuleles, a small Casio keyboard, virtual phone app synthesizers, two microphones and a loop pedal. The sessions were an attempt by Māpura to expand out into new parts of Auckland, but the programme never attracted enough people to sustain it, which meant the three or four regular attendees ended up receiving a lot of quality time and space to really engage with the instruments and develop their own modes and approaches. The attendees were asked to come up with a name for the programme, and a woman named Tara suggested **PomPom**, so these sessions are always referred to as 'the PomPom recordings'.

The only participant who came every week was Ela Tukuhaukava. **Ela** has lived in Auckland for over 40 years, grew up singing in the church and regularly sings along to the radio in order to de-stress. Ela benefited from many PomPom recordings where she was the only one who turned up. She would sometimes play the keyboard and often sit down with the ukulele, using a small battery-powered fan to strum the strings, but mainly chose to sing. She would direct Stefan, asking for certain rhythms or moods to sing to, and then sing a pop hit she had heard on the radio set to his (or the group's) often chaotic backing track rather than the original tune. Whitney Houston, Madonna and Tina Turner were the artists she was listening to most at the time, so Ela would sing soprano versions of 'What's Love Got to Do With It' and 'Crazy for You' over the top of an instrumental performed by Stefan or her fellow classmates. She'd sing as much of the song as she could remember and then improvise the rest, replacing any words that'd slipped her mind with whatever felt right. Ela would also perform her own doo-wop variations, introduce her Tongan culture into sessions with dancing and singing, and include storytelling while on the mic, sometimes autobiographical, sometimes fantasy and fictional.

Stefan recorded every PomPom session. Everything went through a mono four-channel mixer into a single PA speaker and was recorded live as it happened in a reverberant room on a stereo digital recorder. Weekly session highlights were edited down and burnt to CD for participants to enjoy, share and reflect upon. A series of albums were eventually uploaded to Bandcamp, compiled of highlights across many recording sessions, the track-list always shaped by the participants' choices and intentions. *My New Music* by **Ela & PomPom** was released in June 2016.

Strange Country

As the week in New Zealand progressed things got easier. I'm not sure if I can attribute this to the albums I bought, but being in Auckland on my own reminded me that I had my own connection with the city (and the country) that was separate from my relationship with BWTGH. I had visited New Zealand for the first time in 2013 and it instantly meant something to me in a way that's difficult to articulate. It felt both familiar and unknown at the same time, like the kind of place I'd always wanted to be. Walking around Auckland in 2017 brought me back to 2013; I had just come out of a relationship then as well and had found the trip to be exactly what I needed, and now, four years later, it was having the same effect despite the fact it logically should not. I love pretty much everything about New Zealand; I love Whittaker's chocolate (the greatest chocolate in the world), I love L&P (the greatest soft drink in the world), I love everyone's accents, the scenery, the comedians there, the people who run the comedy festival, and I love that I fell in love there. Being in Auckland that week reminded me of everything I loved about BWTGH in a way that made me feel more at peace with things than I had been up until that point. So it was a good trip.

Feeling a connection with a country or a place is special, although it is weird that the country I feel a strong connection with isn't my own. I envy people who do feel strong connections to the country they grew up in, I'd love to feel fondness for where I'm from and pride in its history, but at the moment I just don't.

•

Joana Gomila was born in Manacor, Mallorca. No one in her family sang except her grandmother, who sang a lot while working in the fields when she was young. Back then nobody had cassettes, so they needed to sing to fight the loneliness of work, and each kind of work had its own song. As a child, Joana would sleep in her grandmother's bed and learn to sing traditional Spanish songs.

Years later, in 2011, Gomila was invited to perform an intimate concert of traditional Spanish music. She recruited a friend she'd met at Taller de Músics (a music academy) to accompany her and began to read a lot about oral-transmission culture, traditional music and its anthropology. The concert was intended to be a one-off performance, but the next day the phone rang and Gomila was asked to repeat the concert at a local festival in Manacor. So she expanded the band, and the songs were performed under the collective title *Folk Souvenir* for the first time.

Gomila then moved around for a few years, first to Brazil, where she became fascinated with improvisation within traditional music, and then to Madrid to work on a theatre piece with the musician Jaume Manresa who encouraged Gomila to finally record the *Folk Souvenir* project. In 2015, Joana formed the definitive *Folk Souvenir* band with Manresa producing the album. They travelled to Mallorca to record for three days, and on the last day a big party was thrown with many traditional musicians in attendance, playing the songs in the way they're usually played while everyone danced and sang. The concept of the project was 'not to recover traditional songs but to let the songs recover us as a human collective'. Joana wanted to play the songs with respect but also with freedom. To try not to interfere with their identity, but to have no fear of creating new melodies and harmonies. Gomila wanted to find the essence of each tune; who began to sing it, when, what were they doing, which words came first, and to try to understand the energy of the song, the connection between now and the moment someone began to sing it.

The songs on *Folk Souvenir* are strung together by a collection of personal audio files. Since she was very young, Gomila had been recording her grandmother talking and singing as well as making recordings of the outdoors, or 'environmental landscapes', as she calls them. These recordings can be heard throughout the album, along with some archive recordings by ethnomusicologist Alan Lomax, who recorded in the Balearic Islands in 1956, capturing people singing while working and discussing their music with him. *Folk Souvenir* wasn't the only 2016 album Lomax's work featured on: his recordings of America in the first half of the 20th century during the time of the Jim Crow laws were also sampled on the Beyoncé track 'Freedom'. His work has appeared on many musical projects over the years and has sometimes caused disagreements over how ethical such recordings really are, but at their best Lomax's tapes serve as historical documents that capture cultures in ways few people have achieved. *Folk Souvenir* was released in May 2016.

•

When Lyons-based guitarist Damien Cluzel was 47 he released two completely unique albums that fused different types of traditional world music with modern heavy rock. *Awo*, with his band **uKanDanZ**, is rooted in traditional Ethiopian music, while the self-titled album by his second project, Pixvae, is centred on Afro-Colombian music. Both records incorporate elements of jazz as well as European rock, and in both instances the execution is so clean that a new and stimulating genre is born.

Awo saw his pre-existing band, uKanDanZ, collaborate with Ethiopian singer Asnake Gebreyes. Cluzel had visited Ethiopia six times between 1999 and 2014, occasionally staying for more than two months at a time, getting to know the country and submerging himself in the culture. The idea behind *Awo* was to create music that fell somewhere in between Ethiopian music and the fusion of hard rock and jazz the band already played. Most of the songs on *Awo* were originally Ethiopian pop songs of the 70s or traditional compositions; they were all completely rearranged by the band, but in every case the lyrics and the melody were kept exactly the same, so lyrically *Awo* is mainly about love. Most of the original Ethiopian songs were about impossible love or based on love poems, as love is one of the only subjects artists can talk about in a strict political regime. Cluzel then introduced elements of early Black Sabbath to the sound, as well as the polyrhythms of South Indian Carnatic music in order to create tension where needed. It's important to note that Ethiopian rock didn't fully exist before this album. In the 60s and 70s Ethiopian musicians mixed their own music with soul, funk and jazz, but rock never happened, so with *Awo* the band set out to prove that Ethiopian rock music was even possible. They had to come up with a name for this new genre but didn't want to use 'Ethiopian rock' as it sounded boring. Also, most of the Ethiopian–European/American fusion projects called their music Ethio-something (Ethio-jazz, Ethio-groove, etc.), and Cluzel didn't want to be associated with these bands either. Finally they settled on 'Ethiopian crunch music' as the word 'crunch' covered the crisp energy of the songs while still conveying their heaviness. The response was extreme and mixed. Fans of rock music adored the record, but the world music lovers felt that uKanDanZ had gone too far and that there are certain types of traditional music which should never be messed with, especially not to this degree.

It's no surprise, then, that when coming up with a name for the genre his **Pixvae** project had invented, Cluzel went with 'Colombian crunch music'. *Pixvae* sees two bands coming together with Cluzel's math rock trio, Kouma, providing the instrumentals and the south Colombian Pacific group Bambazú performing the vocals, and this new band set out to specifically confront the traditional music of the Pacific coast of Colombia. Despite the fact it's also categorised as 'crunch music', the music on *Pixvae* is completely different in many ways to the songs on *Awo*. *Pixvae* features three vocalists singing together in a brilliant, powerful chorus as oppose to the wailing acrobatics performed solely by Gebreyes, and there's something innately positive about each song as a result. The rock aspect of the record draws more from math rock than *Awo* does, it's much more technical, with unpredictable stops and starts and the south Pacific Colombian rhythms drag all of this into new and unfamiliar territories. *Pixvae* is named after the hybrid peach palm tree native to Colombia (the tree also features on the front cover). One explanation I found for the name, besides the hybrid element, is to do with the tree's gnarled roots, something the band bears also, not just in regard to the roots of their music but also the roots of the musicians themselves as individuals: the band is made up of people from multiple territories coming together to create something that feels true to them and expresses who they are. This idea of a tree with misshapen, contorted roots that bears a unique fruit fitted so easily with the band's ethos that surely there was never any discussion about calling the project by another name. But when I asked Damien Cluzel himself about this, he said it was because the fruit of the tree is used to make an instrument the band like to use. Fair enough.

Live + Direct

At the end of May 2017, Matthew Crosby invited me to go and see Jeff Rosenstock perform at the Camden Underworld. I came straight from doing my own show in Central London and arrived at the Underworld ten minutes before Rosenstock began his set. I was still wearing the blazer I'd worn on stage earlier that night (I went through a very brief blazer phase) and looked like someone's dad. Matthew was wearing a cool T-shirt with a logo on it and looked like my son. Rosenstock's 2016 album WORRY. was already one of both Matthew's and my favourite albums of all time, and this gig was one of my few high points of 2017. It was one of the best gigs I've ever been to in my life, and whenever the audience sang together I felt connected to other people in a way I'd not experienced in years. I realised at that show that it wasn't just recorded music I'd been neglecting but live music as well.

I used to love going to gigs. As a teenager, watching live music felt like a religious experience, and that's saying something considering how fully Christian I was. One of the first bands I ever saw live were **My Vitriol**. They were supporting a band called Cay at the Bedford Esquires in the year 2000, I was 15 and it was the second gig I'd ever been to. Their blend of rock and shoegaze got them weirdly labelled nu-gaze (it was around the time of nu-metal so calling things 'nu' was still acceptable), and they'd not even released their debut album when I saw them. They were my own personal discovery, the first band I'd been into 'before anyone else', making me better than anyone who came to the party late or jumped on the bandwagon. I saw them three times that year: in Bedford to hardly anyone, opening the main stage at the Reading Festival and finally to a packed room on their own headline tour, their popularity rapidly increasing as the year progressed. But it was short-lived: after the release of their debut album, a record that frontman Som Wardner felt he'd been rushed to finish, the band went on an indefinite hiatus and vanished.

Fifteen years later, My Vitriol released their first studio album since 2001, *The Secret Sessions*. It was only available for download on their website and had been funded by their fans via PledgeMusic. Everything about the album from the title to the way they went about funding and selling it pointed to a band that didn't want to be the centre of attention or out in the field of competition ever again. They'd unarguably nurtured and honed their sound over time and done so exclusively in front of a dedicated fan base who had stuck with them during these self-imposed years in the wilderness (not the fans who assumed they'd split up and then rediscovered them because they're trying to buy as much music as they can from 2016). *The Secret Sessions* was released in October 2016.

•

When Arcade Fire decided to wind down a little after the release of their fourth album, *Reflektor*, guitarist **Will Butler** took the opportunity to pursue some personal projects. He released his debut solo album, *Policy*, in 2015 and in order to promote the album wrote a song a day for the *Guardian* newspaper, with each song being inspired by a news story. Butler started playing the *Guardian* songs on tour for fun and they improved with each performance, making him wish he'd released these updated versions instead of their first drafts. After a show at the Sasquatch! Music Festival, Butler and his band drove to a winery in Yakima and Butler got drunk for the very first time in his life. He'd never drunk as a teenager or throughout his twenties and now found himself tipsy and talking to the owner of a winery in the desert. Will offered the owner a record, but this guy, roughly in his fifties, turned the offer down, saying, 'I only like live albums.' So because he was drunk and he'd been trying to figure out a way of releasing these improved *Guardian* songs anyway, Will decided to make a live album for this winery owner and went on to record that album over two nights during his ongoing tour.

Butler was accompanied on tour by the comedian Jo Firestone, who also ended up appearing on the live record. Every night on tour, Butler and Firestone would introduce each other's sets and would have fun trying to make it difficult for each other. Will once told an audience that Jo was extremely shy so when she came on stage they needed to turn around, crouch down and be totally silent, then when she said her first word they needed to gently turn around and whisper, 'Hi, Jo' in unison. In return Firestone once told the audience that Butler had requested to be booed onto the stage and encouraged the audience to boo him as harshly as possible when he walked out. This was the intro she gave on the night of the live recording and it worked so well that the booing, along with Firestone's introduction, remained on the record. But it's not how the album starts, Firestone's intro is actually the second track, because the first track is the encore.

Will wanted the audience to be thrown into the heart of the gig and feel the warmth and the sweat immediately, so began with the encore before flashing back to the opening song and then progressing through the evening, eventually ending on another encore from another night on the tour. The opening encore is a song the band had never played before, not even in practice. Will had quickly shown them the first chord offstage and then they'd walked out and performed it for the first time. The song is called 'Tell Me We're All Right' and contains a moment when Butler shouts the title and the audience respond, 'We're alright!', something he didn't even know was going to be part of the song and puts down to Firestone's act involving plenty of call-and-response lines. What makes this such a great live album is that the audience feel like another instrument, like they're in the band also. There are several points on the record where the audience are either invited to join in or take the initiative themselves, sometimes just throwing in a cheer or a whoop but timing it just right so the listener at home connects with the energy in the room. The set is made up of songs from *Policy*, the updated *Guardian* tracks and two previously unreleased songs – 'Tell Me We're All Right' and 'Friday Night', a song about the kind of evening Butler hoped to capture on the record. This track was written specifically for the album, to be the title track and to get played as an encore to round off the evening. *Friday Night* was released in June 2016, and it wasn't until the album was mixed and ready to go that Butler realised, at the start of 'Take My Side', he loudly tells the crowd that it's good to see them all on this lovely Thursday.

•

Born in 1942, Hawaiian-shirt enthusiast **Mike Cooper** has never stopped learning, evolving and reinventing when it comes to music. Starting out as a blues guitarist in the 60s before progressing on to free jazz in the 70s, Cooper has mastered several genres, forever accumulating knowledge and influences along the way. The lap steel (specifically a 1930s metal-bodied National Tri-Plate Resonator guitar) became the focal point of his music from the mid-70s onwards, Cooper fretted the instrument with a steel bar and drew influence from numerous styles of world music, experimenting by taking different objects and sliding them up and down the strings to achieve a wide range of glissando effects. In 2015 he decided he wanted to buy an instrument he could transport more easily, something he could take on holidays, stow in the overhead compartments on planes, something small and light. He bought himself a wooden-bodied Yamaha short-scale travel guitar (a standard acoustic guitar), the first wooden guitar he'd owned since 1958. This new guitar was meant to just be for fun, but he kept on returning to it, finding that this new instrument caused him to play differently and discover new sounds, techniques and ideas. In the winter of 2016, Cooper went on a European tour with the travel guitar, performing with it for the first time on stage and improvising what he calls 'Spirit Songs'. All of Cooper's lyrics around that time were made up of rearranged text from Thomas Pynchon novels, using a cut-up technique pioneered by 60s writer William S. Burroughs. He played with his fingers on the frets for the first time in decades as well as with a bottleneck and his signature lap steel method, earnestly singing over hypnotic noisescapes that were somehow soothing despite their frenzied nature. No two shows were the same. One date on this tour was at Cave12 in Geneva, where Cooper's sound technician, Eleanora Puzzle, recorded the set. Cooper would later release this show online, although you would never know this was a live album as you never hear the audience, just a clear guitar and a clear voice improvising for 51 minutes. *New Guitar Old Hat Knew Blues* was released in September 2016.

Special Night

I came out of the Jeff Rosenstock show feeling wired and not wanting to go home. Matthew and I went to a pub down the road, drank and relived the gig. It wasn't long before I started chatting to some strangers at the bar about music – I hadn't bothered having a proper conversation with strangers in years! I used to talk to strangers all the time: when I first started stand-up I'd sit on the train to London hoping that someone sat next to me. I used to love getting the late train because that meant there'd be loads of eccentric types with no filter who would gladly sit and talk at me. But over the years I wanted to be left alone more and more. I started sitting on the train with my headphones on and my head down. But now here I was, in a *pub* chatting to *strangers*!

The strangers were my age, three women and a man, and they were in a band. Matthew had to go home but instead of leaving with him I decided to stay and hang out with the *strangers*! Half an hour after Matthew left, as if by magic, Jeff Rosenstock and his bandmates walked into the bar! I was hammered and decided to tell Jeff Rosenstock how amazing the show had been because it felt like an important thing to do. I walked over and gushed about how connected I'd felt to everyone in the room and he was very patient, listening to me describe his own gig back to him. I got a photo with Jeff Rosenstock and texted it to Matthew, then returned to the strangers, feeling amazing. The pub closed and the strangers and I stayed out; we went to another bar and danced drunkenly to British indie rock for an hour before that bar also closed.

The Tube had now stopped running, I was wasted, and for some reason the Uber app on my phone wasn't working, so the strangers invited me to stay at their place. When we got back to their flat I learnt that the strangers all slept on one big bed together; the bed didn't have covers or a sheet on it – it was just a bare mattress that they slept on top of like *Where the Wild Things Are*. I didn't want to sleep on the bare mattress in a big pile of strangers so I convinced them to let me sleep in their flatmate's bed as they were away for the night. I got into bed in my boxers and had fallen asleep by the time one of the strangers got into bed with me. She was fully clothed, we were both tired and we just went to sleep.

In the morning my hangover was awful and I started to feel extreme dread about everything that'd happened the night before. I was now convinced I must've annoyed Jeff Rosenstock, I remembered going on and on at him about the gig and he'd told me he actually hadn't enjoyed the show that much because people were fighting on the front row, but I kept insisting it had been incredible regardless. And then I'd got a photo with him and sent the photo to Matthew! Matthew must've thought I was rubbing his face in it because I'd met Jeff Rosenstock and he hadn't! And now I was in bed with a woman I didn't know, in my underwear while she was fully clothed. Last night, due to the alcohol and the exhilarating show I'd just been to, I was ridiculously full of love for all people and adored this group of strangers like they were my best friends, but now I was hungover and they were simply strangers again and I didn't want to be in my underwear in front of strangers. I said goodbye and left the flat, realised my phone was now dead and I'd somehow lost my oyster card, so I had to walk home from Camden to Shepherd's Bush, which took well over an hour on what turned out to be a really hot day, and I remember thinking to myself, 'Well – last night you felt more connected to people than you've felt in years, so you carried on going until you've never felt more alone.'

WORRY.

Jeff Rosenstock grew up in Baldwin, Long Island. He picked up his dad's guitar aged four and started bass, guitar, piano and sax lessons when he was six. He would always write songs in his head inspired by Debbie Gibson and Paula Abdul, and dance around his backyard singing them. Jeff had a hard time transitioning out of elementary school to junior high and high school. He never felt like he fitted in anywhere until he formed a ska punk band with a kid named Joe Werfelman who was friends with Jeff's brother. A thriving local music scene had sprung up in Baldwin, and everyone was booking catering halls, church basements, lodges and bars that would look the other way when under-agers performed there. He thought the bands in his school were amazing and could have been legendary if they didn't keep breaking up. This meant that Jeff was determined that his band, The Arrogant Sons of Bitches, stay together after high school was over, which they did. They stayed together and toured the world and Jeff became a musician, going on to form the much loved Bomb the Music Industry.

By 2015, Jeff was releasing music under his own name and had also produced a few records by other artists. He was temporarily living in Australia while producing *Throw Me in the*

River by The Smith Street Band when he started to write his own new set of songs. He had weekends off, which gave him time to explore Melbourne, and he'd walk around the city recording ideas into his phone. The next album would be the last record of a two-record deal with SideOneDummy, the only record deal Jeff had ever had, so it felt like it might be the only opportunity he had left to say 'some basement punk shit' to a wider audience. When the Smith Street record was done he returned to Brooklyn with his fiancée, Christine, living in an apartment with windows that didn't open up properly, black mould in the bathroom and shoddy plumbing, to start making this album.

On past records Rosenstock had sung about his depression and anxiety, but this time round he wanted to avoid mentioning these themes directly. He didn't want to talk about it in interviews any more and he didn't want to keep discussing it with strangers after shows. It had become this thing the public knew about him even though he still felt too self-conscious to talk about it with the people he loved. He needed a little space from it verbally, but also believed the best way to make art is to throw your whole self into it, so decided that trying to represent these feelings as a musical arc would feel like a less obvious approach. An unlikely inspiration for the record was Quentin Tarantino's *Death Proof* – a homage to grindhouse movies that slowly builds, giving you an idea of setting and characters at first and then BANG! – there's a flurry of car crashes, violence and revenge. Jeff wanted to re-create this journey on the album so made the middle section of the record feel like the sudden fear of a car crash coming on, the adrenaline as it's about to happen, followed by the destruction of the crash itself, and then made the final run of songs the act of picking up the pieces afterwards before burning the world down. Musically, he wanted it to feel like a slow build into an anxiety attack and to capture the panic that comes with the knowledge that, actually, everything isn't fine.

Lyrically, that left him needing to dip his toes into something he viewed as trite, something that almost no one is good at – writing love songs. He'd always believed that love songs ignore the 'orb of dread' inside all of us and he wanted to understand why he felt this way. He also wanted to sing about the external forces of capitalist greed and fear that drive us away from co-operation and towards competition. He wanted to figure out for himself, over the course of writing the record, if it's possible not only to love your partner without restraint, but to genuinely care for anyone in a world that drives you away from deep personal relationships at every turn – whether it be through forcing oneself to work unpaid extra hours to make more money for a person who already makes ten times as much as you, or returning home to try to relax but being assaulted by non-stop advertising that makes you feel incomplete unless you spend the money you made at your job, or the exhaustive state this endless cycle of modern capitalism and social media puts you in. Jeff was about to commit to love and get married, and was asking himself the question, how can love thrive among this inhumanity, where love is just assumed to be something that will eventually happen for everyone, completely unspecial, something to be ignored and eventually discarded?

Towards the end of the writing process, Jeff was talking to his old friend and occasional collaborator Tim Ruggeri one New Year's Eve about some songwriting frustrations. He had nearly finished writing the new record but had a bunch of songs that felt like they should go at the end, and while he didn't want to get rid of any of them necessarily, they all felt too long. Among them was a song Jeff was writing for a musical with comedian Chris Gethard, a song about a cute elderly couple that got married in the courthouse when Jeff and Christine were getting married, a ska song and about five more tracks on top of those. Tim's advice was, 'Why don't you just *Abbey Road* it?', boil the songs down to their essential parts and connect them all together. It felt like a revelation. Having this final run of songs, about different states of being, all merge into each other as if they were one escalating track perfectly conveyed the concept of experiencing everything at once – love, fear, joy, sadness, greed, generosity, anxiety, emptiness, freedom, hopelessness, anger, pride, shame . . . It became clear that what Jeff was writing wasn't about feeling one particular emotion and moving on to the next. It was about the weight of feeling it all at once, which is what love is.

The band recorded the album in the spring of 2016, in a beautiful studio in Stinson Beach called the Panoramic House, directly after watching two old friends get married in Las Vegas. It was the only time Jeff had ever had a record label fronting the cost of recording, and since the contract was up after this record he thought they might as well go somewhere nice. After the first day of vocals, Rosenstock went to 1-2-3-4 Go! to record a hundred friends and fans, collectively referred to as The Hundred Voice Choir, who would sing all the group vocals on the record. No one in the choir (aside from Jeff and the band) had heard the album yet – they read the lyrics off of zines that Jeff and a friend were still photocopying as the doors were opening – and sang as though they were in a bar, half singing half yelling, as one unified crowd. The following week Jeff had to record the rest of his vocals on the album but had totally worn out his voice during the choir session. When he tried to sing, Rosenstock felt like he was trying to paint an impossibly magical picture with a dried-up Sharpie, but in the end this worked to his advantage. It's rare to be able to hear a singer throwing everything into their performance on a record, but Jeff's distinctive, open-throated, all-or-nothing delivery instantly connects – it feels real, and any so-called imperfections are what makes everything resonate so deeply.

The reaction to the record was huge, bigger than anything Rosenstock had done in the past. To begin with audiences were connecting with the music, specifically the countless hooks and the lyrics about love. But when Trump got elected the band experienced an entirely different reaction from their fans. The parts of the album that address the systemic issues inherent with American capitalism – police brutality, gentrification, advertising culture, and the sad and confused mental state that puts everyone in – really hit home with people. Jeff suddenly found that speaking to fans about the record after the election made him feel less alone in his thoughts, and feeling less alone gave him hope that the next generation wouldn't let this happen again. Ultimately, this album started to make him feel like he was no longer screaming into the abyss, and that if he was going to be on the right side of a long fight, he wouldn't have to fight alone. The more they played those songs live and crowds sang along, the less it felt about him as an individual and the more it felt about everyone all at once. WORRY. was released in October 2016.

Telefone

Whenever I tell people that 2016 was the greatest year for music of all time, they always ask me what the greatest album of 2016 was and I never know what to say. There are so many 2016 projects that mean a great deal to me, and it feels vulgar to rank them because they all scratch different itches and comparing them seems silly and downright disrespectful. But I still need to convince these interrogators that 2016 is indeed the greatest year for music of all time; I can already tell they're sceptical and I'm not going to win them round by giving some cop-out answer like, 'Oh, there's just so many, I can't separate them really, I just like them all!' I gotta give them *something*, it needs to be something they're unlikely to have heard before and it must have the potential to change their entire life. So every time someone asks me what the greatest album of 2016 was, I give them the names of *two* albums. The two 2016 albums that without a shadow of a doubt are going to be in my favourite albums of all time for ever. The two albums that have already permanently altered me in some way and for the better. One of these albums is WORRY. and the other is *Telefone*.

•

In 2016, Chicago rapper **Noname** self-released her debut mix-tape *Telefone* as a free download, but by the time I heard about it in 2017 it was no longer free because it was widely regarded as one of 2016's best albums. Ten tracks painting a vivid picture of her home city of Chicago, a distinct feeling of summer running through the entire project, *Telefone* instantly felt like a record that would outlast its contemporaries and stay with its fans for a lifetime. With every element so on point it's easy to question why it was initially released as a humble mixtape and not an official album. But part of what makes Noname different from other rappers is her withdrawn onstage persona and overall modesty despite possessing the sort of game-changing talent most musicians would kill for. So releasing an instant classic with minimal fanfare actually fits.

Noname was born Fatima Warner, and her parents were both involved in literature. Her mother owned a bookstore and her father was a book distributor, so, as an adult, Warner draws most of her inspiration from writers and poets. This has contributed to her distinctive flow whenever she raps, her lyrics reading so close to literature that her style often gets likened to spoken word. After guesting on other people's mixtapes for a few years Noname started thinking about recording a solo record in 2013, but life got in the way and in the end the entire project happened within the nine months prior to *Telefone*'s release in July 2016. She brought in producers she was friends with and had worked with before: Saba, Cam O'bi and Phoelix were all contemporaries she could be open with and who understood her, they would provide these soulful, lazy-jazz-sounding instrumentals, and then Noname would compose all the lyrics. At the time she was living in an Airbnb in LA and would write out on the balcony or in a nearby park and then record her vocals in the apartment itself. She wanted the whole album to feel like the first phone conversation with someone you've got a crush on, full of nervousness, laughter, silence, excitement and awkwardness, but the tape took on further meaning the more she continued to work on it. These days, the name *Telefone* refers to how Noname's entire life is on her phone, how she interacts with and learns about the outside world as well as friends and family, so she explores that idea in great depth: her personal relationships, social issues, love – it's an album about being connected to so much, so constantly.

Due to the sunny instrumentals, many didn't pick up on the verses about police brutality and abortion the first time round, but these subjects are tackled with eloquence and provide a stark contrast to the hazy synths and finger clicks surrounding them. There's a positivity to Noname's lyrics also: she raps about nostalgia and friendship and sometimes you can hear her smile at her own phrasing through almost closed lips. Her first verse on the opening track, 'Yesterday', is one of my favourite beginnings to any rap album. Warner sums up universal truths one after the other, from the conflicting desire to be both happy and successful to the final half-hurried line before the chorus, 'I wish I was a kid again'. It's an introduction to an artist who's plugged into the human experience, the heart and the soul of us all, and has the ability to make you feel seen.

The moniker 'Noname' comes from a reluctance to be in the spotlight, as well as not wanting her art to be categorised or pigeonholed. Warner rarely grants interviews and, especially around the time *Telefone* was released, has always been very private. This need for privacy makes the openness of Noname's lyrics way more impactful; she's choosing to let us in because she has something she genuinely wants to say and has thought carefully about how she wants to say it. And the entire album feels that way; deeply considered and executed with care, intent and precision. Records like this are the main reason I keep falling in love with music: they change your expectations of what an album can be and have an unprecedented effect on you that renews your enthusiasm for life and living in general. I love introducing people to *Telefone* and I can't ever see myself not loving this project.

•

The biggest mixtapes of 2016 all came out of Chicago. **Chance the Rapper** arguably had the most successful mixtape of the year with *Coloring Book*, 15 upbeat gospel rap songs that cemented his place in mainstream hip hop. He'd been steadily rising through the ranks over the years, but now there was no doubting him as a relevant and essential voice in the genre. *Coloring Book* won Best Rap album at the Grammys and charted high on the Billboard charts despite the fact that it was only available to stream (the first album ever to do so). He had been living in an LA mansion prior to making the album and spent most of his days on Xanax being unproductive. So he moved back to Chicago and reconnected with things he felt he was missing from his life, namely an ex-girlfriend and his religion, and recorded *Coloring Book* in just one month. Chance also guested on fellow Chicagoan **Jamila Woods'** album *HEAVN*, another record that technically falls into the mixtape category as it was released as a free download (then re-released the following year by a label but it came out in 2016 first, thank you very much, Ed Gamble). Woods is an incredibly gifted musician, poet and activist, and on *HEAVN* all her strengths are brought to the table. Musically, *HEAVN* is equal parts jazz, hip hop and R&B, with occasional nods to some unlikely songs by other artists ('Stellar' by nu-metal band Incubus and 'I Don't Want to Wait' by Paula Cole, aka the *Dawson's Creek* theme tune, are both paid homage to). Spoken-word interludes set the scene for many of the songs, whether it's about how she got her name, the things she loves about being black, resilience among the black community or personal loss – these voicemail-like messages introduce different trains of thought and prompt us to pay attention to the forthcoming lyrics. When she's not making music, Woods teaches kids in Chicago as part of an organisation called Young Chicago Authors – which makes perfect sense when listening to this record as she communicates ideas in ways that educate and encourage, inspiring the listener to participate and improve.

Telefone, Coloring Book and *HEAVN* were easily the most talked about free downloads of 2016, and it's crazy to think they not only came out of the same city but the same peer group, with the artists guesting on each other's projects (listen to *VRY BLK* by Jamila Woods featuring Noname) and bringing in other Chicago alumni too. Thanks to this 2016 challenge I now find myself in the position where I'm excited to see how a specific group of artists progress as a collective and as individuals in the years to come, and having music to look forward to, even before it's been announced, feels legitimately great.

For This We Fought the Battle of Ages

June 2017 and I had to go to the US again. I had some gigs booked in LA, along with my very first American TV appearance. I'd be performing stand-up on *Conan*, a show I'd been a huge fan of for some time. I had been looking forward to this for ages and this trip was just what I needed – a welcome respite from the unfortunate year so far.

•

Cate Le Bon was born in Penboyr in Wales and moved to Los Angeles, California, in 2013. She's a musician who thrives most when she appears out of place and suits being the self-assured odd one out. There's something so innately Welsh about Le Bon's music, and taking that energy and placing it in the middle of the desert, where it's offset by Hollywood of all places, plays to her advantage wonderfully. In 2016, Cate Le Bon released her third studio album, *Crab Day*.

Crab Day is a day spent searching for crabs and drawing pictures of crabs. You are encouraged to give the crabs you draw a variety of hairstyles and the whole thing takes place every year on 1 April. Crab Day was invented by Cate Le Bon's niece because she didn't like how mean-spirited April Fool's Day was and felt an alternative was needed for those of us who don't enjoy practical jokes at the expense of others.

Here are some drawings of crabs I did on Crab Day this year:

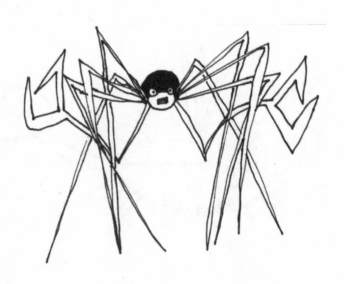

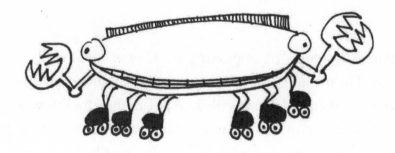

Those were nice crab drawings weren't they? I particularly liked Roller Buzzcut. Ok, I've put this next story off long enough. I was in LA and things were looking up. I couldn't wait to shake off this rough patch and get on with enjoying life.

•

Within 30 minutes of appearing on *Conan* I'd literally shat myself. The previous night I'd eaten a chicken quesadilla from a food truck, then woken up with food poisoning. But this was my first appearance on American television and there was no way I was going to cancel so I soldiered on. Personally, I'm proud of not shitting myself sooner. I spent the whole day focusing on not shitting myself, including the five minutes spent performing stand-up in front of a studio audience (you can probably find it online: it's a man trying not to shit himself for five minutes while an audience don't 100 per cent connect with his humour but he sticks to his guns anyway, mainly because if he loses confidence in his material he will probably lose confidence in his bowel control and shit himself). I walked off set and into my dressing room and was greeted by my agent giving me the thumbs-up: 'Well done, let's go and get a steak dinner to cele-brate!' I didn't really want a steak dinner for obvious reasons, but he said he'd been wanting to go to this steakhouse for a long time, and I didn't want to let him down, so I agreed.

Once in the car I felt fine, I no longer needed a shit at all; maybe it had just been nerves about performing on TV and now I was back to normal. I did need a piss though, so as soon as I got to the steakhouse I went to the bathroom. And while I was pissing I shat myself. I'm not the first and I won't be the last to mistake a shit for a fart. Fortunately the bathroom was empty so I finished my piss and swiftly sidestepped into a cubicle. I was wearing a backpack at the time, containing a change of clothes (the production team had asked me to bring wardrobe options) and some makeup wipes for after the show. This meant that I was able to carry out a way more efficient clean-up than most people who've just shat themselves. I managed to make-up-wipe myself down and change into the clean clothes but it still wasn't ideal and I knew I had to get home asap. I ditched my soiled underwear in the bin (bad luck whoever had to deal with that) and exited the toilets. I walked straight up to my agent who had now been seated at a table and said, 'I have to go, I've shit myself' (from the age of 30 onwards you tend to stop skirting around the main issue when you've shit yourself). But my agent didn't want to leave, he really wanted to stay and have a meal, and asked me to please stay because he'd heard the food here was meant to be amazing. And so I stayed because I didn't want him to be disappointed. Even though I'd shit my pants. I sat down and ordered a meal that I then didn't eat because I still had food poisoning from the night before. I then started to feel really gutted about my performance on *Conan*. I was convinced I'd been awful, plus I had now shat myself, so I felt double gutted. I then sat there, definitely still with bits of shit on me, with my head in my hands, telling my agent how I didn't think I was cut out for stand-up and felt like I should quit, how comedy didn't make me happy and I was worried about what it was doing to my wellbeing. Throughout this he told me that everyone thought I was great while he gamely attempted to enjoy his long-anticipated steak dinner in an LA steakhouse with multiple sides. It was a low point in a year of low points. I've never wanted to quit my job more than I did in LA that week. In fact, sometimes imagining giving up for good is weirdly comforting and seems like the only sane option.

The End of Comedy

Even though I was buying these albums just one year after they came out, some of the bands had already broken up. LVL UP released their third and final record, *Return to Love*, in September 2016, an American indie rock album that wore its influences on its sleeve (Neutral Milk Hotel, Mount Eerie) in the best possible way. There's no dramatic story as to why the band split: they'd been together since university and their interests had just changed over the years. Most of the time that's all it comes down to with bands; they don't have huge fights and stop talking – people just stop caring about the same things and agree to do something different. They had achieved a lot in five years, integrating themselves into a thriving musical community that each member had found their own home in, but lately they'd each started pursuing separate projects outside the band.

Bassist Nick Corbo had started playing drums in modern-AOR band **Crying** along with New York musicians Ryan Galloway (guitars) and Z (vocals). Crying make music for stadiums and pretty much everything I've said in my description of them is unhelpful. AOR stands for Adult-Oriented Rock (bands like Toto, Journey and Boston), and while Crying aren't pure AOR, I think it's fair to say they've updated the sound and are carrying the torch for AOR in the 21st century. They've mixed its sensibilities with indie and even some pop punk, but the guitar solos, big synths and power riffs are unmistakably AOR, and Ryan was listening to Airplay's self-titled AOR masterpiece a lot while writing this record, so calling it modern AOR stands to reason. Oh man, I said AOR a lot just then. Also saying they write music for stadiums isn't helpful as they don't actually do stadium gigs, but their songs sound like they're made to light up a stadium and fill that sort of space, specifically a stadium set in an 80s version of the future.

In October 2016, Crying released *Beyond the Fleeting Gales*. On previous EPs they had incorporated Gameboy noises into their music, but they wouldn't be able to achieve the sound they wanted on this new album by sticking to the old format, so they went down the traditional rock route of guitar, bass, drums and vocals. You can hear the Chiptune influence lingering though, and some of the guitar and synth patterns wouldn't sound out of place on an 80s video game soundtrack. Z has a voice made for sugary pop songs, and the way she can make herself sound small and unassuming one second then bold and commanding the next is essential to the band's character. Her vocal parts were recorded with Emily Sprague of **Florist,** which makes perfect sense; Florist released *The Birds Outside Sang* in 2016, an indie pop album that never shied away from stripping everything back and letting Sprague's melancholic vocals dominate a song. This meant the lyrics were exposed in a way few vocalists usually dare, and Sprague and Z achieved the same intimacy on *Beyond the Fleeting Gales* while matching the energy of the album's ever-expanding instrumentals. Another detail about *The Birds Outside Sang* by Florist is that it was released on Double Double Whammy, a record label started by university students Dave Benton and Mike Caridi in 2011 as a way of putting out albums by their own band, LVL UP. Satisfying.

Ears

After shitting myself in a steakhouse I returned to my Airbnb and went to bed, waking up every hour or so to do an awful food-poisoned shit in the toilet, and when I woke up the following morning I was unable to hear out of my left ear. I hoped it was temporary, but not only did my hearing not return, my ear soon started to scream with intense pain. I made the decision to go to the ER, called a cab and travelled to the emergency room still very much suffering from food poisoning and now deaf in one ear. I was worried I may be overreacting and hoped the ER staff didn't think I was wasting their time. I've mainly only had experience with British medical professionals and, if I'm honest, they've not liked me very much. I used to be a proper hypochondriac and visit the doctor at the slightest suggestion of illness, often convincing myself there was something wrong when there wasn't. I remember a doctor once scowling at me and through gritted teeth saying, 'That is your HIP.' I was literally showing him my hip at the time, convinced it was a tumour. He pointed out that I also had one on the other side and I shut up.

I was eventually cured of my hypochondria, though. If you're a hypochondriac, sooner or later you're going to become convinced that something is wrong with your reproductive organs and you're going to unnecessarily ask somebody to examine your junk. After many nights sat in bed staring at my own dick like a magic eye drawing until I saw the horrific image I wanted to see, I was ready to go to the doctors and drop trou' in front of another person and hear the bad news from someone else, 'Mr Acaster, you're right, that dick is awful', or words to that effect. I didn't deliberately book an appointment with a female doctor but a female doctor is what I got. She told me that legally she was not allowed to examine 'it' by herself. I still don't know if this is true; I've asked other doctors and some have said it sounds plausible but most have said it's not a law. Either way, what happened next was definitely not routine procedure. She got another member of staff to stand in the room with us and that member of staff was – the receptionist. The receptionist, who, I might add, was also a lady, stood with the doctor and they looked at my penis together. The doctor said it was fine. The receptionist offered no opinion. I was still worried, though, and knew I never wanted to come back to this practice ever again, so I asked one more time, 'Are you absolutely sure it's ok?' The doctor rolled her eyes and said, 'Hold on, I'll get another doctor in here so you can get a second opinion.' She left the room briefly and then returned with the same doctor I'd shown my hip to that time. He entered the room, took one look at me and gave me an angry look as if to say, 'Of course it's you. Only you would have three people in here looking at your not-diseased dick.' He stormed up to me and roughly handled my penis with, I'd say, the least amount of respect anyone has ever shown for somebody else's genitalia. He lifted it up, shook it left and right like a joystick, flung it back down and disdainfully said, 'That's fine!' while pointing at it like he hated it, then left the room. From that day forth, I've never worried about my health because I would rather be dead due to an exploded dick than go through that again.

•

Law Holt was training to be a nurse and working in a home for the elderly when she recorded her debut album. *City* came out in July 2016, and since its release Holt has continued pursuing a career in nursing, working long shifts and not dwelling too much on the possibility of a future in the music industry. She used to live in Edinburgh and via the scene there became involved with the group Young Fathers, joining them for numerous shows and occasionally guesting on tracks. In many ways it was the Young Fathers' producer, Tim London, who really pushed Holt to record an album, writing a selection of unconventional instrumentals with her in mind and leaving her in a room with them before recording whatever she'd come up with later the same day.

When it comes to music, nothing about what she's doing, how she's doing it, or what it's achieved seems remarkable to Holt. She regularly shrugs off praise and focuses on more pressing matters in her day-to-day life as music doesn't pay the bills, so she can't afford to become consumed by it. That's not to say she's not passionate: music means a great deal to her, but she's naturally modest, humble and maybe even shy when it comes to discussing her own talent. This isn't the character portrayed on the record, though. Holt decided to filter her lyrics on *City* through a fictional diva, an arrogant, selfish figure who cheats on her partner and takes pride in the hurt she's caused. This diabolical menace is the polar opposite of who Holt really is (in reality she's in a committed long-term relationship and is drawn to jobs that involve caring for others). She's not playing this role because she secretly wants to do terrible things but because she doesn't see why people would want to hear about her actual life, so she conjured up an unhinged alter ego to bring the necessary drama to proceedings. The nature of the character meant that Holt was able to cram several different voices into this one warped persona, so most songs see her constantly switching moods, having conversations with herself and answering her own questions. This choice transforms *City* into a twisted reinvention of a pop record, taking the genre and distorting it with lo-fi electronic beats and sordid stories told from the perspective of a comic-book baddie. And since her approach to the industry is more nonchalant than most, there's currently no way of knowing if this is the first of many Law Holt albums or all we ever get.

Give a Glimpse of What Yer Not

Alter egos popped up a lot in 2016: on jazz-rock monolith *Emily's D+Evolution*, Grammy-winning bassist and singer **Esperanza Spalding** played a character called Emily for the entire album. Spalding said that Emily enabled her to let go and do some proper damage when necessary, but dodged most questions about her alter ego in interviews, only revealing that the name came from her own middle name. But there is one track on the album, a cover song originally sung by another fictional character, that maybe answers everything. The closing track of *D+Evolution* is 'I Want It Now', originally performed by Julie Dawn Cole, aka Veruca Salt, in the 1971 film *Willy Wonka & the Chocolate Factory*. Veruca Salt is probably the most spoilt of all the spoilt kids in that story: she pushes everyone around and barks orders to get what she wants, and in this particular scene she's stomping around the golden-egg room busting up all the Oompa-Loompas' kit and being proper bratty because she wants her own golden egg and Willy Wonka won't let her have one. So maybe Emily is a Veruca Salt kind of figure, a bratty tyrant bossing everyone around in order to get her own way or else she'll scream and destroy stuff. In the film, Veruca Salt gets her comeuppance at the end of this song and disappears down the bad-egg chute never to be seen again. This is maybe why Spalding saved 'I Want It Now' until last on the tracklist, so she can flush Emily out in the finale, freeing herself of the character and moving on to what's next.

It seems that every time an artist chooses an alter ego it tends to be a more extroverted, selfish one. Esperanza Spalding and Law Holt are both prime examples of this. Apparently, something about being an introvert or always being aware of other people's feelings makes us want to have a little holiday and play the monster for a while. I haven't yet seen a wild anarchic musician adopt the alter ego of a shy, kind person for a whole record, and if those albums do exist they're few and far between. The one exception to this rule is, of course, the Ned Flanders-themed metalcore band Okilly Dokilly. You did not misread that sentence, so please stop rereading it.

Howdilly Doodilly

Head Ned, Thread Ned, Bled Ned, Red Ned and Stead Ned are **Okilly Dokilly,** a Phoenix-based metalcore group devoted entirely to *Simpsons* character Ned Flanders. They released their debut album, *Howdilly Doodilly*, in November 2016. They all dress like Ned Flanders in dark-green jumpers, pink polo shirts, spectacles and slacks, all of their song titles are Flanders references and their lyrics are mostly made up of quotes from Ned Flanders. Also, I called them a metalcore band earlier, while they refer to themselves as a Nedal band. I don't think I need to explain why. Anyway, I own this album due to my 2016 project. Thanks to this project, I own a Ned Flanders-themed metalcore album.

It was when I bought *Howdilly Doodilly* that I knew this project had got out of hand. Not just because I bought it but because when I found this album online I instantly knew that I NEEDED it. I had become so determined to build a vivid picture of a single year in music that I now NEEDED a metal album devoted entirely to *Simpsons* character Ned Flanders. I'd crossed the line between hobby and lifestyle – this was my identity now and I had no choice. If I'd not bought *Howdilly Doodilly* by Ned Flanders-themed Nedal band Okilly Dokilly, then I wouldn't possess an accurate representation of the year 2016 in music because you can't just sweep something like that under the rug. I couldn't say, 'Here's everything you need to hear from an entire year in music . . . oh, and also there was a metal band who dressed like Ned Flanders from *The Simpsons* and sang songs about him, but I don't see why that matters, there are plenty of similar bands out there, listen to these two blokes playing a washing machine instead.'

What's that? You don't think an album exists where two blokes play a washing machine for the entire duration? You sure about that?

•

The Whirlpool Ultimate Care II is a 27 Cycle, Super Capacity Plus washing machine. The easy-to-use console makes it simple to select the desired wash and spin speed combination and the enhanced agitator vanes ensure clothes roll over for consistent cleaning. It's also the sole instrument used on *Ultimate Care II*, the tenth album by electronic duo **Matmos**. Every sound on the album is made using the washing machine in the pair's apartment. From the shunks and gurgles it naturally makes during a cycle, to the beats created using the washer as a percussive instrument, Matmos utilise the machine in every way possible, often sequencing and manipulating the noises to achieve the desired effect. The album consists of one 38-minute-long track, the same length as a standard wash cycle, and was released in February 2016.

While we're discussing some of the more unusual projects I own from 2016, let's not forget *One* by **Be**. *One* is intended to simulate the sound of British summertime as heard through the ears of a honey bee (I don't even know if bees have ears; I don't think they do). It consists of four tracks, each between five and 19 minutes long, of drone improvisations accompanied at all times by an audio recording of a 40,000-strong active beehive. It was originally composed as a soundtrack to an art installation by Wolfgang Buttress about the importance of pollination – the sound of the hive was actually streamed live from Nottingham to Milan so people could get a feel for the day-to-day experience of a bee. Recorded by Kev Bales and Tony Foster (who have played in Spiritualized among others), *One* features many guests, including Youth from Killing Joke and Sigur Ros's string section, Amiina, as well as some improvised vocals by Buttress's 14-year-old daughter, Camille, and some classical cello by Deirdre Bencsik, the wife of Nottingham beekeeper Dr Martin Bencsik, owner of the featured beehive. It was Deirdre who figured out the bees were humming in the key of C and laid down the bed for the rest of the record. I highly recommend *One* to anyone who's ever wondered what it feels like to be a bee.

All Wet

Back to ER in LA. As established, British doctors and nurses tended to treat me with disdain, but in their defence they do this while using professional medical language recognised by the World Health Organisation. The American healthcare professionals I met in LA treated me like I was their long-lost friend: they were delighted I'd arrived and made me feel completely at home, while using language that would fail any medical exam. The nurse looked in my ear and exclaimed, 'Woah! That ear is hella waxy!' She said it into my blocked ear but I heard her all the same and the message was clear – I had a lot of wax in my ear and I was gross. It was decided that I would have my ears flushed out to wash all the wax away so I'd no longer be in pain. They handed me one of those hospital gowns that's open at the back and told me to strip off. 'But my ears are on my face' I protested. 'If I was you I'd at least take your T-shirt off but I'd recommend your pants [trousers] too because you're about to get hella wet.' I was pretty sure my trousers weren't going to get hella wet so I kept them on (besides, they were corduroy and I had to stay on brand), but I did take my top off despite the fact it made me feel even more wretched. I also should point out that the entire ER staff were stupidly attractive. They all looked like they could've starred in the TV show *ER*, and I felt like all these beautiful people were judging the waxy-eared English guy who'd now got his pigeon chest out. She asked me to lie on my side in the foetal position so she could commence the flushing. This was not an ideal position to be in while still suffering from chronic food poisoning. In fact I'd say that lying on your side and pushing your knees towards your chest is a good way to make yourself do another shit. But the hospital bed was too short for me to lie flat on, so I had to go foetal and focus on not publicly shitting myself for the second time in 24 hours.

She was right about taking my trousers off. The water filled my ear up, poured down my cheek and neck, then cascaded down my back and soaked my arse. Not the rest of my trousers – just my arse. And the water was warm. When you're focusing on not shitting yourself, the last thing you need is for your bum to become warm and wet, thus telling your brain that it may as well do a shit as sensationally it's already happened. Once the flushing was done I dried my body and put my T-shirt back on but still had to leave with a soaking-wet butt. I don't know if you've ever shat yourself before (you have), but the shame doesn't leave your eyes for at least 48 hours, so as I was walking out of the hospital not only did I physically look like I had shit myself, but my eyes were telling people the same story because they were still riddled with guilt from the day before. I was staring at everyone shamefully with eyes that said, 'I have disgraced myself', and once I'd walked past they'd look at my soaking-wet backside and put two and two together pretty quickly. I was far from living the LA highlife.

•

In 2015, **Katie Gately** was living in the heart of Hollywood right by the strip and working on her debut full-length album, *Color*. In her spare time, she was repeatedly watching interviews with Robin Williams and Martin Short, always marvelling at how beautifully absurd both of them were, and was deeply in love with the movie *Who Framed Roger Rabbit*. In general, Gately is drawn to art where both serious and silly energies can coexist simultaneously, so she's always hunting for a sadistically whimsical, mischievously tart energy in her music. The idea with *Color* was to make an antisocial pop record. Something that attacks you and even threatens you but with a wink and a trot to it. For this, she needed to have faith in the listener's ability to ride a wave and take a turn; to nosedive and head-thrash and essentially trust in her. She also wanted the album to be playful and feature moments of light but dangerous fun, housing creepy giggles within it. But the road to achieving this goal was riddled with obstacles.

While recording *Color*, Gately had an outbreak of shingles after kissing a street dog in Chile (something she admits she deserved). The problem was that the shingles developed in her ear, and since shingles almost never develop in the ear, her doctor gave her the wrong medication as he assumed she had an ear infection. This delay in diagnosis led Katie to developing Bell's palsy. The virus attacked a facial nerve so she 'looked like a sad clown' while recording vocals. She had to wear an eyepatch because she couldn't blink and sang the vocal parts out of one side of her mouth because she couldn't move the other half of her face. She also developed tendonitis in her arm from all the sound editing, so her arm was basically nerve-damaged and paralysed for a good chunk of the year. This led to Gately having to learn to use her left hand for the rest

176 PERFECT SOUND WHATEVER

of the editing process. Unsurprisingly, Katie had a number of panic attacks during this time period and, due to the palsy and the tendonitis, got legally addicted to benzodiazepines. To make matters even more stressful, Gately had to move house in the middle of working on the record because there was a homeless woman outside the apartment screaming 'I'll kill you' for six hours a day. Fortunately, the change of location ended up being a huge help: it was more peaceful and she felt more clear-headed and able to finish the record the way she wanted to. *Color* was released in October 2016, and the songs sounded every bit as antisocial as Gately had intended.

I Feel Magic

I didn't shake the food poisoning for a whole week. I just lay in bed watching *Orange is the New Black* and feeling ill. My Airbnb was a tiny apartment on the side of a big house where a family lived, and my bedroom adjoined a room in the main house that I assume was simply known as 'The Telling-Off Room'. Every time the kids needed to be told off they were taken to the spot directly behind where I lay in bed and then got yelled at for being awful kids. Obviously I downloaded a ton of 2016 albums that week, if only to drown out the scoldings. I had recently sailed past the 150 mark and couldn't believe I was still uncovering so many gems on a daily basis; it was starting to make me think that maybe 2016 was the greatest year for music in my lifetime or something ;). I remember lying in bed one morning while one of the kids got yelled at for touching the other one's phone, and searching for 'best experimental R&B 2016', which threw up both *Princess* by **ABRA** and **serpentwithfeet**'s *blisters*. Those EPs are by far and away the best thing that happened to me that entire trip. ABRA is like that kid in the playground who's a loner by choice, confidently at odds with the popular crowd while simultaneously coming off cooler than they do; meanwhile serpentwithfeet marries bewitching vocals with theatrical instrumentals, lyrics about the need to be valued are set to 'Marche au supplice' by French Romantic composer Hector Berlioz, creating a contemporary opera of sorts. Both EPs are right up my street (wacky) and are therefore perfect for exacting revenge on noisy families. I played them so loud.

After a week of not leaving that room I decided to go to CVS and get some bottled water and ammonium (niiiiice). I couldn't lie in the same room all week – I had to experience the city while I could. I had a shower, got dressed for the first time in seven days, loaded up my backpack with supplies and took one step outside the apartment into the sunshine, when a teenager flew past on a bike and yelled, 'HEY RON WEASLEY!!!!!'

There was nothing I could do about that kid – I knew as soon as he shouted it that I was defenceless against his dark arts. Because if I had responded, no matter what I'd said, my English accent would only back up the fact I was Ron Weasley the wizard. So, yeah. LA didn't go too well for me and soon it was time to fly back to London.

•

In 2015 **Open Mike Eagle** travelled from LA to London to record an album with English producer and multi-instrumentalist

Paul White. He'd only ever spoken to Paul over the internet after hearing a project he'd done with Homeboy Sandman and had never visited London before. Mike had always been pretty anxious about travelling, especially internationally: he regards himself as culturally lazy and doesn't like being somewhere where he doesn't know the language. He gets very uncomfortable in new places, preferring to know how to get and communicate exactly what he needs, and even though some people find immersing themselves in unfamiliar cultures thrilling, to Mike it's completely intimidating and sometimes a little too much to take on all at once.

He started his trip off on a very bad foot. He usually travels with edibles, and because he was going to be in Europe for a few weeks (he would be embarking on a short European tour prior to settling in London), he had a few weeks' worth of edibles in his hand luggage. He got to the airport and through security to find the airport was virtually empty. He was sitting alone waiting for his flight to be called when a policeman appeared round the corner with a sniffer dog. Because of the way sightlines work, he knew he couldn't make it to the trash to ditch the comestibles – he was literally the only person sitting in that area, so if the dog started barking at anything, the cop would clearly see it was Mike that put it there. So he freaked out, made a snap decision and ate it all. He ate a few weeks' worth of edibles in one sitting. And that was the worst flight of his life. He spent most of it trying to hold the molecules of his body together, wrapping his arms tightly around his torso, because he felt like he was about to explode and die all over the other passengers. When the plane landed he was very much not ok. Luckily the tour manager had built in two days for Mike to get acclimatised before the first show, but during those two days, due to a combination of jet lag and being on a huge comedown, he felt beyond terrible, like he hadn't slept in for ever and had to climb out of that hole before he could even get to his base level of cultural anxiety.

From there, Mike travelled around Europe on tour with experimental rap group **clipping.** (who came out with *Splendor & Misery* in 2016, an Afrofuturist concept album about a slave astronaut who escapes his slaveship and flees across the vastness of space), and once the tour was over he moved to London for two weeks to make the new project with Paul. His wife and child joined him at the start of his stay and they hit all the tourist stops as a family – Buckingham Palace, the Houses of Parliament, Big Ben, everything tourists are meant to see. Mike found these epic buildings to be weirdly intimidating as well as captivating; he would sometimes find pockets of calm when standing among these iconic landmarks with legacies that had lasted generations. But, mainly, Mike didn't feel relaxed in London. It was a lot all at once: being in a new city for the first time, meeting Paul White for the first time and recording in a way he wasn't really used to, in which they would write a song and then immediately record it that day. A lot of it was overwhelming but that's not to say it wasn't also inspiring.

Before Mike flew to London, Paul had sent him a bunch of basic beats, drum loops and songs that he'd wanted to sample; they'd identified the ones they were feeling the most and then wrote and recorded to those. Then Paul would take those beats and re-create whatever the sample was himself – he would manually play each instrument over the top of the original, laying down guitar, drums, whatever, until he could remove the initial sample and have his own version sit in its place. Other times he would just play bass or replace the keys, and keep the original as the bed. But he never left it as it was. He would always find ways to make everything sound more his own and three-dimensional.

The way Paul would take someone else's music, put himself in the track and become each instrument until the whole thing was his wasn't too dissimilar to how Mike was writing lyrics around that time. While in songwriting mode he found himself being hypervigilant and trying to note things down that were happening around him like they were short films. In a cafe in London he saw a guy clearly in a third-wheel situation a few tables over. It looked like he'd shown up thinking he was going on a date, but the woman he was meeting had brought along another guy, and it didn't look like the man who'd just arrived was prepared for that. Mike started writing this story out, not from his own perspective, looking in from the outside, but from this uncomfortable guy's point of view. He put himself inside the situation, internalised it and tried to empathise with what this stranger was going through. A lot of the lyrics on the record were written this way, where Mike would observe other people's everyday interactions and swap bodies with the most awkward person in that story to try and relate and tell their side of it. This is the kind of persona he likes to explore in rap music; a vulnerable character, whether it's himself or somebody else. He likes exploring specific kinds of social anxiety and finds that even when he thinks he's got nothing to write about, he always has a different take on this subject in his reserves at all times.

Hella Personal Film Festival by Open Mike Eagle and Paul White was released in March 2016. The use of the word 'personal' in the title really stands out with this project. While some songs are written about Mike's own experiences ('Smiling' is about how nobody smiled at him during the French leg of the tour due to his race), a lot of them are imagined through other people's eyes, and yet they still feel like personal tracks because we all feel this way when confronted with certain social dilemmas. I could be wrong about that, but whatever the intention behind it, I found the idea of referring to someone else's experience as 'personal' to be oddly affecting.

Body War

When boarding the plane from LA to London I felt like I was getting ill but dismissed it. Then I had to sit on said plane for hours on end breathing recycled air. On the train from Heathrow airport to my London flat I noticed I'd developed a cough. When I got back home my flatmates informed me that there had been a leak in the shower that had seeped into the walls of the flat and made them damp, so from now on we would have seven dehumidifiers, all on full blast, in the flat at all times. Two of the dehumidifiers were in my bedroom and were turned on as I slept, so my throat got dried out even more. Long story short, this guy got himself a chest infection. You're right, I was ill a lot in 2017.

•

At 38, **TW Walsh** decided he was finally going to get in shape and get his act together. He went from doing no exercise at all to lifting weights four days a week and playing 90 minutes of basketball on his days off. He did this for about six months without ever listening to his body and ended up overdoing it. He pushed his body to the point where he had a physical breakdown that centred on his nervous system, so it couldn't self-regulate. His temperature was all wrong, he was overheated the whole time, he couldn't sleep and had extreme anxiety, all related to this overworking of the nervous system that he had initiated with this intensive period of working out. It was incredibly debilitating: he was barely able to function for about 18 months and to this day still feels some of its lingering effects. He was grasping at straws for a long time, trying to find a remedy: endocrinology, diets, different types of therapies, but once he started to home in on the autonomic system it became apparent that meditation would be the best way to rehabilitate everything. Once he started regularly practising meditation Walsh entered a period of reflection, healing and spiritual growth. He did a lot of searching, trying to figure out how to get himself back to a place of equilibrium.

Around this time he started to record his latest album in his home studio, but this illness was still hanging over him. His stamina was massively affected, and he also started to experience significant cognitive effects, so had trouble concentrating. He would want to be creative but even sitting up at a computer was too draining. He'd be dizzy and would resort to lying on his back for large chunks of time. Knowing that he might not be able to get this album where he wanted it to be on his own, he reached out to friend and musician **Yuuki Matthews** (of The Shins, among others) to help get the project over the finishing line. Walsh had a vision in his mind: most of his previous records had been more traditionally rock'n'roll-based with live drums, guitars and bass, but this time he wanted to try something different, something that felt timeless but futuristic. He wanted it to include elements from all the music that he liked, from classic rock to weird hip hop and synth pop from the 80s.

Matthews had a huge impact on how everything turned out; there were a handful of songs on which he rewrote the chords underneath the vocal melody, and there wasn't a track that he didn't make a significant contribution to. It should be pointed out that the majority of the instruments were still played by Walsh, who did most of the composition also, but the record would not have turned out the way it did if Matthews had not joined the project. Matthews tried a lot of unconventional techniques when recording. He'd experiment with children's toy instruments, resample them and manipulate the sound, and he'd typically mix a song then run it through two channels of his old cassette four-track, so it produced a blown-out, compressed, gritty sound, reminiscent of the way Walsh grew up listening to music as a child.

The album was called *Fruitless Research* and was released in February 2016. The title is a reference to how Walsh was feeling at the time, taking stock as he approached 40, with only a short list of achievements after a lifetime of work. So he wanted to poke fun at this with a humorous title that described how it feels to put so much work into something then have nothing to show for it – much like the relentless exercise regime he'd once prescribed himself only to make his own body ill.

•

The chest infection floored me. I had to cancel all of my gigs in July, some of which were in countries I'd never visited before (Japan and Canada, respectively), and spent a month in bed feeling sorry for myself and coughing so hard I was unable to sleep. The dehumidifiers roared all day and all night as I continued to cancel work and stay in bed. I had spent too much time in 2017 trapped indoors and was fed up. After lying in my Airbnb bedroom in LA for a week with food poisoning, I was now lying in my bedroom in London for a month with a stupid chest infection. Not to mention the week in Auckland when I was a prisoner in my own hotel room. To cheer myself up I downloaded *Colossal Squid*, a solo drum record by **Adam Betts**. Betts uses a bunch of electronic pads to trigger samples and synth patterns, meaning he can play the accompaniment to his own drumming *while* drumming, producing animated instrumentals full of rhythmically driven melodies. I also treated myself to **Róisín Murphy**'s *Take Her Up to Monto*, a curious electronic album all about architecture, *Midnight Run*, a superb collaboration between Houston rapper **Siddiq** and vaporwave producer **Vektroid**, and *Outer Edges* by experimental drum & bass trio **NOISIΛ**. NOISIΛ are called NOISIΛ because when you turn it upside down it says VISION. Yes. Please. I absolutely love that sort of shit.

But, ultimately, lying in bedrooms was boring. I despised bedrooms by the end of 2017. Honestly, I never wanted to be in another bedroom again as long as I lived. I swore that once I was better I'd sleep outdoors and get changed in the bushes before I ever set foot in a bedroom again. I hated bedrooms so much. I was officially anti-bedroom. Bedrooms were the worst rooms of all time. Apart from all the bedrooms where amazing musicians have written and recorded entire amazing albums. Those bedrooms are cool. But all other bedrooms stink.

Wide Asleep

In 2016, **Sadie Dupuis** rented out a friend's bedroom in Philadelphia and started to work obsessively on a solo record. She did this not out of necessity, but because she specifically wanted to work this way. The first album by her regular band Speedy Ortiz had been a solo venture recorded in Sadie's bedroom and lately a part of her had become nostalgic for those times. So since this was effectively her second solo album she decided to return to a bedroom setting even though 'proper' recording studios were now an option.

Sadie had spent most of 2015 feeling inspired by the amount of incredible self-produced female projects on offer and wanted to make her own pop record while still retaining the rock elements of Speedy Ortiz. She would often stay up all night recording drum machines, synths and guitars directly into the computer, and finished the whole album in just two weeks. Many of these bubblegum grunge songs are sung from a feminist standpoint: the song 'Hype' is about the way women are written about in the media, how they're constantly being pitted against each other (Dupuis experiencing this first hand having regularly featured in lazy articles about women in music) and 'Get a Yes' is a feelgood dancefloor filler about consent, focussing on victim blaming and how bad society has been at tackling and teaching us about such issues. Sadie released *Slugger* under the name **Sad13** in November 2016. Sad13 is pronounced as it's written – 'Sad Thirteen' – and not 'Sadie' like some smart arses (me) might've assumed and then said out loud to Sadie herself during an interview over the phone (also me).

•

Katie Dey grew up in a small town on the east coast of New South Wales near beaches and tourists, surfers and retirees. Unfortunately she could never swim, so didn't participate in most activities and opted instead to stay inside on her computer. When she was 11 years old, an uncle gave her a Wurlitzer organ and she taught herself to play – messing with the different sounds, operating the volume pedal like a sewing machine, speeding up the programmed drum beats as fast as they'd go and making the whole instrument work the way she wanted it to.

In 2015, Katie was living in Melbourne and sharing a house with two friends. They were all totally broke and lived above a salon owned by a secret meth addict who would occasionally ask to smoke in their kitchen to hide it from his wife. Katie would spend most of her time shut in her bedroom, writing and recording music, and from mid-2015 to mid-2016 she wrote and recorded *Flood Network*. She wanted to make an album that made the listener feel like they were moving through something; she had been listening to a band called The Brave Little Abacus, whose album of home recordings, *Just Got Back from the Discomfort We're Alright*, had a beautifully stitched-together flow to it, full of detailed sound collages. She would work on the album in short bursts, two to three weeks of feverish non-stop writing and intense recording followed by months of nothing, then another two weeks of intense work. She puts this down to her bipolar disorder, which has always caused her problems with time management: she'll get too depressed to do anything for long periods and then write manically for a short amount of time.

The theme of mental illness made its way into the lyrics

along with how mental health can be affected by spirituality, the internet and sexual abuse, although Dey deliberately tried to give the album as ambiguous a tone as possible. Both *Flood Network* and her debut, *Asdfasdf*, featured unclear images of Katie on their covers, and her voice was often pitched way up throughout. Her social media presence, however, provided a notable contrast to this. Open and frank tweets about her mental health, as well as her political and social views, increased over the months and years following the release of *Flood Network*, which Katie puts down to Twitter never feeling 100 per cent 'real'. In 2018, Dey began tweeting about being transgender and sharing photos of herself without any filters clouding the image for the first time. She also released a collaborative project, *Some New Form of Life*, with Canadian artist Devi McCallion, which featured an unedited photo of Dey on the cover and songs that contained her natural singing voice without any effects being added. The reason Katie hadn't been forthcoming about her transsexuality until now was that she didn't want it to distract from the music, but she had gradually felt different about this over time, due to having a supportive network of friends around her who encouraged her to proudly and openly be herself both in her music and with her fans.

The fact that Katie is a trans woman could never distract from her music because it's naturally a part of it anyway, the same as anyone's identity unavoidably becomes a part of their art whether they're open about it or not. Even before she publicly came out, many people, including myself, would listen to Katie's albums and experience a strong feeling that this unique music had been made by a transgender woman. Obviously a cis man like me has no idea what it's like to be transgender, so this feeling wasn't based on anything informed or logical – something unexplainable just spoke through the songs somehow. I've never experienced this before: to listen to a song and get such a strong sense of the person creating it is like gaining a new and intense emotion out of nowhere. So this is another aspect of *Flood Network* that makes it stand out in Dey's discography. Along with the innovative songwriting and unconventional production, it also signals the end of a chapter in Dey's journey as an artist. Her follow-up solo record, *Solipsisters*, came out in 2019 with all lyrics focusing on Katie's life as a trans woman, very firmly signalling the end of everything that came before it.

Flood Network

In 1999 my family home flooded. The water tank in the attic had overflowed due to a cracked ballcock (at 14, I was the perfect age to be told this piece of information), and for some time the entire attic had been steadily filling up with water. One Easter weekend while we were away visiting friends, the ceiling caved in and a waterfall flowed through the entire house. It took three months for the house to be refurbished and during that time we lived in a much smaller house without a television. Having to go without television at 14 was a daunting prospect, plus we'd not got the internet yet so our options were limited. I began listening to the radio for the first time and became hooked on Radio 1 (I would listen to Chris Moyles when I got home from school and John Peel as I went to sleep), as well as an obscure Dutch station called Radio Dingo. My brother and I loved Radio Dingo because they were so lively and every so often they'd say a word in English (like that *Fast Show* Channel 9 sketch), and we used to record Radio Dingo onto cassette and then listen back to the funniest bits. We had a little tape player with a mic on it which meant we could record anything onto tape, including our own voices, and now that I was a fan of the wireless I wanted to record my own radio show. I recorded countless episodes of James FM while living in that house. I don't know where any of the tapes are now, and the fact that I don't know where they are fills me with anxiety and dread. If anyone ever found and listened to those tapes I would be beyond mortified: hours of me speaking in an American accent for no reason – 'Howdy, ladies and gentlemen, welcome to James FM, y'all. Today I'm interviewing Ruth, who may or may not be my sister . . .' – and then interviewing my younger sister and pressing funny sound effects on a keyboard while she's patiently trying to talk to me about her day. Embarrassing now but at the time I loved it. I had a lot of fun in that little house and three months flew by, largely thanks to the shows I listened to on the radio.

Radio International

After coming out with a few avant-garde indie projects, in 2016 musician and conceptual artist Dean Blunt, under the name **Babyfather,** released an experimental UK hip hop album set in a pirate radio station. The record was called *'BBF' Hosted by DJ Escrow*, an epic concept album examining life in London and the UK music scene. With sirens and ringtones interrupting songs and a front cover featuring a hoverboard adorned in the Union Jack, this was a project that prompted a lot of discussion, even though it never took itself too seriously.

The album opens with a looped quote by Craig David stating, 'This makes me proud to be British' over the top of some soothing classical guitar. The more this message is repeated, the more it gets under the skin and feels passive-aggressive, losing its original meaning and assuming a darker tone. There are songs on this album that, for a moment, feel like standard garage tracks, but they nearly always evolve (or devolve) into something more self-aware. Occasionally, the music feels like it's messing with you, with the instrumentals sometimes being manipulated to the point of unlistenable noise, and at times the dub beats and lyrical content feel like parody as Blunt makes a statement about the UK scene by showing rather than telling.

The official members of Babyfather are Dean Blunt, DJ Escrow and Gassman D, but when the album was released nothing was known about Blunt's collaborators. It was unclear whether they actually existed or were just aliases used by Blunt himself. Escrow talks throughout the entire record, hosting the album as our pirate radio DJ. His voice has been pitched up, further concealing his identity, and he speaks freely about what it is to be an MC and to live in London in 2016, and how we need unity – how North, South, East and West are divided and need to link up. Sometimes he's played for laughs, sometimes he's employed to convey a sincere message, but he holds the whole thing together and signposts any details we may have missed in the lyrics by monologuing at length about the album's key subjects.

The humorous side of the record prompted many people to claim the whole project was just a joke and that anyone who liked it at face value or took it seriously was falling for a huge prank – a theory reinforced by the fact that the album was released on April Fool's Day. But as well as being silly, '*BBF*' does speak to the people whose life it shines a light on and takes you on a genuine emotional journey from beginning to end. So it's maybe a bit of both: the people it's written for can relate to it and laugh with it, and the people it's not written for will look stupid when they take it too seriously and over-intellectualise it. And seeing as I've just analysed it in a book, I think I fall firmly into the second category.

•

One of the songs I remember hearing for the first time on the Chris Moyles show in 1999 was **Baz Luhrmann**'s 'Everybody's Free (to Wear Sunscreen)'. For those of you who don't know, it's a speech given by Luhrmann to 'the class of '99', in which he dispenses advice on how to live a worthwhile and rewarding life: appreciate your family, do your stretches, drink some milk – all the important stuff.

I was a very earnest teenager. I hung out with the 'alternative kids' but didn't drink or smoke; I spent most of my weekends walking around the woods or nearby quarry with my friend Jake, talking about 'life', mainly because I was secretly terrified by all the life I had ahead of me. So when 'Everybody's Free' came out I took it very seriously. It wasn't just a song to me – these were literal instructions on how to get life right and I honestly lived by them for longer than you'd expect. I kept my old love letters and threw away my bank statements because Baz had told me to. I genuinely had a box of letters from ex-girlfriends at the back of a cupboard but no record of my finances whatsoever. As the years rolled by I became self-employed and began to keep my bank statements in a ring binder and I gradually left the love letters alone because it felt creepy to store them away in a box like a serial killer. Life got less whimsical and more sensible, as it tends to.

In 2017 I found myself thinking a lot about 1999, a year I enjoyed perhaps more than any other. I saw a solar eclipse in '99, Manchester United won the treble, not to mention Millennium Eve being the best New Year's ever. Millennium Eve was spectacular, a milestone for humanity, and everyone on Earth felt like they were shifting into a bright new era, together as one. At least that's how it felt to an optimistic 14-year-old. I was very glass-half-full as a teenager. Somehow my entire house flooding in 1999 had been a fun little adventure, but a tiny leak in my shower in 2017 now felt like a total disaster. As I lay in bed with a chest infection and seven dehumidifiers screaming throughout the flat, I felt like this shitty year was all my fault, that I wasn't living a full and decent life because I'd strayed from the original guidelines set out by Baz Luhrmann when I was 14. I had become an adult. I wasn't dancing and singing enough like he'd told me to, I worried too much and I certainly hadn't worn enough sunscreen in my life (some sources say you're meant to wear it even when it's not sunny for god's sakes). That's why I kept getting ill and strangers were starting fights with me, that's why I couldn't sustain a relationship – I'd ignored Luhrmann and now I was paying the price.

Very few generations have the perfect manual for life fall into their lap as a teenager (I know there are plenty of religious texts but who's got the time to unpick any of those). I was given all of life's cheat codes on a plate with 'Everybody's Free' and I still ended up lonely, unhealthy and bored with only myself to blame. I often wonder how Baz Luhrmann's doing these days, if he's happy, if he stretches every day and has a box of old love letters stashed away somewhere, always being kind to his knees and drinking big glasses of milk. I bet he does none of those things. I bet he goes against his own teachings all the time. I bet he's sunburnt right now. Really badly sunburnt.

I don't listen to songs like 'Everybody's Free' any more. They make me feel bad about myself for not doing everything perfectly. Now I listen to albums where the singer adopts an alter ego of a scumbag so I can go easier on myself. In 2017 I was exhausted from trying to get everything right all the time and I felt liberated by artists who'd stopped trying to please everyone, especially if those artists deliberately pissed people off and didn't seem to give a shit.

Guilty of Love

Literally nobody else seemed to like the **Död Mark** album *Drabbad av Sjukdom*, but I loved it. It's a navel gaze punk album made by Swedish rapper **Yung Lean** (who provided backing vocals on the song 'Godspeed' from Frank Ocean's *Blonde*) and producer Yung Gud. All the criticisms levelled at it are the reasons why I love it. I love that the songs feel aimless, I love that you can tell it's being made by a rapper and not a punk band; there's something about Död Mark that I haven't heard anywhere else because I think you could only achieve this sound by asking a Swedish rapper to make a punk album.

I just love that *Drabbad av Sjukdom* exists and that it managed to wind so many people up. They're deliberately doing everything 'wrong' and owning it with every single track, and it's this refusal to cater for anyone that unquestionably attracts me to this project, along with its counterintuitive approach to songwriting. Just to be clear – I genuinely love this record at face value and am not being contrary by liking a 'shit record'. It's a great record and feels more punk than most punk albums do these days. More than any other project released in 2016, *Drabbad Av Sjukdom* felt like my own personal record; I almost didn't want anyone else to like it. It was hard to put the effect it had on me into words, the nerves it touched: it just connected with something that's been inside me for very a long time. I instantly felt sentimental about this album but I didn't know why, like it took me back to a childhood I'd never actually lived. It was an album that came across as unassuming and belligerent all at once, both naive and robust, and despite the fact it was a punk record made by a rap artist it managed to be one of the most vulnerable releases of the year. It was like they'd decided to make a punk record without properly researching or listening to a great deal of punk music – it's a half-remembered interpretation of a genre as opposed to a bunch of musos following all the rules to make a by-the-book punk album. I'm sure I'm wrong and that Död Mark would tell me to go fuck myself if they ever read this, but, to be honest, that'd only make me love them even more. And if you don't love an album that everybody else hates, then I don't believe you truly love music. We can intellectualise all day long but, really, true fandom is about you having a personal connection to an album and it's impossible to only enjoy critically acclaimed cult classics that everyone approves of. Albums like this are how you know you're not just liking stuff because you're told you have to like it. Some people are told a certain year from the 70s is the greatest year for music of all time so adopt the same perspective, without stopping to consider whether they genuinely feel that way themselves. These people think they love music but they don't, they're a bunch of robot zombies and I am the coolest.

Anyway . . .

Being in bed on my own for a month was the loneliest I felt all year. I got really down during that time, obsessing way too much over how isolated I felt. I was fed up of needing to be around other people in order to feel happy, but was also fed up of behaving awkwardly in social situations due to spending so much time on my own. I bought a lot of albums from 2016 during the chest infection month and a lot of them were related to either solitude or togetherness. For example, *Id Vendor* by **Yeah You**, a father-and-daughter duo who go by the aliases Elvin Brandhi and Mykl Jaxn. *Id Vendor* was their first album since Elvin had moved to Vienna to study. Before this they used to improvise and record their electro-punk songs in the car on the way to the supermarket (I presume someone else was driving). So, for the first time, they weren't hanging out every day and could only record when Mykl was able to pay Elvin a visit. This meant the songs came out way more intense and it's easy to get swept up in the urgency of each track as a father and daughter adapt to not seeing each other as often as they used to.

Too Much of Life is Mood

Adam Torres released his first record, 'Mr Noman', in 2006, it was a big cult hit, but afterwards he was unsure about what he wanted to do with his life. So he moved to Austin to go to graduate school and take Latin American Studies, became a Spanish Literature teacher and got married, all at the same time. In total, he was working 48 hours a week and then on top of that had to finish homework and conduct further research for his papers. He was extremely busy and needed some kind of release valve for all the stress he was under. So he inadvertently rededicated himself to music and started writing songs again.

Around this time he felt incredibly isolated and doubted whether all of this esoteric work and research had any bearing on reality. He didn't feel connected to anyone at the school, when he was teaching he didn't feel like he was connecting with his students, or maybe they weren't connecting with him, or both. He kept returning to the typical academic ivory tower argument, that academia is too far removed from the rest of the world, something he was starting to feel in a very real way, and he would often find himself standing in the school corridors having no idea what he was doing there. A combination of things were pulling him in different directions but he never had any intention to return to being a musician and make that his life. It just sort of happened because, after quitting his teaching job and his classes, he was inspired to finish some songs he'd been working on in his spare time. This was in 2013.

One summer Torres started to read a book by activist writer Edward Abbey called *Desert Solitaire*. Set in the late 70s, when

Abbey was a seasonal park ranger for a National Park in Utah, the book is made up of his thoughts and ponderings during the summer season. The subtitle was *A Season in the Wilderness*, and the whole thing resonated strongly with Torres, mainly because of where he was in his life. He had been working for the State of Texas for a couple of years now and a lot of his work had to do with environmental conservation, so some of the environmental and cultural subjects covered by Abbey (decay, decline and society) struck a chord with Adam. He tried to put a similar energy into writing songs, and, in an abstract way, you can hear this influence throughout his second album. Intentionally or unintentionally, Torres had a desire to capture landscape within his music: a lot of that had to do with his upbringing in Ohio and the feeling he got through being part of the outdoors – the romantic moods of isolation and the experience of being infinitesimal in a vast and sprawling space. After years of steady work, *Pearls to Swine* was released in September 2016.

Two months before the album's release Torres was involved in a serious motorcycle crash. He was out on a ride by himself, going down a highway access road in Bastrop, Texas, 30 miles east of Austin. A passenger truck recklessly came off the highway, which ran parallel to the access road, and tried to make a sharp turn into a grocery store, sweeping in front of Adam. He remembers the second before the impact and then suddenly being on his back underneath the truck, surrounded by paramedics with everybody telling him not to move while they tried to figure out his injuries. His head was about 6 inches in front of the rear left tyre, and his body was diagonally placed underneath the truck. A witness said that he flew through the air and once he'd hit the ground the truck had run over him.

So he was taken to the hospital but somehow didn't have any organ damage or broken bones. No one understood how he'd got so lucky – he had been travelling at 50 miles per hour and the truck was going a lot faster. It was unclear whether he'd be able to go on tour to promote the record as he wasn't in great shape and was taking a while to recover. Then, shortly after the album's release, his marriage ended, the biggest loss he'd experienced in his life so far. The split was on his mind throughout the *Pearls to Swine* tour, which wasn't a happy period for him anyway as while he was on the road his grandmother died and Trump was elected. The election result was a devastating blow to Torres, who found it hard not to take it personally. And so he moved out to the country.

Torres now lives in Driftwood, Texas. All there is in Driftwood is a post office and a graveyard. He moved in with some friends who owned a plot, about five acres of land, and it's peaceful. He likes the country a lot, especially the desert. He feels a visceral comfort in being able to see for miles on the horizon, to look out and to only be able to see mountains or hills. In Cincinnati the winters were extremely bleak, cold and dark, but in Driftwood it never really gets cold so much. It just stops being hot sometimes. There are coral snakes and mountain lions in the area, and Adam spends a lot of time alone writing his songs.

•

Javan St Prix grew up in East London around a thriving grime scene. He started to MC at an early age but had to keep it a secret from his cousins, who didn't want him to become an MC. He used to do dealings with them, so if he got big in the scene he'd draw unwanted attention to their business. But he was having problems with some of his cousins' associates, and one night when they'd heard Javan would be making an appearance on local radio, they made a plan to ambush him when he turned up at the station. They phoned his cousins for backup, unaware that they were related, simply stating that this MC was on his way, they were gonna fuck him up and his name was Javan. His cousins obviously figured out it was him so called off the ambush and confronted Javan at the station about his MCing. There was a lot of back and forth, but eventually Javan demonstrated his abilities and his cousins agreed he could continue, but he had to keep his distance from them. Javan respected this and was free to pursue music out in the open as **Trim**.

He decided early on to adopt a variety of different styles and to accompany these styles with corresponding egos and names. Trim, Trimble, Trimothy, Trimetheus, Taliban Trim, Osama Trim Laden and many more. The names came from different places. One of his favourite characters is Lord Sith Flow, which he reserves for his darkest, coldest tracks. He's a big *Star Wars* fan and prides himself on being from the dark side, which he also relates to the colour of his skin, as growing up in a predominantly white area he was always made aware of colour. Even though he had a sense of humour regarding his egos, he knew they all came from a personal place, often tied to more negatives than positives. The bottom line with all of this is that he was insecure and scared to be himself, so just created loads of different people he could pretend to be instead. He didn't want to be the man he'd grown up to be and felt like he wasn't meant to be living this way. Some of those characters were Trim trying to be someone living a decent life, others were the bad side of him and people probably liked them more because that's who he was in E14. But he never wanted to be that person. Trim hopes that anyone who grew up in that life understands that all the ego he puts into his different aliases are really and truly about being scared. Everything you do comes from fear because you feel like you're backed into a corner and want to fight the world.

Trim knew he wanted to establish his own style. He was looking around at a lot of grime MCs at the time who were talking about selling drugs and carrying a gun and he didn't believe them. He felt like grime was starting to become too catch-phrase-orientated with a lot of MCs doing one-line flows, which can work but some of it was becoming too comedic and formu-laic. He felt like British rap was a joke to rappers in America, where everyone actually has a gun, and in comparison UK rap seemed gimmicky. But he wanted to show the US that life is not easy in Britain, that some people are living in a shithole and fighting to get out or even fighting to stay alive, and if he could put these facts in ways that other grime MCs hadn't done, then he stood a better chance of standing out and being heard. He wanted to take his time and make something artistic, but the strength of a lot of grime is that it's so powerful and so immediate, the people making it are often not well off and they know they've got to go out and make this music count. There's no room for the university-art-school 'Let's hang about for six months and make a weird esoteric sort of album' attitude. There's an urgency to it that you don't find in other music. But Trim didn't want to make pop grime – he was raised by a Rastafarian mother, listening to Dennis Brown and John Holt, and knew he couldn't look his mum in the face after delivering a pop performance. He never wanted to sound mainstream so making the sort of album he wanted to was always going to be hard.

For many years as a solo artist **James Blake** had felt a bit like a mad scientist alone in his studio making beats, getting up close with his work and never bringing in anyone else. But lately he'd gone through some personal changes and wanted to step back from everything and learn how to produce other people, how to collaborate, and learn when to back off and not be involved.

Blake discovered Trim by stumbling across an online video. The footage was filmed on a camera phone: Trim was freestyling in a car with an associate of his called MC Obese, over a beat that really appealed. So Blake scoured the internet for any Trim song he could find that didn't have a beat under it and found an interview with Trim out on the street freestyling about what was going on around him. There was some background noise but Blake sampled it anyway and made a song out of it called 'Saying', which led to Blake producing Trim's single 'Confidence Boost', with 'Saying' as the B-side.

When Blake contacted Trim a couple of years later, proposing they make an album together, Trim was going through a rough time. Life in E14 was getting even more complicated and dangerous, plus he was struggling with his family, homelessness and his girlfriend. It was a time in his life when everybody was on his back, and he was under a lot of stress due to being the main source of income when it came to his family. The grime scene was weighing on him also; he felt like a lot of people were stealing his lyrics, some of his peers had got famous and now thought they were better than him, he felt like everyone was taking the piss and he felt disorientated. So, while excited about making an album, Trim felt a lot of pressure.

The lyrics flowed pretty easily, with Trim trying not to over-think what he was writing. He would record himself a cappella and send it over to Blake and Rob McAndrews (aka AirHead, an affiliate of Blake's label, 1-800 Dinosaur), who would match it to an instrumental. It was a novel way of working, starting with the voice and building the music around it. Three tracks were made more traditionally, with Trim and McAndrews in the studio coming up with the beats and vocals together. Rob grew up playing guitar and was largely into indie music, so when making the tunes for Trim's album, although he was trying to make grime, it naturally got warped through the prism of everything he'd made before. So while he didn't intentionally do anything different, it still ended up sounding controversial to the purists. They spent a lot of time experimenting: at one point Trim sang a chorus (something he'd never usually do) on a track called 'Waco'. The vocal was meant to be a placeholder as far as Trim was concerned, but Rob and James loved how he sounded on it and kept trying to convince him to let them use his take. In a lighthearted way, Trim maintains that they tricked him: he wanted someone else to come in and sing it but time just ran out, so it was released with him singing the chorus instead. Trim didn't even hear this track, or most of the beats for that matter, until the project was coming to an end. He felt like 1-800 Dinosaur had heard his story in the lyrics and strung it together themselves in a way that made sense, giving the listener a full and clear narrative.

Once it was finished, the album as a whole felt more like a collaboration than a Trim solo project, like an excursion they'd all taken together. So the project was released under the name *1-800 Dinosaur Presents Trim* in July 2016. It's a simple name and one that didn't grab me until I learnt the story of the album and how it came to be. When you know that both parties contributed to every track and the work was split almost perfectly down the middle, then the title takes on more significance: a collaboration between an artist and their label is either rare or never admitted to, but I love that in this instance it's how the entire project is presented.

Nothing More to Say

I shook the chest infection just in time for the Edinburgh Festival in August. I performed the four different shows on rotation for the month and brought my 2016 album total up to 216 (I nearly stopped at 216 because it looks a bit like 2016 but then decided 366 would be more satisfying as there were 366 days in 2016). That month I bought the wonderfully Americana *Eric Bachmann* by **Eric Bachmann**, **Comfort Food**'s rhythmical jazz venture *Waffle Frolic*, **Kojey Radical**'s semi-conceptual, grime/ spoken-word project *23Winters* and *Soft Hair* by Australian sex-pop duo **Soft Hair**, to name a few. I returned to London in September, just in time to launch the book I'd been working on during the tour. But, in true 2017 fashion, the book launch didn't go quite as I'd envisioned. The launch of my first book should've been a special moment in my career as it's nice to be able to take a break from work and enjoy your achievements, but instead I froze up and openly told people that I wanted to jump off the roof of the building.

Things had reached crisis point with my agent and I was no longer able to handle it. After a lot of hard work on everyone's part we had found a home for the live specials, but I publicly announced this news before the contract stated I could, which caused my agent to stress out for fear that we could now lose the entire deal. I became convinced I'd ruined everything and felt like I'd humiliated myself by announcing a project that was no longer going to happen – I'd look like a liar or, at best, someone who doesn't understand the industry he's in. I wanted to quit my job and start a new life somewhere else – I was spiralling out of control and catastrophizing hard.

The book launch occurred four days after I'd fucked up and by then I could barely talk. The launch was on the sixth floor of a building in Blackfriars with a roof garden that guests could walk around while taking in an amazing view of London. I wanted to jump head first off that building and kept blurting it out to people, trying to frame it as a joke but then receiving a reaction that told me they knew I wasn't joking. The colour had drained from my face and I stood in the corner for the most of the night, stressing out. My editor gave a wonderful speech about the book and then everyone looked to me to follow it up, but I was unable to say anything and just looked back at them while giving a feeble thumbs-up. There was a confused silence as people realised there would be no speech from the writer and then everyone gradually resumed milling around while I felt like a dickhead. As I was leaving, my agent asked if I was ok and I said I wasn't. I told him how I was feeling and said I currently felt like I was completely on my own. He responded by saying, 'It makes me feel bad when you say that', and I mumbled something and left.

•

In 2014, **40 Watt Sun**'s Patrick Walker announced that the band were starting work on their second album and anticipation started to build among fans, but then everything went quiet. It wasn't until October 2016 that the band finally released *Wider Than the Sky* on their own label, Radiance Records. The years in between had been something of a battle: the band had sent some early demos to their then label Cyclone Empire, who didn't care much for the new direction the band was going in; a scaled-down sound where only the core elements remained, the cleanness of the instrumentation seeing them move even further from the doom genre Walker's previous projects had been associated with. But, despite the lack of support from their label, the band recorded the album regardless, retreating to a small farm in the Welsh countryside, miles from anywhere else. The three of them would work all day and spend the evening eating a home-cooked meal outside together. The label still wanted an album from them, though, and refused to let the band go until they got a record that *they* wanted to release. And so the members of 40 Watt Sun spent the next 18 months trying to get out of their contract in order to be free to release *Wider Than the Sky*, the album they wanted people to hear, on their own terms.

The album consists of six glacial-paced minimal rock songs, most of them over nine minutes long, that exist in a state of terminal melancholy due to Walker's mesmerising, and at times heart-wrenching, vocals. He's a man who lives deep in the Devon countryside, on the edge of Dartmoor near the coast, and spends much of his time walking alone outdoors. But he refuses to connect this need for space in his personal life to the sound and content of his music. In fact, Walker insists there is no connection between his lifestyle and his writing, despite the abundance of natural imagery throughout his work and the fact that this record makes you feel in awe of something far greater than yourself. But sometimes what an album means to you isn't what it means to its creator, and there are some things we impose on the album ourselves. Having that said that, when listening to songs that beautifully embody the towering solitude we can sometimes experience during adulthood, it is nice knowing they were written by someone who regularly spends time alone in the grey British countryside.

Toss

The morning after the book launch I rang my agent to explain exactly why I felt stressed and on my own, but the phone call quickly turned into an argument. I said no one had told me I wasn't allowed to announce the specials and asked for more support, he said I knew I wasn't allowed to announce the specials but had done it anyway, and that I wasn't making sense. I also told him about the suicidal thoughts I'd been having. So the phone call went badly.

Shortly after this phone call we had to film the specials, so naturally the filming was very intense. I still didn't know if these specials would be going out anywhere and I had many unresolved issues with my agent. I was filming all four shows in a day and then filming all four again the following day. I had half an hour between shows to get changed and ready for the next and I spent much of that time with my head in my hands because I felt like I was mentally and physically falling apart. Fortunately for me, the entire team working on those specials were incredible and held the whole thing together. The audience who turned up were amazing too and I was able to get the performances I wanted on camera. I still feel incredibly privileged to have been able to rely on so many people that weekend. I can go on about how alone I felt in 2017, but there were also so many wonderful people in my corner and in this instance we achieved something I'm incredibly proud of together.

I wanted to schedule a meeting with my agent so we could talk about this phone call face to face. Lines had been crossed and this had to be addressed. The meeting started well but quickly devolved into a standoff where I complained about his behaviour and he complained about my behaviour and he blamed his behaviour on my behaviour. The day after the meeting I was on my way up north for five days to promote the book. I got a phone call from my agent and was informed that the company no longer represented me. He then informed me that once we'd finished this phone call, he would be sending an email to all of his clients informing them that the company no longer represented me.

•

Laura Mvula got dropped by her record label, Sony, by email after her 2016 album *The Dreaming Room* didn't sell as many copies as her debut record. *The Dreaming Room* won an Ivor Novello Award and got nominated for the Mercury Music Prize but didn't break the top ten – that seems to be its only crime as far as I can tell.

Mvula sounds iconic on this album – the way that artists like Prince sound like they're meant to be a star. Something in her delivery commands respect and attention and dropping that presence over email seems counterintuitive and shortsighted to me. It's a revealing album too. While not all the lyrics are personal, Mvula does touch on the breakdown of her marriage, part of which she attributes to her longstanding battles with anxiety. But once again she still manages to convey these challenges while radiating strength, determination and a rare type of magnetism that you *do not drop over email*.

What's most notable about *The Dreaming Room* is that it's an orchestral record without being *about* the orchestra. I honestly didn't even realise the London Symphony Orchestra were on this album as they're essentially used as Mvula's backing band on every song. Obviously, now that I know there's an orchestra involved I feel like a fool, because if you listen out for it then there is clearly an orchestra playing almost all the time. But every sound *belongs* so much that it wasn't the first thing I noticed – Mvula's not using the orchestra to patch up some mediocre tracks, she's using it to enhance songs that already contain their own grandeur. Mvula tricked me elsewhere on the album too. There's an interlude called 'Nan' which on first listen is just a recorded phone call between Laura and her grandmother. But Mvula is actually doing both voices, delivering a convincing impression of her nan and re-creating both sides of a conversation they had during the making of the album. The affection with which she impersonates her nan, how believable and real she is as her, emphasises how close they are. Her performance as herself also takes on new meaning: she sounds weary after a day at the studio, maybe a little too tired for the phone call, but is making the effort anyway.

The Dreaming Room only bound Mvula's fans closer to her idiosyncratic brand of pop, and Sony's actions failed to even slow her down. She actually found the separation quite liberating, continuing to write music, performing further with the London Symphony Orchestra and composing the score for the Royal Shakespeare Company's production of *Antony and Cleopatra* in 2017. Ending the relationship with her label seems to have allowed Laura to assess who she is as an artist and prioritise the projects she most wants to do, following her own self-made path with more purpose than before.

•

For the first time in eight years I was without management and I decided to manage myself for a bit, because the stress of finding a new agent didn't seem worth it. My first action as my own agent was to enforce a deadline on the 2016 project and I decided that I needed to meet my goal of 366 albums by the end of 2017. Buying a year's worth of albums in a year sounded much neater than buying a year's worth of albums in a non-specific amount of time and it felt good to establish a finishing line. It was a good managerial decision on my part.

During my first week of being a lone wolf I received an email from a man I'd never met, asking if I would voice a cartoon character in a Christmas film he was making. The film would only be watched by his family, it would feature his daughters in the lead roles, I would not be getting paid and would be required to record all my parts myself on my phone and send them over to him. And I said yes.

I said yes because he seemed very nice and was making the film to encourage confidence in his daughters. I had just been dropped by my agent and had gone through a breakup earlier the same year, I was emotionally, mentally and physically exhausted and just wanted to be involved in something positive for a bit. So I accepted the role of head elf, Jiminy Jodphurs.

Jiminy Jodphurs is a jolly soul full of boundless enthusiasm and Christmas cheer. And I had to voice this happy little fella when I was at my most miserable and stressed as hell. So the character was a bit of a stretch. The first line I had to record in a spritely elf voice was, '*HOWDY, TINY VIEWERS! JIMINY JODPHURS HERE! WELCOMING YOU TO ANOTHER FABBY DOOBY EPISODE OF TOYMAKING WITH EMILY THE ELF!*' I wish I could shed some light on what that means but I'm afraid I was only sent my lines and nothing else, so I can't fully explain what's happening in this scene or in the film as a whole. But it sounds like Jiminy Jodphurs is a TV host. Oh, and all my lines were in caps lock for some reason.

I should add that I recorded my part while sitting under a duvet in a hotel room in Derby (I was still on the book promo tour, the duvet was meant to block out all external sound) and it was boiling under there. But I soldiered on, ignoring my body temperature and, while massively depressed, delivered such lines as:

'*EMILY THE ELF! YOU HAVE 30 SECONDS TO TURN THESE THREE OBJECTS INTO A LOVELY LOVELY TOY. READY! STEADY! GO!*' – Toymaking with Emily the Elf seems to be a toymaking show in the same vein as *Ready, Steady, Cook*. Which makes Jiminy Jodphurs the elf equivalent of Ainsley Harriott. So just the happiest being that has ever lived, then.

'*YER DARN TOOTIN'!*' – This line took me about 50 takes. Next time you're feeling depressed, try and deliver a convincing 'yer darn tootin'!' It's honestly impossible.

'*WOW! YOU HAVE REALLY EXCELLED YOURS-ELF, EMILY. WHAT DO YOU THINK, FRANÇOISE?*' – As if 'yer darn tootin'!' wasn't hard enough, I had to deliver a goddamn pun. I deserve an Oscar for this. Also – no idea who Françoise is.

'*AND SO, IT'S GOODNIGHT FROM ME, JOLLY JIMINY JODPHURS! BE SURE TO TUNE IN NEXT TIME FOR*

ANOTHER HUGELY HAPPY HELPING OF "TOYMAKING WITH EMILY THE ELF" – BYE!' – I'd been Jiminy Jodphurs for an hour at this point, my energy levels were going haywire and I threw everything into this final line. When I shouted, 'Bye!', it sounded so manic that I may as well have been saying it while looking back over my shoulder and stepping off a building.

I sent the audio files over but, to this day, I've never seen the film. The writer/director/dad says the family had a screening at home which went down very well. Lovely to hear, but also a real kick in the gut not to get invited to the premiere. What a start to being my own agent.

•

In 2016 **Wes Borland** released *Crystal Machete*, a soundtrack to a movie that only exists in his mind. I first became aware of Borland in the late 90s/early 2000s when he was the lead guitarist in nu-metal outfit Limp Bizkit. While the other three members of the band dressed in white T-shirts, baggy jeans and backwards baseball caps, Borland would cover himself in body paint and wear contact lenses that would either magnify his pupils or completely change his eye colour – always looking like he was in a different band entirely. I went to see a Limp Bizkit reunion gig in 2015 (ironically at first before having the night of my life) and once again he had set himself apart from his bandmates, this time dressing up like an American tourist in a Hawaiian shirt, sunglasses, straw trilby, incredibly short shorts and a lei, while drinking out of pineapples all night and discarding the empties by tossing them into the crowd, all while standing in a self-made tiki hut. I love Wes Borland.

Judging by the music on Crystal Machete, this imaginary

movie is an 80s anime about a hero on a noble quest who rides a trusty steed. The song 'White Stallion' came about when Borland read an article exploring how all hit singles followed the same formula, so he followed that formula as a cynical joke and produced his most streamed solo song. I'd now like to take a moment to hammer home the fact that the guitarist in Limp Bizkit wrote a soundtrack for a film that doesn't exist and it's called *Crystal Machete*. On top of this, it's better than most soundtracks for real-life films and because there's no knowing what official story is being told, we're free to project our own beginning, middle and end onto the tracks and decide for ourselves. I've frequently put this album on when having friends over without telling them who it is – they always ask at some point, prematurely showing their hand and saying it's excellent. And then I get to tell them it's a soundtrack for a film that doesn't exist called *Crystal Machete* by the guitarist from Limp Bizkit. And not once has anyone ever responded by saying, 'Oh yeah, thought so.'

•

Before we move on, I'd like to mention my favourite detail in the Jiminy Jodphurs story, and I don't know why it pleases me so much, but I later discovered that due to my involvement in the film Josh Widdicombe accepted the role of 'The Judge'. Little is known about the character, but, as far as I can tell, he's a judge who keeps throwing people in prison for farting. My favourite Judge line has to be, *'Who dares to contaminate the King's seat of sweet justice with noxious rear-end emissions of the gaseous variety? Lock that vile polluter in the cells until such time as he doth repenteth of his trouser-based sins!'*

I continued to manage myself for the rest of 2017, sometimes getting paid, sometimes not, and had to re-learn how to fend for myself and hustle as an independent artiste out there in the treacherous world of showbiz.

•

The Tuts are a working-class, all-female DIY punk band from Hayes in West London, operating within the middle-class UK punk scene. They create music that brings women together as well as people from all races and cultures, and refer to themselves as Three Tone (singer/guitarist Nadia Javed is South Asian, drummer Bev Ishmael is black Caribbean and bassist Harriet Doveton is white British). In the early days promoters would assume they were the girlfriends of the band and not the band themselves, then after gigs the phrase they'd hear most was, 'That was *actually* really good.' They knew they had to hustle for themselves from the very start. Early on, Harriet's sister made a music video (filmed at a funfair) for the band's song 'I Call You Up', a video The Tuts then tweeted at Kate Nash on the off chance she might watch it. This resulted in the band being invited to Brighton, where they watched Nash's show, hung out backstage after, sang an a cappella version of one of their songs to her and secured a support slot at her next gig, which then turned into an entire tour. When Kate Nash was playing Glastonbury she brought The Tuts along as her backing dancers, and as soon as they'd got into the festival they were trying to make contacts and get their name out there. One of the people they gave a demo CD to was Billy Bragg, who subsequently booked them to play a tent he was curating the following year. But next year's Glastonbury didn't go as planned. A huge storm started just before the band's set, which was helpful at first because it meant everyone piled into the tent for shelter and had to watch them play. The first two songs went amazingly, but then the organisers were forced to pull the show due to extreme weather conditions. However, one of the people in the crowd was Pauline Black of ska legends The Selector, who later went on Steve Lamacq's Radio 2 show and praised the band's performance. The Tuts took this opportunity to send Black some merch, and she in turn invited them to support The Selector on tour. The Kate Nash and Selector tours were huge for the band, meaning they gradually amassed the loyal fan base they'd wanted from day one, a diverse audience where no one feels alienated, and in turn that audience helped them finance their first record.

In 2016, The Tuts released their debut album, *Update Your Brain*, an album crowdfunded by their fans with no support from any record label or management. During the recording process they were living in the producer's house, who was an amazing chef and cooked for them every night. But there was a personality clash, specifically between him and Nadia: playful piss-taking would frequently get out of hand, resulting in someone getting upset or offended and he soon started going on multiple bike rides a day to de-stress. Things eventually came to a head and he kicked the band out of the studio with over half the material yet to be recorded. For weeks it wasn't clear how they'd finish the record, but after a reconciliation they were allowed back, this time with a new producer, who pushed them harder in order to get the best performances out of them. During the break the band had written more guitar parts for the songs and improved them, adding way more detail and texture to the overall sound – what had initially seemed like a disaster turned out to have been the best thing that could've happened for the album. *Update Your Brain* broadened their fan base even further: a passionate and authentic melodic punk record that manages to progress the genre while retaining the traditional values at its core, full of songs expressing their frustrations with the music industry, personal relationships and British politics. One track that got the band attention early on was a cover of the Spice Girls hit 'Wannabe' (a one-off single, not on the album), the original version of which was embraced by a lot of punks due to the similarities between the 'punk' ethos and the ethos of 'girl power'. I think this song illustrates the spirit of the band nicely, although The Tuts have since discovered the Spice Girls are 'a little bit Tory', so have declared their cover of 'Wannabe' to be the superior and definitive version.

West

Shortly after being dropped by my agent and hiding under a duvet pretending to be an elf, I received a rather encouraging and much needed surprise. Back in July, I'd got so carried away with the music of 2016 that I had added a page of 2016 album recommendations to my website. One November night, while sitting in a hotel room in Leeds thinking in circles about all the things my agent had said to me, I decided (probably out of neediness) to check my emails. A guy named Pedro Zina had contacted me saying he'd browsed my website and thought I should give his band's album a go, providing me with a link to their Bandcamp page. This was the first time a band had reached out to me and not the other way around. I clicked on the link, hoping to hear something I liked but fully prepared for disappointment. It was a very good album and I liked it a lot.

It was like the 2016 Music Gods knew I needed a pick-me-up and sent a guardian angel to rescue me, restoring my faith in humanity and the kindness of strangers. Yer darn tootin'.

•

Portuguese indie band **Cave Story** named themselves after a Japanese platform video game. The game took place on a floating island, featured a race of rabbit people who went crazy when they ate a red flower and an army of robot soldiers trying to capture an artefact called the Demon Crown. The band used to play the video game frequently, and bassist Pedro Zina emailed the creator of the game, Daisuke Amaya, to see if using the name for their band was ok. Amaya responded, 'Hi, Pedro. I don't know about legal well. I don't mind it.'

In 2016, Cave Story released their debut album, *West*, an album that takes the slacker indie sound made popular by bands like Pavement and uses it to paint a picture of the place they grew up in, Caldas da Rainha. Caldas da Rainha is a quiet city near the beach, located in a region called Oeste, which translates from Portuguese as 'West'. For the band, thinking about west Portugal turned into thinking about the Western world as a whole and the way it'd turned into an anxious yet comfortable mess. During the rehearsal process frontman Gonçalo Formila wrote a song featuring the lyrics, 'I'm a western boy so I'm worried about the weather'; the song didn't get finished, let alone make the album, but the idea behind that line – being afforded the luxury to invent concerns for yourself – made its way all over the record. I listened to *West* throughout that book tour and it kept me afloat. The constant sense of activity on this record, the lazy vocals, tight rhythmic drumming and off-kilter guitars are exactly what I want from this genre, but so few bands manage to deliver at this level.

It also made me believe, if only for a second, that bands would contact me from now on and I'd never have to go looking for music ever again. This has proved not to be the case.

I Thought You Didn't Even Like Leaving

My counsellor was very helpful when my agent dropped me. She put things in perspective and made me feel like I was better off without him. Then, one Tuesday in November, she didn't turn up to one of our sessions.

I waited for quite some time and, as I began to leave, she arrived on a bicycle, apologised and asked me to come back in 20 minutes. I later returned, she apologised some more and I said it was ok. But she wasn't happy about this. 'You're allowed to be angry with me.' 'I know but it's ok, honestly.' 'You can be angry.' 'Yep. I'm alright though.' 'You're allowed to be angry right now.' I nearly got angry at being told to get angry but didn't, because that would have been playing right into her hands.

From that day onwards she was always a little off; she didn't listen to me as intently and her responses to anything I told her were weirdly obsessed with fame and what I was going to do when the specials came out and my popularity increased (the specials would still be airing by the way; me prematurely announcing them wasn't an issue). I wasn't worried about 'fame' in the slightest, I wanted to talk about my relationships, but she always brought it back round to celebrity. She then told her son about my comedy and one day, as I was leaving, she briefly introduced me to her husband. It was time to leave.

Things got out of hand when I texted her saying that I would be ending our sessions together. What followed was a string of unprofessional messages from her that I had to navigate while still dealing with my own anxieties in my personal life (being dropped by my agent had caused me to obsess over the breakup with my girlfriend all over again). It was the last thing I needed, if I'm honest. It'd been a rough year, a year I'd told her about in great detail, and I wasn't ready for my counsellor to transform into my stalker. It took a week, but in the end I managed to send her a text outlining why her behaviour was inappropriate and why I wouldn't be seeing her again, and she agreed to leave me alone. The texts from my counsellor stressed me out so much I remember actually laughing out loud and getting hysterical because I couldn't comprehend what was happening. Just a really unfortunate surreal addition to a stupid year.

•

Doomsday Student formed in Rhode Island, a loud and fast-paced state full of tough love that can barely take care of itself but always manages to take care of its residents. From the beginning, the band set out to sound the way Rhode Island feels. The minimal, obnoxiously noisy songs on their 2016 album *A Self-Help Tragedy* are invasive and confrontational and never let up; at times it even feels as though the songs themselves are bullying you.

While working on the album, Doomsday Student were getting harassed online by an ex-bandmate. He had locked them out of the old band's social media and email accounts and was using them to spread rumours and lies about them. In addition, he was trolling them with fake accounts and using those accounts to email people more lies about the band. His behaviour didn't surprise them – this is why they stopped playing music with him in the first place – but what was surprising was how much time and energy he would devote to undermining the band and how persistent he was. Many of the songs on *A Self-Help Tragedy* are centred on this experience since the band were forced to go through it together as a group and, at times, found it deeply disturbing.

Online stalkers aren't the only theme on the album, though: many songs are about the birth of lead singer Eric Paul's child and written during a period of total sleep deprivation. The lyrics for 'Angry Christmas' are about Eric standing in the delivery room, holding his wife's hand while his son was literally being sucked out of his wife's body by a strange, white vacuum contraption that looked like something out of a sci-fi movie. The lyrics recount a few of the more memorable thoughts Eric had in that moment. He remembers marvelling at the power and beauty of creation and the divine quality his wife possessed while giving birth and continues to possess as a mother. He also felt such an intense love for his wife in a way he had never felt before. He obviously always loved and admired her, but witnessing her literally creating a life was overwhelming. The last line in the song, 'We've just taken our first breath', recounts the beginning of his son's life but also the beginning of the 'three-headed angel or monster' that the entire family were about to become together.

Because many of the songs originated from a place of stress, stressed is often how this album makes you feel – it's a record that actually makes you feel more anxious than you did going in, but I love it for that. In the same way that it's enjoyable to watch *A Clockwork Orange*, it's enjoyable to sit down and listen to *A Self-Help Tragedy*.

Am I Home?

After being dropped by my agent and my counsellor going loco on me, I badly needed a break, and fortunately one came around at just the right time. The highlight of 2017 without question was that I got to turn on the Christmas lights in my hometown of Kettering. I had launched my campaign a year previously after the palaver that was the 2016 Kettering Christmas Lights Ceremony.

Like most things in Britain during 2016 (and since 2016) the Kettering Christmas lights had been negatively impacted by Brexit. On 24 June 2016, the night of the referendum results, many of us decided to stay up late and watch the outcome unfold live on television, including Hollywood icon Lindsay Lohan. The Mean Girls star was in an English hotel and, like many but not all of us, was anticipating a victory for Remain, so couldn't believe her eyes as more and more constituencies announced they'd voted to leave the European Union. Sixty-one per cent of the people who voted in Kettering, my sweet hometown, the place I grew up, the people I cherished, voted to leave the EU. Lohan was furious, so took to Twitter. '#REMAIN Sorry #KETTERING but where are you&why is this woman @BBCNews speaking on people rather than TELLING us what happens if UK LEAVES?' she mercilessly tweeted. And my timeline went haywire. I have publicly associated myself with Kettering all too frequently to not get dragged into things like this: everyone was sending Lohan's tweet to me and asking what I was going to do about it, Remainers and Leavers for different reasons – would I challenge Lohan or would I challenge

Kettering? What an ordeal. To be honest, at the time, I had bigger concerns (as a Remainer), so I stayed silent LIKE A COWARD. But, fortunately for the people of Kettering, one man did not stay silent, one man had the guts to stand up to the Lohans of the world during these trying times and that man was Kettering's Conservative MP and committed Leave campaigner, Philip Hollobone.

Within a week of the result, Philip Hollobone had stood up in the House of Commons, in front of his fellow MPs, many of whom were raising issues regarding the fallout of the referendum result (how best to conduct negotiations, what the best deal for the UK was, how to tackle the rise in hate crimes across the country), and he'd done what was best for the people who had elected him as their MP. He bravely said, in a clear and wealthy voice: 'On referendum night a week ago, the pro-Remain American actress Lindsay Lohan in a series of bizarre tweets slagged off areas of this country that voted to leave the European Union and at one point she directed a fierce and offensive tweet at Kettering claiming she's never heard of it and implying that no one knew where it was. Apart from the fact that it might be the most average town in the country, everyone knows where Kettering is, it's famous as the home of Weetabix breakfast cereal, Cheaney's and Loake's shoes and Kettering Town Football Club has scored more goals in the history of the FA Cup than any other football team in the country. So would my Right Honourable friend support my invitation to Lindsay Lohan to come and switch on the Christmas lights in Kettering this Christmas, thus redeeming her political reputation and raising money for good causes.' At this point, a lot of you might be thinking, 'Come on, James, he's clearly just joking, get off his back', and you'd be right;

he was just joking and that's the problem. He'd campaigned for the Leave vote in Kettering, he'd now got the Leave vote in Kettering and instead of doing everything he could to make sure that Britain's separation from the EU went as smoothly as possible and his constituents were delivered the things he'd promised them, he was using his seat in Parliament to make a joke. And that was all he said that day. He went to the House of Commons and told a joke. Nigel Farage had already declared that the Leave Campaign's promise of £350 million a week to the NHS wasn't going to happen, members of the public had taken it upon themselves to vandalise the Polish Centre in Hammersmith, the pound had immediately taken a nosedive, David Cameron had resigned and left the country without a leader, and Philip Hollobone was making a joke about how mean the cast of *Herbie Fully Loaded* had been to Kettering in a tweet instead of using his platform to push for positive change and give Kettering the future he'd guaranteed them. And instead of telling Hollobone he was unfit to do his job and should be ashamed of himself, Commons leader Chris Grayling supported the plea, joking that it might reinvigorate Lohan's career. What a bunch of piece of shit country run by over-privileged dickhead wankers.

And then the unthinkable happened – Lohan responded. On Twitter, naturally. '@MPChrisGrayling and #philiphollobone Direct message me about your offer. Would be happy to light the Christmas tree in #Kettering 🙏.' She'd changed her tune. Kettering wasn't in all caps any more, she wanted to accept the invitation and was using the prayer hands emoji. Obviously this was the worst thing that could've happened as it just distracted the people of Kettering from Brexit even more because it was exciting to have a Hollywood celebrity turn on the lights in

Kettering. I think situations like this really sum up the British public – absolutely outraged that a celebrity said something trivial about them and then absolutely exhilarated at the prospect of getting to lay eyes upon that very same celebrity. Only British people treat celebs like this – with equal parts hate and idolisation. It makes no sense. If I was Lohan I would've suspected something. I'd have been certain that this was a trap. If I'd just openly slagged off a town and now they'd invited me to pay them a visit – alone at night with all the townspeople gathered together in the square before me – I'd smell a rat. It feels too *Wicker Man*, everyone huddled in the town square, speaking in monotone. 'We do this every year . . . it's a tradition . . . Happy Christmas, Lindsay . . .' I'm astonished she agreed to it but agree to it she did.

BUT DID SHE AGREE TO IT, THOUGH?!?!?!

Things went quiet for a while after Lohan's second tweet. As the months rolled by, more and more Ketteringers were asking what'd happened with Lohan – was she 100 per cent confirmed? No one had heard a definite answer yet. Eventually Philip Hollobone, with a heavy heart, announced, 'Despite everyone's best efforts, it's simply not possible to track her down.' You might be confused at this point in the story. In Lohan's acceptance tweet she had simply said 'Direct Message me for details', so they should've just DMed her and booked her there and then, right? But, alas, on Twitter you can only DM someone who follows you back, and even though Kettering Borough Council followed Lindsay Lohan, Lindsay Lohan did not follow Kettering Borough Council. Therefor DMing Lohan was an impossibility for KBC. What a way to remind someone of where they stand in the hierarchy. Philip Hollobone had called Lohan out in public and she had responded by subtly reminding him that he is a poor excuse for an MP and she is a global superstar who eats giggling little Tories for breakfast.

Obviously there are other ways that you can contact people like Lindsay Lohan besides DMing them on Twitter, but Lohan's team claimed that no attempt had been made by Kettering Borough Council or Philip Hollobone to do this until very late in the day, by which point nothing could be done and Lohan was off the table. So just to recap – Kettering Borough Council were unable to get Lindsay Lohan to turn on the Kettering Christmas lights because she didn't follow them on Twitter so they were unable to DM her and they didn't attempt to contact her by any other means until it was too late. And yet Philip Hollobone still maintained that leaving the EU was going to be an enormous success. Even though he couldn't figure out how to book someone to turn on his own town's Christmas lights, despite the fact the person in question had already publicly agreed to do so. Anyway, I'm writing this sentence in June 2019 and we still haven't left the EU. Great joke, Philip.

Lohan was replaced by Cheryl Fergison, aka Heather from *EastEnders*, who was appearing in the local panto that year. Cheryl was a blast, just what the people of Kettering needed. On the night of the ceremony she took to the stage well in advance in order to entertain the masses in the lead-up to the big event. The crowd were worked up into a frenzy, but right before Cheryl got to flip the switch a short film was played on the huge screen behind her. It was a video, shot on a phone, from none other than Lindsay Lohan. She had a message to the people of Kettering – 'Hi, everyone in Kettering, it's Lindsay Lohan. I really wanted to make it there to light the tree but with my busy schedule I wasn't able to and I appreciate the offer. Happy holidays.' She spoke really fast and filmed it in selfie mode using a filter that made her eyes sparkle and added cartoon flowers in her hair. She also filmed herself in portrait and not landscape. Everyone knows in order to make a video look good you should film in landscape, unless you don't care, in which case definitely film it in portrait to send an extra message to the people of a town you frankly couldn't give a shit about. She may as well have sent a video of her giving Kettering the finger and saying, 'Hello, you English nobodies, this is Lindsay Lohan telling you to go ram yourselves for ever and ever, hahahahahahaha – Remain 4 Life, bitches!!!' before throwing her phone in a toilet and flushing, as we watch the screen spin and flood and descend into darkness. To be honest, I'd have loved it if she did that and I'd watch it every day for the rest of my life. Anyway, Lohan's video weirdly turned out to be more of a buzzkill than a spirit lifter, and poor Cheryl had to turn the lights on to a deflated crowd who felt stood up and unwanted. Merry Christmas.

Shortly after this mess, I appeared on Radio 4's *Now Show* to do some topical stand-up comedy and decided that the perfect news story to talk about was the Lohan/Kettering debacle. I explained to the listeners what had occurred and then stated that, apparently, if you ever want to turn on the Christmas lights in Kettering all you have to do is slag off Kettering. I then spent a few minutes slagging off my dear hometown in an attempt to be invited to turn on the lights the following year. I mainly focused on the fact that once, for two weeks in 2009, there was an area of Kettering that smelt like hot sick. I also may have said that I hope Kettering drifts away from the UK and becomes surrounded by acid and I hope everyone's hair catches fire and they can't stop having nosebleeds for ever. I really gave them both barrels.

And then I got the gig.

Kettering Borough Council have never confirmed whether or not they asked me to turn on the lights because I had slagged off Kettering, but they certainly haven't denied it either. To say that turning on the Kettering Christmas lights was the best day of 2017 would be an understatement; I got given a free meal at Mexican restaurant Chimichanga, the Mayor of Kettering allowed me to wear his chain and Wicksteed Park mascot Wicky Bear was even in attendance (a big friendly brown bear in a blue cap and blue dungarees), along with many proud Ketteringers. I had to be interviewed on stage in front of the crowd prior to the lights being switched on and really wanted to get everyone jazzed, just like Cheryl Fergison did, so I made sure all my answers ended with me shouting 'Kettering' really loud because I knew that shouting 'Kettering' usually got a cheer in Kettering. When it came to flipping the big switch I prepared myself for another 'apology' video from Lohan but none came. In a way I was relieved, but on the other hand it was sad that she'd totally forgotten about us now and there was a chance she wasn't even thinking about Kettering on a night as special as this. I'd half hoped for a video from Lohan wishing me good luck, telling everyone in Kettering that I was the coolest and that they should respect me. She could've still ended the vid by throwing the phone in the toilet, I wouldn't have minded. But, all in all, it was probably a good thing to be able to turn the lights on out of the shadow of Lohan. The events of 2016 had come to define the town, and indeed Christmas, a little too much. We had to put the Age of Lohan behind us. And enter the Age of Acaster.

They didn't warn me that as soon as the lights were turned on fireworks would go off millimetres from where I was standing and then 'All I Want for Christmas is You' would play in its entirety and I would have to dance for the full duration. But that's what happened. I just danced the Mash Potato for the entire song and replaced the word 'Christmas' with 'Kettering' when singing into the handheld mic they'd given me. The whole experience was weirdly emotional. Just like Lohan, I was saddened at the referendum result and I imagine it meant more to me than it did her because of how much I love my hometown. So being able to celebrate something positive back home, to meet all the locals who turned up that day and stir up the old feelings of childhood Christmases in Kettering together, felt important. Even if I was acting like a nob the whole time.

Don't Call It a Christmas Album

Run the Jewels surprise-released their 2016 album *Run the Jewels 3* on Christmas Eve. First of all, surprise releases are cool. If you can afford to drop an album without announcing it, then that means you don't have to worry about album sales because everyone thinks you are great and the public will do the promo for you by word of mouth. It's also cool to 'drop' an album because dropping something is pretty careless and not caring is cool. On top of this, surprise-dropping an album on Christmas Eve is the ultimate cool move because you know most people are busy. It's the epitome of confidence, surprise-dropping an album on a day where we've all got stuff on. Very few artists could pull it off without looking like idiots when no one buys their album because they were busy wrapping presents and singing carols. But Run the Jewels (a duo consisting of producer/rapper El-P and rapper/

activist Killer Mike) have always been this self-assured. Long before most artists they were self-releasing high-quality albums for free online, bypassing record labels and PR and relying solely on the strength of their music. *RTJ3* is arguably their best album yet, with everything stepping up a notch: the production, the rapping and the message all seem sharper than before, making RTJ one of the rare groups who perform even better the more people are paying attention to them. The album was digitally released on Christmas Eve 2016 after everyone had announced their 'best of 2016' lists. The physical release didn't come out until January 2017 so some people (Ed Gamble) shamefully tried to include it in their 'best of 2017' lists but were only kidding themselves. Another big release that sidestepped everyone's end of year lists was **Childish Gambino**'s *'Awaken, My Love!'* which saw Donald Glover unexpectedly branch out into funk and gospel, reducing the amount of hip hop in his sound by a significant margin. It was released on 6 December and made all the list dweebs cry because by the time they'd adjusted to his new sound it was too late and their beloved lists were already up on their blogs. The bottom line is, if these dweebs really wanted to include *RTJ3* and *'Awaken, My Love!'* in their best of 2016 lists, then they should've continued to buy music from 2016 for at least another year before eventually compiling their official top 50, ensuring they hadn't missed any albums and were making the most informed and correct decision possible. But very few people bother to do things right these days.

•

Another surprise release in 2016 was **Kendrick Lamar**'s *untitled unmastered.* – a collection of songs that didn't make it on to *To Pimp A Butterfly*. It just appeared one day, unannounced, with a plain dark-green cover, the title written in one corner and a parental advisory sticker in another. It was eight tracks long, the tracks didn't have names, they'd not been mastered properly and the whole thing lasted 35 minutes. There is so much folklore behind the songs on *untitled unmastered.* and fans love to trade tales about how the tracks came about. Kendrick debuted two songs from the album on *Late Night* in the US (for Jimmy Fallon and Stephen Colbert, respectively). The story goes that the reason he did this is because he was bored of playing old songs, so decided to literally write new songs especially for these TV appearances. Everyone will tell you that Thundercat forgot how the bassline to 'untitled 03' went (because the song had only been written that morning), so just improvised it on *The Colbert Report*, or that the crew on Fallon were told Kendrick would be playing a song from *TPAB* and had no idea he was doing anything different until he performed 'untitled 08' live in the studio during the show. Either way, these songs had never been heard before, so when the performances aired, everyone lost their shit trying to figure out what they were and where they'd come from. While *untitled unmastered.* still contained songs that would've felt at home on *TPAB* lyrically and musically, there were also tracks that saw Lamar and his collaborators goofing around in the studio, improvising as they wound down between recordings and took a break from playing intense jazz. If *TPAB* seems like a bit of an undertaking to you, then I'd recommend listening to *untitled unmastered.* first – it's in the same vein but it's shorter and easier to digest, and the hype around it isn't as prevalent, meaning you can unwind to it rather than worrying about being an idiot if you don't get it. Every song is impeccable and will train you up for *TPAB*, like a gateway album of sorts.

Biscuits for Your Outside Man

It was Ed Gamble's idea to go to New York for New Year's. He knew I'd had a bad year so suggested doing something special to send it off. Four of us flew to New York on 29 December 2017: Ed Gamble, John Robins, Lloyd Langford and myself. Four stand-ups going on holiday together – as you can imagine, the flight was hilarious (it wasn't, we watched films and drank whisky). We were staying in an Airbnb in Williamsburg and planned to eat and drink a lot every day for five days. Over the holiday we ate roast potato and brisket poutine, sweet potato fries covered in clam chowder, tater tots covered in vegan cheese and tofu scramble, the best steak I've ever had, the best pizza I've ever had, amazing Szechuan food that numbed my tongue followed by soup dumplings that woke it up again – I could write an entire separate book about these meals. I was obsessing over buying an ice cream cake from the moment we arrived. I'd never eaten an ice cream cake before and desperately wanted to know what one tasted like. One night while drunk I ran into a Baskin Robbins, bought an entire ice cream birthday cake and spent the rest of the holiday eating it. The USP of an ice cream cake, in my opinion, is the fact that you get to experience the taste of cake icing iced directly onto ice cream. Everything else isn't that spectacular, but the fact that they've basically iced some ice cream for you is very special.

Looking back, food cheered me up in 2017 almost as much as music did. The one saving grace during that disastrous week in LA was that at one point I ate Clint Eastwood's cookie. It was the same day a teenager had called me Ron Weasley. My friend Aisling invited me out for a meal, and after a week of food poisoning and lying in bed I decided it was important to try and eat something. I accepted her invitation and was star-struck when I noticed Clint Eastwood was sat on the table next to us. We tried not to make a big deal out of it, but when his party left the restaurant I noticed he had neglected to take his cookie with him (there was a buffet and Clint had selected but not consumed a chocolate chip and oatmeal cookie). I snapped that cookie up so fast. To be honest, whenever anybody, celeb or not, leaves their dessert in a restaurant I want to run over to their table and eat it up, but it's never acceptable. Fortunately, this particular dessert had been abandoned by Clint Eastwood, so my fellow diners totally understood why I had to steal and eat it. I would like to add that before I ate Clint Eastwood's cookie I burst out laughing because I had thought to myself, in my own head, 'Go ahead cookie, make my day.' I know that's not very funny but I also imagined Clint Eastwood saying it to every item of food before he eats it, and in my post-illness delirium that was amusing to me. 'Go ahead, butterscotch, make my day', 'Go ahead, shepherd's pie, make my day', 'Go ahead crab puff, make my day.' You get it.

One of the most iconic moments of 2017 was when I dis-covered my favourite ever food was cold lasagne. I had bought a ready-meal lasagne from a supermarket, heated it up in the oven and taken a bite only to discover I hated it. So I put the remaining lasagne in the fridge because I'd feel guilty if I put an entire lasagne straight in the bin, knowing that I would most likely just end up leaving it in the fridge until it went off, thus allowing me to bin it without feeling guilty a few days later. I then went into the living room and started drinking whisky and binge-watching *Queer Eye*. I'm using the word 'binge' before the word 'watching' there, but I concede I could also have used it before the word 'drinking' because I got absolutely smashed. The combination of the booze and *Queer Eye* made me cry like crazy. I then started to reflect on all my past relationships and convinced myself they all failed thanks to me and if I'd only had the Fab Five around to help me then none of this would've happened. I then remember hitting myself in the face. Just slapping myself between the eyes while crying. I've never done this before or since, it really hurt and, for some reason, it gave me a craving for cold lasagne. I returned to the kitchen and grabbed a serving spoon (an optimistic spoon choice considering I didn't even like the lasagne when it was hot) before digging into the refrigerated lasagne. It was the best meal I've ever had. When a lasagne is cold it becomes a brand-new dish. The beef is somehow more plump and succulent, the edges are crispier and the bechamel sauce congeals, taking on the consistency of a Haribo foam dinosaur. My mood flipped when I tried that cold lasagne – I instantly became euphoric and went straight onto a WhatsApp group and told everybody how delicious it was, but because it was now 3 a.m. I had the group to myself and was able to do a WhatsApp solo. This is my favourite time to go on a WhatsApp group: I can let my stream of consciousness flow and just get everything out. And not in one big long text – in short bursts, one thought after another: 'I love cold lasagne' 'the beef plump' 'brchenak' 'bechensj' 'FUCK' 'benchmark sause so tasty' 'I love you guys'. It sounds tragic now but it was nice to feel happy for a bit. Incidentally, a week later I got a craving for cold lasagne again, so I bought another ready-made lasagne from the supermarket, heated it up (I don't have time to include the full recipe/cooking instructions for cold lasagne in this book but always make sure you heat it up first before refrigerating it – do not eat it frozen out of the box like a savoury Solero), then put it in the fridge and later on ate a huge serving spoon full and it was absolutely revolting. I should add that the second time I tried the cold lasagne I was sober but I doubt that's relevant.

•

Rapper **Denmark Vessey** first heard **Gensu Dean**'s production in 2014 when Dean collaborated with Mississippi rapper 7even-Thirty. Shortly after becoming a fan, Vessey coincidentally heard from Dean himself with an invitation to collaborate. The time spent making this record is something of a blur for Vessey, but his clearest memory is of finding the album's cover. They had already decided the album would be called *Whole Food* so searched a range of food terminology on Google images and hit upon a photograph by the Russian artist Dimitri Tsykalov entitled *Eggplant Skull*. The piece looks exactly as it sounds: Tsykalov had fused an aubergine (sorry to switch to British-talk but I couldn't bring myself to say 'eggplant' again) with a skull – the aubergine acting as a tall crown. This image resonated with Vessey for a number of reasons – a lot of the lyrics on the album were about race and one racist term for black people that he'd been thinking about was 'eggplanters', a slur he'd only ever experienced from Italians around his neighbourhood. He'd also been reading the works of Dr Frances Cress Welsing, an American Afrocentrist psychiatrist who had previously inspired artists such as Public Enemy (their album *Fear of a Black Planet* was based entirely on her work). Dr Welsing passed away on 2 January 2016, at 80 years old, and in her lifetime wrote many influential essays and papers about race and white supremacy, including white people's fear of black people involving penis envy and how that's been a motivator for violence. This made the aubergine/eggplant in the photograph significant again because, thanks to emojis, this vegetable has now become the universal symbol for a penis. This photo represented so much of what Denmark had been thinking about: food, racism, the hypersexualisation of black men, violence and death in the form of a skull. No other image was considered for the album cover. *Whole Food* was released in July 2016.

Longest Day, Shortest Night

It was really nice to have a second attempt at visiting New York after the terrible trip at the start of the year. It felt quite fitting – the perfect city to end 2017 in. On New Year's Eve itself we went to a bar called Battery Harris and stayed there for quite some time despite being the only customers. Even though it was New Year's Eve the bar was empty at 10 p.m. as the staff stuck balloons up on the walls around us. I was drunk by this point (way drunker than my friends) and had taken a trip to Negative Town, quickly becoming convinced that our waitress hated us. This would become a pattern for the entire holiday. No matter where we went I would become convinced that the staff absolutely despised the lot of us for no reason. I don't remember much of what happened at Battery Harris but apparently I kept lecturing my companions about how much this waitress hated us and how she was going to go home and tell her friends that she waited on a bunch of absolute suckers tonight and make fun of us with them. I then went on to inform my friends that about once a day I fantasise about slamming my head on a spike (I apparently told them this like it was a cool thing). I paid for all our drinks at Battery Harris because I was fully aware I'd been a dickhead and then we headed to a bar that was also an arcade, called Barcade.

Once in Barcade I played, and very quickly gave up on, Metallica-themed pinball, then went into the bathroom for quite some time before Lloyd came in and fetched me because I was standing on the toilet, peering over the cubicle and offering people at the urinals pep talks. I was literally looking down at them and saying, 'Do you want a pep talk, mate?', then getting turned down before offering a pep talk to the next person without letting the previous rejection faze me at all. I have no idea what the pep talk was going to be because, surprisingly, everyone turned down the offer of a pep talk from an incoherent Englishman standing on a toilet. Then we went back to the Airbnb and watched an episode of *Black Mirror*, I ate a ton of ice cream cake, John did a dance for us all (the *Harris Dance* from Michael Flatley's lesser known *Skydance* show) and we all retired to our bedrooms at 00:23 because we were still jet lagged. I sat up in bed searching for one last 2016 album before the project was officially over. I'd already achieved my goal of 366 downloads and it technically wasn't 2017 any more but I was drunk and feeling rebellious. So I bought *Blood Bitch* by **Jenny Hval**, a concept album about blood, periods and vampires, fell asleep in the glow of laptop, and, with that, 2017 was over.

Golden Sings That Have been Sung

I woke up on 1 January 2018, staggered into the living room and sat on the sofa staring at the TV even though it was turned off. My mind wandered and I looked back on the previous year the same way anyone does when hungover on New Year's Day. Reflecting on the highs, lows, how I'd changed etc. Obviously, I was glad to see the back of 2017, but there were still positives among the negatives – all in the form of music – and there were some albums in particular that had altered me in ways I hadn't anticipated.

The 2016 album that changed my music taste more than any other was *What Now?* by **Jon Bap**. Bap has since stated on social media that he felt like he was compromising his sound on this album, which makes me laugh every time because, while not impenetrable, it's hardly an easy listen for the majority of us. *What Now?* is essentially an experimental R&B record that draws heavily from free jazz, pulling from various other genres along the way. The first thing that grabbed me about the record was the tumbling, skittish drums that seemed to exist almost independently from everything else while still somehow binding each track together. So it was satisfying to learn that the entire project began life with these drum beats. In 2015, young jazz drummer Mike Mitchell was travelling through Buffalo, where Bap was living at the time, and made a brief stop to track a bunch of drums for him. There were no songs to speak of at this stage, nothing else had been written, Mitchell just improvised for a day and then left. Bap then listened back to these improvisations, edited them and gradually built songs around Mitchell's untethered drum tracks. What we're left with are songs where no two instruments are playing in perfect time with one another, with lagging bass and funk guitar moving in and out of 'sloppy' drum beats while soulful R&B vocals keep everything anchored both emotionally and structurally. I would not have given this album the time of day a year earlier but now it's one of my favourite records of all time. After months of listening to new music every single day I needed something unlike anything I'd listened to before and I needed to hear melodies delivered in an unfamiliar fashion. It was like someone had taken what I knew an album to be and jumbled it like a Rubik's Cube so it still made sense without anything being in its usual place. The opening to *What Now?* is a 9-minute-and-52-second-long track entitled 'Guided Meditation', which is literally 9 minutes 52 of guided meditation, presumably so we can clear our minds completely before listening to the rest of the record. It's actually not a bad idea – trancing yourself up a bit and then listening to a bunch of songs that erratically fire in several directions at once. A calm disposition helps when listening to this record, and this is aided further by the addition of ambient field recordings and spoken-word segments, both of which give the album a grander sense of shape – rigid walls for the songs to run around in. The most traditional song on the album, 'Don't Run into the Dark So Quick', sees Bap singing softly to a compressed electric guitar, the whole song in 4/4 and both instruments in time with one another. It's the kind of track we may never hear Bap perform again, but here it serves as a novel breather and shows another side to the man we've just spent so much time with, before the album draws to a close. Jon Bap opened a door to countless other bands and records I would never have bothered with beforehand. What I used to disregard as noise had turned into an infinite goldmine and suddenly there were geniuses at every turn.

My tastes also expanded in the opposite direction during 2017. I immersed myself in some of the poppiest and most accessible albums I've ever enjoyed and found depth in places I'd been ignoring for far too long.

•

Jess Cerro grew up in Sydney in a place called the Hills District, a cluster of Christian suburbs situated upon an undulating land mass. Being removed from any kind of bustling life fostered a strong streak for introspection and self-awareness in her, and she would often fill any sort of void with music. In 2013, during her final year of high school, she began to write the songs that would end up on her debut album, *Glorious Heights*, a bold and emotive pop record fronted by an array of sharp, thick synths and Cerro's passionate vocal delivery.

Jess wouldn't actually enter the studio until 2015, though, when her life was neither stable nor consistent. She was 19 and a chain of events had forced her to suddenly move out of her home and stay in a series of spare rooms for two months before finally settling on the couch of Joji Malani, lead guitarist of Australian band Gang of Youths. During all of this she was working three jobs: a waitressing job at a pizza place, a news agency job where the management inexplicably hated her, and as a waitress in a stuffy cafe. She was fresh out of breaking up with her first boyfriend (they'd been in an open relationship by his request, even though she had wanted monogamy), but had moved quickly into a new relationship with a man 15 years her senior who was obsessed with his now married ex-girlfriend and who had another girlfriend of four years that he'd not told Jess about.

While writing *Glorious Heights* Jess didn't think the events in her personal life were particularly getting to her. She didn't consider herself an anxious person, she saw herself as happy with good self-esteem, unafflicted by any deep-seated emotional turmoil. As far as she was concerned, she just happened to have drama in her life to write songs about and a bad day was simply a bad day. Looking back now, she feels that this emotional repression actually had a positive effect on the way she wrote about her experiences. This sense of detachment allowed her to be forthcoming and completely open in her lyrics, which developed a yearning, pained, but self-mocking tone. It felt like she was writing about a different person, so didn't fear revealing what to a lot of people are deeply intimate details about a whole manner of dysfunctional relationships. Because of this, a lot of the lyrics come from a place of empathy and never stray into self pity, while the vivid instrumentals give every track a sense of empowerment, so anyone who sees themselves in these songs can also envisage survival, recovery and victory. Jess released *Glorious Heights* in 2016 under the name **Montaigne**, after the philosopher Michel de Montaigne, a man who shared a great deal of his private life in order to 'create a mirror in which other people recognise their own humanity'.

Let's Lurk

I began 2018 by getting stranded in New York. The day before we were meant to fly home a snow storm/bomb cyclone hit the city and all flights the following day were cancelled. We all responded to this differently: Ed Gamble immediately got on the phone to the airline trying to get us home asap, Lloyd was feeding Ed Gamble updates and information from his laptop, I ate more of the ice cream cake and John went to Battery Harris. The airline were being even less helpful than John and I were – it wouldn't surprise me if on the other end of the phone they were all shovelling ice cream cake into their mouths before popping to Battery Harris to celebrate winding Ed Gamble up. And Ed Gamble was *wound up* – he was so wound up he did something drastic and tweeted the airline publicly (just like Lindsay Lohan would do) so everyone could see how unhelpful they had been. He tweeted at American Airlines: 'My flight tomorrow to LHR from JFK (142) has been cancelled. I've been on hold for 25 minutes and the call has just been hung up. We have nowhere to stay and the only flight you have suggested via email is on Monday and takes 20 hours. Please contact me ASAP.' Now firstly, yes, Ed Gamble is an absolute square-o-zoid of the highest order, a true dweeb getting all hoity-toity on Twitter with the airline, but, to be fair, their response was even madder than Ed-Gamble-the-Nerd's initial tweet. 'We wish Winter Storm Grayson would take it a bit easier on us too, Ed. We'll take it up with Mother Nature.' Blimey. What a bunch of wankers. Being all sarcastic with a poor stressed man who doesn't know where he's going to sleep tomorrow night. And so, as the snow storm rushed round our little Airbnb, a war began between Ed Gamble (official nerd) and American Airlines (official wankers), with members of the public constantly chipping in, favouriting and retweeting to their hearts' content – sparks flew, temperatures ran high, it was drama of the highest order.

•

TEEN are a technical synth-pop group consisting of sisters Lizzie, Katherine and Teeny Lieberson. In January 2015 the band rented a house in Woodstock for a month to hibernate, write, cook and hang out in. This was meant to be a relaxed way of writing a new record, but it turned out to be oddly challenging. The weather was insane, they got snowed in constantly and the driveway would ice over, so they couldn't leave because it was impossible to drive. Inside, the carpets were thick, the ceilings were low and it was extremely claus-trophobic. There were dead mice everywhere (they were in the walls and were being poisoned) so it always smelt awful. Also, the house was haunted. There had been two separate deaths in the house within the last year, and although no one in the band ever saw a ghost, they all agreed the whole place felt very haunted all the time. It was the most miserable they'd all been – Lizzie especially was hugely depressed and kept getting migraines all the time. One day she had to get out of the house, so went for a walk in the snow and while walking started, almost absentmindedly, writing a song about their dad. Their father was a classical composer, and when they were kids he would teach them to sing Broadway standards round the piano. He'd breezily say, 'Try this easy piece', before tasking them with something impossible, full of counterpoint and things most adults would struggle with. But the three of them enjoyed these 'games', and over time singing and harmonising with each other became second nature. Out in the snow that morning, Lizzie wrote lyrics in her head about how her dad used to worry about her, how she'd feel guilty about that and how she still wishes she could talk to him now. When she arrived back at the haunted house, she sat down at her keyboard and completed the song in a day – it was called 'Please' and was the first song written for the new record. *Love Yes* was released in February 2016.

•

Nænø*ĉ*ÿbbŒrğ VbëŕŕHõlökäävsŦ (pronounced Nano-Cyborg Uberholocaust) consist of two research scientists performing under the aliases Wavanova and Dark Dude. They met in Antarctica while working together in a South Pole research centre. Both being bass players, they discovered that they had similar music tastes, so decided to record an experimental drone album together. They travelled to the actual South Pole to do it, recording the whole thing outdoors, and then in 2007 they released their debut album, *The Ultimate Fate of the Universe*. Since then they've regularly recorded in this manner and always upload their music onto their website for free download. In 2016 they released two albums (appearing to be sister albums) named *Solar 2* and *Lunar 2*. They run at an hour each and contain some of the most intimidating and thunderous ambient drone metal tracks you're ever likely to hear. I'd now like to take a moment to hammer home the fact that there are two actual research scientists recording ambient drone music outdoors at the actual South Pole.

Letters to Home

The day after Ed Gamble's tweets we were a front-page story on the BBC News website. I'm not even joking. I suppose in early January not much is going on so you may as well write about four comedians whose flight got cancelled and now have to hang around New York for a few more days. 'COMIC CAPERS OF FOUR BRITISH COMEDIANS STUCK IN NEW YORK'. Not the punchiest of headlines but accurate. They detailed Ed Gamble's Twitter spat, included photos of us on our holiday that Robins had posted on Instagram and even included fan art (John's fans, admittedly) based on the event (mainly a bunch of photoshopped images of us in various film posters: *Home Alone 2: Lost In New York* being a highlight, with me as Joe Pesci and Robins as Culkin, even though I look more like Culkin than Robins does, but they're his fans, so of course he was bound to land the lead role). The news story made us out to be victims of misfortune, but in reality getting stranded was the best thing that could've happened to us. Our holiday doubled in length, we got a new Airbnb and we continued having a fantastic holiday.

Pretty soon other news outlets wanted to talk to the four of us: newspapers, TV shows and radio programmes, all wanting the scoop on our holiday for no good reason. John and Lloyd did a live interview with Sky News during which Lloyd unintentionally looked like a mobster. He thought it'd be funny to wear a USA medallion he'd found in the Airbnb, but the camera framed him in such a way that you couldn't see the USA pendant. Plus he's watching himself on the living room TV while the interview is taking place so he looks confused and angry throughout. The comedian Andrew O'Neill tweeted a photo of Lloyd's face on TV (see below) with no context provided, and that image still makes me laugh to this day. Getting stranded was a bona fide riot. But even though we were having a swell time, all this fuss quickly became infuriating for the British public. A lot of people were expressing their disbelief and outright anger that this nothing of a story, this inconsequential tale, this half-an-anecdote-at-best, was considered actual, proper, legitimate news.

Lloyd Langford – January 2018

•

The *New York Post* once ran a cover story about a new cemetery that allowed people to be buried with their pets. Until then, the only option for pet owners when it came to being buried with their best friends was for the human being to be cremated and buried in a pet cemetery. So this would be the first human cemetery in New York that would also welcome dead animals and the *New York Post* were incredulous about it. It wasn't clear if the corpses of the pets would be in the same coffin as their owners or if the ashes of the pets were simply allowed to be buried in the family plot, but either way the *Post* found the whole thing outrageous and ran with the headline 'REST IN FLEAS' in big bold letters. Stephen Cooper, a musician who lived in Queens, saw this edition of the *Post* and loved the expression 'REST IN FLEAS' so much that he immediately bought a copy with the intention of keeping it indefinitely so he never forgot this absurd story. A couple of years later when writing a new collection of songs with his band **Cloud Becomes Your Hand**, Cooper found himself returning to this stupid headline, wanting to incorporate it into his music somehow, and in the end 'REST IN FLEAS' inspired a surreal song of the same name with lyrics that made as much sense as the original news story. Written by Cooper and lyricist Isobelle Martin (a frequent collaborator – Cooper would often give her a song title and she'd produce poetic lyrics almost instantaneously), the song wasn't about pets being buried with their owners but more about nothing at all. Cooper sings about a man with teeth for eyebrows and an apple for a head who lives in the sewer and eats his own vomit, oddy summing up the hysterical tone of the *NY Post* article and how ludicrous it was to make such a silly story front-page news. *Rest in Fleas* quickly became the name of the entire project, a collection of weirdo indie prog songs that showcased the band's versatility and took itself as seriously as Cooper took the article of the same name.

Before the release of *Rest in Fleas*, Cloud Becomes Your Hand embarked on a short tour in the summer of 2015 with tech rock experimentalists **Wei Zhongle**, whose frontman, Rob Jacobs, had just started writing the band's next release, *Nice Mask over an Ugly Face*. The tour had been in the diary for a while, but Jacobs kept procrastinating about writing new music until two weeks before the first show. At the time he was befuddled by an expanding personal life that was getting out of control, he was dissociating constantly and in a place where nothing mattered. He kept taking psychedelic drugs even though he was having horrifically disturbing trips and he was living in a tent in his friend Phil's living room. He'd recently come out of an abusive romantic relationship, after which his ex had begun to stalk him, so he'd moved into the tent in the hope she'd now be unable to track him down. It was a third-floor apartment, and the tent was situated in a corner where there was a turret with four big windows and Rob would regularly leave the windows open so they'd fill the tent with wind. Rob describes this ex-girlfriend as an expert manipulator – he felt that she wore a mask of bravery and pleasant eccentricity to hide her true self. After the breakup, he had to change his phone number and couldn't go to shows or certain parts of town for fear of running into her.

But the title of the record doesn't just refer to this individual; it also refers to the music itself. Around that time, he didn't enjoy listening to dark or heavy-handed music because he was in a bad place and wanted to feel better, so he tried to make music with a light and playful touch to mask the terrible feelings lurking behind it all. However, Jacobs felt downtrodden and had lost confidence as an artist, feeling too scared to attempt these new ideas and progress in a new direction. So he put together a band of musicians whose performances he found continually inspiring (Pat Keen on fretless bass, John McCowen on clarinet and Phil Sudderberg on drums), and being surrounded by these people helped him pull through and move past his fears. He wanted to stop being fancy and write some straight-up songs with proper lyrics, vocals and melodies – pop songs done his way. *Nice Mask over an Ugly Face* is the perfect cocktail of smooth jazz and fidgety pop, full of wobbly guitar lines and clarinets fed through fx pedals, with Jacobs' curiously enunciated vocals playing the role of some peculiar tour guide helping us navigate the general oddness at the heart of every track. The tour with Cloud Becomes Your Hand was up and down – some shows were sold out, others had to be cancelled due to poor attendance – but both bands released their brand-new projects the following year: *Rest in Fleas* in May 2016 and *Nice Mask over an Ugly Face* in August 2016.

Through the Dark

One day, while we were stranded in New York, Ed Gamble discovered that a sludge metal band he liked called EyeHateGod were playing a matinee show nearby, so I decided to accompany him because I'd never been to a matinee metal show before.

Ed Gamble dressed up in his best metal clothes, while I dressed more practically and wrapped up warm in my big coat and gloves, complete with jolly bobble hat. The bar was one of those cool bars that doesn't have a sign outside and basically looks like it's shut. We were very unsure if it was the right place, so I walked up to a metal man who was smoking outside and chirped, 'Good afternoon, is this where EyeHateGod are doing a gig?' and he begrudgingly said yes while glaring at my bobble as it jiggled around with every word I said. Once we were inside we could no longer tell it was daytime because daylight was not allowed into the venue. The windows were blacked out and there was very little light in the bar, just a lot of upside-down crucifixes dangling from the ceiling and the rich smell of back sweat hanging in the air. Ed Gamble and I decided to have a beer but agreed we wouldn't get drunk, and then obviously got drunk, because once you've had a beer the most appealing idea in the world is to have a second beer. I don't know why we even considered not getting drunk, looking back – we had been stranded in New York for five extra days, there was nothing we could do about it and we were currently attending a matinee metal gig. Sounds like an appropriate time to get blasted. Maybe not 100 per cent appropriate, though – Mike Williams, the singer of EyeHateGod, had recently had a liver transplant after a lifetime of heavy drinking and drug use, so getting blasted probably wasn't the number one vibe of the show. Williams was sober now: the liver transplant made him give up drinking and he had already given up opiates due to a bizarre set of circumstances that started during Hurricane Katrina in 2005.

When Katrina hit, Williams and his girlfriend were at home in the Lower Garden District of New Orleans. The power went out and the couple were confined to their home for the duration of the storm, but once it subsided and the waters went down, the streets were no longer safe. People quickly began committing acts of violence and robbing their neighbours, so Williams and his partner fled to a friend's apartment before leaving town in a borrowed car. They drove for 90 minutes to Morgan City, and by the time they arrived, Williams' house back in New Orleans had burnt down. They checked into a hotel with their New Orleans IDs and were promptly arrested because of where they were from (many criminals had recently fled the city after the lootings). Williams was then convicted of drug possession and thrown in jail with a bail set of $150,000. After a spell in prison, with bandmates and fans sending him letters of support and trying to get him released, Williams had his bail paid by Pantera lead singer Phil Anselmo, who let him move in with him until he got back on his feet. But his time in prison without any access to drugs had started him down a new path and he decided to give up opiates for good, remaining clean to this day.

The EyeHateGod show was exactly what Ed Gamble and I needed. I now think every metal band should exclusively perform matinee shows: it felt very upside down in the best way. It was also nice to be among an audience who clearly loved and cared so much for someone they'd come to see. There was a lot of support for Williams from the band's devoted and loyal fan base, and now that his operation had been a success and his health had improved, the show felt like a celebration. Albeit one that'd been crashed by a man in a bobble hat.

•

In 2016, San Diegan multi instrumentalist Rob Crow released *You're Doomed. Be Nice* under the name **Rob Crow's Gloomy Place**. He came out with this record because his family missed him making music. Prior to this he was broke, was away a lot and was drinking three bottles of wine a day to six bottles of Jameson a week. So he quit drinking, social media and certain friendships, started exercising, lost 100 pounds and formed a new band in order to make the best record he could. The album was his way of getting healthy through purging all of his misery and impotent anger; he wanted to make people who share his problems regarding deep bottomless depression feel less alone. He still doesn't feel like it worked. He does see way more of his family, he's sober, productive and not as broke as before, but he still maintains a pessimistic outlook and only has nightmares. The album toured to mainly empty rooms, with the band sleeping on floors most nights, but for Crow's existing fan base *You're Doomed* was celebrated as a return to form with its blend of pop-punk and prog hitting a very narrow mark. Crow currently lives in California, is a stay-at-home dad with five kids and recently got his driving licence.

•

Norwegian avant-garde noise group **Årabrot** based their sixth album, *The Gospel*, on lead singer Kjetil Nernes's treatment and recovery from throat cancer. He felt like he was at war with himself, so war became the record's running theme, with the band setting out to paint a picture of 'a warrior looking over a battlefield in silence as smoke drifts from shell craters'. Drowning became a theme also, the feeling of being pulled to the bottom of the ocean and dragged back up again, suddenly breaking through the surface of the water, breathless and gasping for air. In fact, Nernes's entire experience is handled in metaphors, whether it's through the panic of drowning, the stillness of a battlefield or the tension of a murder trial (the song 'Rebekka' is inspired by the Hitchcock film of the same name that Nernes watched while recuperating) – he never sings literally about what happened to him, choosing to escape into tales of fantasy in order to create a more vivid account of how it felt to be so ill. *The Gospel* is also Årabrot's most vocally orientated record and Kjetil's performance sounds gymnastic. He disdainfully flings words out of his throat, his voice often spiralling through the air, deliberately wobbling and breaking through growls and battle cries, as if he's cockily taunting the disease that couldn't defeat him. *The Gospel* was released in February 2016.

Next Thing

Having our flight delayed very much set the tone for the beginning of my 2018. I spent my birthday on the plane home, five days late, and within 24 hours of arriving back in London I was in a recording studio with two friends, continuing a music project we'd paused a decade ago. Graeme and I had followed through with our plans to revamp the old Wow! Scenario album, and revisiting a project I'd last worked on during a transitional time in my life seemed like a fitting start to the year. Once again, Chris produced all the songs and, in just one week, a group of generous and talented musicians had recorded cello, saxophone, fiddle and clarinet for us. Because I'd gone straight from the airport into the studio where we then worked non-stop, I didn't really have time to stop and indulge in my usual sentimental 'isn't this weird' reflective stuff, which is a shame because I absolutely love doing that. I obviously couldn't allow myself to miss out on this completely, though, so I saved all my sentimentality up for the following week, when I went to mix the album in Chris's flat in Amsterdam. Going abroad to work on music had been a lifelong dream and now I was finally able to fulfil it. I was looking forward to lounging around in an unfamiliar country, pretending to be a cool musician and overdosing on nostalgia.

•

In 2013, Canadian DIY pop singer **Veda Hille** decided to move her husband and son to Berlin for three months to write a new record. She hadn't done very much writing since her son's birth, and it seemed plausible that she wouldn't have any songs to write or anything much to say as motherhood felt so much more important than making music. For two weeks she went to a little room with a rented piano in it and napped on the couch. She read some books, and listened to people walking around outside in Neukölln. She thought about Bowie and Eno and the great records they made in Berlin, then learnt to play some songs by them on the piano, as well as songs by Hindemith and Gilbert and Sullivan, and then she started writing.

She was wrong about having nothing to say. *Love Waves* is an album of diverse love songs, an indie dance album of sorts that examines every version of love, giving each relationship equal worth and importance. Many of these love songs are for her son, others are dedicated to the middle of a marriage and some are for old friends. Hille felt like the world was overrun with gorgeous love songs about love between people in their twenties and was now happy to find some passionate love songs from her own mid-life corner of the world. *Love Waves* was released in May 2016.

•

My mindset in Amsterdam wasn't as sentimental as I'd hoped. I wanted to take this opportunity to reminisce fondly about the old days with Chris but actually spent most of my time fretting over the future. Working on a hobby in Holland halfway through January immediately made me feel uneasy. I'd put off a lot of big life decisions during 2017 because I was too stressed to take any of them on: getting a new agent, a new counsellor, writing any new comedy material – it'd all been delayed in order to quell my anxieties. But now 2017 was over, it was time to move forward and get things done, and here I was in Amsterdam mixing some songs with my friend. This week in Holland suddenly felt like a buffer I'd put in place before needing to take any action on anything. Buffers can be useful if you use them right. You can use a buffer to relax and switch off or you can use them to gently worry about everything you have to do once the buffering time is over, spending the entire buffer period in a state of melancholy and maybe even feeling guilty about the fact you've put a buffer in place immediately after being on a holiday that got extended due to a snow storm. One of the things I had originally planned to do in 2017, a sort of New Year's resolution, was to move out of shared accommodation and into my own flat. But after BWTGH and I split up I suddenly didn't feel stable enough to move house, much less live on my own, so I'd put it on hold. But now, in 2018, I felt like I needed to at least start thinking about moving again and it was weighing on my mind the whole time I was in Amsterdam. I was really scared of living on my own but equally scared of not progressing forward with my life, so I put 'Move House' at the top of my To Do list and allowed the panic to simmer away in the background throughout 'Amsterdam Buffer Week'.

We Have Always Lived in the Harolds

In 2010, **David Thomas Broughton**, originally from Otley, West Yorkshire, moved to Pyongyang in North Korea. His wife worked for the Foreign Office and only intended for them to stay a year, but they ended up there until 2013, at which point she transferred to South Korea and they moved there together. In total the couple lived in Korea for eight years, and while in Pyongyang David wrote and released the album *Crippling Lack*.

North Korea as a country had a huge effect on David's approach to writing the album. Any musicians he met there were technically phenomenal because they'd been raised to excel from a young age, but no one was encouraged to create regardless of technical ability and art was never viewed as 'whatever the artist wants it to be'. When Broughton met these proficient, trained musicians he would always feel humbled and embarrassed by his own output, and became convinced he shouldn't be making music at all. So he would constantly find himself in a cycle of self-doubt, occasionally receiving a boost from someone who would tell him what he does has value, inspiring him to continue. He also imposed restrictions on himself: he didn't want to disrespect the culture or offend anybody by playing his untrained music, understanding that it's important to maintain the diplomatic notion of North Korea in order to make any sort of progress with them. So he would always be tip-toeing around and playing his music really quietly in the spare bedroom where he'd set up a little studio – all of the recordings being sent straight to Europe and certainly not reaching the people of North Korea for a second.

While touring around Europe, Broughton was able to record a few songs in a tiny village in France with an engineer called Raphaela Duquesnoy. All of Broughton's guitar and vocal parts were recorded together in one take with him using a loop pedal, then he would record the bass parts as overdubs in one take with the mistakes kept in. He tended to stay on each section of a song for as long as it held his interest, which means a lot of his songs are lengthy but always warrant the amount of time spent on them. The album ended up clocking in at an hour and 41 minutes – one long folk behemoth of a record – so Broughton decided to take a more novel approach to its release. The album was divided into three separate volumes, then three different record labels (located in Leith in Scotland, Le Mans in France, and New York) released a volume each. There were about three or four tracks on each volume, and Broughton wanted the act of compiling the full album to feel like a treasure hunt for the listener. But this was short-lived because most of us are lazy, so all the songs were released together as one massive album in June 2016.

•

Best known for playing guitar in art rock legends Deerhoof, John Dieterich moved to Albuquerque, New Mexico, in the summer of 2010 because his partner needed to be situated there for her PhD programme. They didn't know anybody in Albuquerque but everybody told them to get in touch with Jeremy Barnes and Heather Trost, a couple who perform music under the name A Hawk and a Hacksaw. They very quickly became friends, clicking immediately, and John and Jeremy began regularly playing music together, improvising for hours at a time. These improvisations gradually took the form of an album, and in May 2016 the duo released *The Coral Casino* under the name **Dieterich & Barnes.**

The Coral Casino was one of many highly inventive and diverse projects John Dieterich was involved in during 2016. **Deerhoof** themselves released *The Magic* the following month, which again was recorded in Albuquerque despite how far flung the band had now become (drummer Greg Saunier was based in LA, singer Satomi Matsuzaki in New York and bassist Ed Rodriguez in Portland). Writing for the album had begun the previous year, when the band were asked to compose some music for a TV show. Greg, John and Ed each wrote songs on their own and submitted them to the show, only for them not to be used. But now they had three finished songs that they liked, and these songs became the foundations for the new record.

But *The Magic* wasn't the only Dieterich project to start with a commission in 2016. An art project in Hong Kong approached John to write a song based on a short story, so he contacted singer/songwriter and poet **Claire Cronin,** asking her to collaborate. Dieterich had seen Claire perform at the Pear Space in LA and had been completely mesmerised, thinking about her set for days afterwards. As she was a poet, her music was often driven by the lyrics, so Dieterich knew writing a song based on a short story would be easy for her. The story was called 'The Unnatural', and offered a comedic look at life without death. Cronin travelled to Albuquerque and the pair wrote and recorded the song in John's home studio, with friends contributing strings to the track also (Heather Trost being one of them). The song sounds like a beautiful funeral waltz: Cronin leads a gloomy procession while Dieterich's arrangements provide drawn-out atmospheric screeches and eerie feedback that engulfs Cronin's folk guitar before retreating. But the funding for the short-story project fell through and Claire and John were left with a song without a home. So, just like with *The Magic*, this song became the catalyst for an actual project – an EP in this case, six songs long, called *Came Down a Storm*.

'The Unnatural' set the tone for the rest of the record: death became a running theme and the songs became loaded with drowning imagery and morbid storytelling. Songs like 'Meet Me at the Undertakers' and 'Dark Water' were so clearly about death, while others were a little more cryptic. 'In the Field' was about the tragic death of Claire's cousin in a hot-air-balloon accident in a field in Richmond, Virginia. The song wasn't written to fit the theme of the project, it just turned out that way, and Cronin didn't realise until after. On the Bandcamp page for *Came Down a Storm* the notes say that the EP is not depressing but 'aims to float', and I like that; there's a sense of gratitude to these songs, and the death imagery and foreboding instrumentals somehow never kill the mood. *Came Down a Storm* was released in May 2016, the same month as *The Coral Casino*.

The final project John Dieterich was involved in during 2016 was *Balter/Saunier*. **Marcos Balter** is a composer from Rio de Janeiro, and while living in Chicago in 2012 he wrote a chamber piece, divided into seven sections, called *Meltdown Upshot*. The piece was inspired by a tough period in his life, full of anxieties and fears. He was about to get out of a relationship, was overwhelmed with work, and was having panic attacks and suffering from depression. *Meltdown Upshot* is about coming through the other end, the light at the end of the tunnel and surviving struggles. Musically, he wanted to bring two worlds together on these songs. He had worked with contemporary classical group **Ensemble Dal Niente** in the past and had met Deerhoof after a show in 2011 after being a fan for years beforehand. Although the two groups were radically different, he knew they shared a lot of core beliefs when it came to music and wanted the piece to become a collaboration between the two of them. *Meltdown Upshot* was debuted on stage at the 2012 Ecstatic Festival in New York; the group (consisting of more than 30 people) performed two pieces that night: *Meltdown Upshot* and a selection of Deerhoof songs adapted as chamber music variations, arranged by Deerhoof drummer **Greg Saunier**. None of this would actually be recorded until 2015, though. Without a record label, the two groups, along with Balter, organised themselves and set up a makeshift studio in a concert hall on top of the Fine Arts Building in Chicago, recording an album that would later be released in April 2016.

I Hope All of Your Dreams Come True

Every morning in Amsterdam, before we started mixing, I'd wake up and cycle around the city while listening to my iPod. The air was brisk, every ride was melancholic and I mainly listened to classics *not released* in 2016. It felt like time to draw a line underneath that particular project now that 2017 was over. I now owned around 366 albums (maybe a little more) from 2016, I'd covered more genres than I'd ever listened to before and I'd bought music from Norway, Japan, Spain, New Zealand, Holland, Cameroon, Australia, China, Argentina, Greece, Israel, Haiti, Pakistan, France, Denmark, Italy, Togo, Sweden, Ethiopia, Iceland, Portugal, Mexico,

Austria, Singapore, Canada, Brazil, Mauritania, Switzerland, Germany, Antarctica, Russia, South Korea, Colombia, Serbia, Chile, Poland, Mongolia, Belgium, India, Gambia, Taiwan, Ireland, Latvia, Hungary, Scotland, Wales, England and the USA. It felt like I'd made my point. One cold morning when the streets and roads were frosted over I decided to soundtrack my bike ride with *To Pimp a Butterfly*. Not long into the ride I took a corner too fast, my wheels locked and I flew off the bike. I had to make a quick decision in mid-air and decided to land on both knees hard. The main reason I chose to land on my knees was because I was trying to protect my iPod in my coat pocket. I remember travelling through the air during a passage where Kendrick repeatedly emphasises the phrase 'this dick ain't free'. I think that in my head I must've replaced the word 'dick' with 'iPod' – such is the value I place on both items – and so protected the thing that meant the most to me. I'm as concerned as you are.

That night I walked for an hour with bruised knees from Chris's house to a restaurant I'd researched online called Ron Gastrobar, while listening to *Relationship of Command*. The meal was one of the best I've ever had. They put tiny pork scratching-like bacon bits in the caramelised butter with the bread. I had an astounding beef wellington for two all to myself with roasted cauliflower and then, as I left, they gave me a complimentary mini-ice cream in a tiny cone. On the way home I stopped in a pub because, in all honesty, I needed an emergency dump due to eating a massive banquet all to myself. I then felt like I needed to buy a beer at the pub because it was empty and the barman had watched me walk in, go straight to their toilet and remain in there for longer than it takes to go for a wee then emerge looking like a man who'd done a shit.

He poured me a locally brewed sour beer and it was one of the most unexpectedly refreshing and exciting beers I have ever tasted. I then continued my walk home, listening to *U.F.O.* by Jim Sullivan, thinking about how much sour beer I'm going to drink in the future, and, while crossing a bridge over the river, I felt ok about being on my own for the first time in a year.

•

Prolific Singaporean producer **Fauxe** started releasing music in 2012. Back then he wore a mask when he performed, but in 2016 he finally took it off for good because he felt like who he was in life and who he was in his music were finally the same. His latest album had been his most personal, triggered by a breakup, and the journey to completion was more painful than usual, but by the end he felt enlightened.

The album took two years; two years of meditating on his failures and disappointments, and as the project drew to a close he found himself constantly listening to the song 'Daydreaming' from Radiohead's 2016 album *A Moon Shaped Pool*. Although Thom Yorke hasn't divulged too much publicly about the meaning behind the song, many have deduced from its music video (directed by Paul Thomas Anderson) that it's about his breakup from long-term partner and mother of his two children Rachel Owen. The video was released on Mother's Day and sees Yorke walk through 23 different rooms (one for every year of their relationship). At the end of the video Yorke curls up next to a campfire and says something important, but, because it's Radiohead, we hear his words in reverse and have no idea what he's telling us. When it's played forward we can hear Thom Yorke is saying, 'Half of my life. Half of my love'. Yorke was 47 when the song was released, so his 23-year relationship with Rachel had lasted roughly half of his life. Radiohead also released their debut album, *Pablo Honey*, the same year Yorke began his relationship with Rachel, so it's speculated that the 'half of my love' line is in reference to his love being divided between her and the band. (At this point I'd like to remind you that I subscribe to YouTube channels dedicated to fan theories, so none of what I've just said about a six-and-a-half-minute Radiohead music video should come as a surprise to you.)

These words from Thom Yorke, 'half of my life, half of my love', helped Fauxe make sense of everything he'd been through in the last couple of years, as he realised that his love had been split between the people who matter to him and his music. It's unclear whether he puts his breakup down to this, but he did name a 17-track album about that same breakup *Half of My Love*, so there's a chance he might do. At an hour and eight minutes, *Half of My Love* might seem intimidating, but the journey veers in new and unexpected directions with every song and never dulls. At times this feels like an emo R&B or emo hip hop album; the music and lyrics are open-hearted and the guests sound like they're earnestly singing about Fauxe's experiences and their own simultaneously, like they're empathising with a friend's recent heartbreak. And yet things never feel wet or whiny, Fauxe's grittier production keeps everything authentic and it's hard to give in to cynicism when an artist is clearly being this genuine. In the liner notes, Fauxe acknowledges that he doesn't always handle himself or communicate well in relationships but states that one of the things he learnt while making this record was that taking care of others meant taking care of himself also. He doesn't elaborate on this, he doesn't say that making music is his way of practising self-care or that taking care of himself means taking a break from the music and making sure he's not too run down, but it's a good conclusion to come to. If you don't like yourself, then being able to accept love from other people is tricky.

I used to take two years between relationships. Although not done intentionally, I think the first year was always spent getting over the other person and the second year was spent learning to like myself again and believe I was worth somebody else's time. When I met BWTGH I had been single for just one year, I definitely didn't like myself enough yet, but I was in love, so I committed to a relationship anyway. We were together for two and a half years and, if I'm honest, I never felt like I was worth her time, so I wasn't the boyfriend I could've been.

Perfect

That week in Amsterdam felt like the end of 2017 even though it took place well into January 2018. I finally felt ready to move forward by the end of it. I'd immersed myself in plenty of my own nostalgia and successfully delayed addressing any of my present-day responsibilities for long enough. I wasn't fully mended, but when does anyone ever really feel like that anyway? On the final day of mixing, Chris and I listened back to everything we'd done and agreed we were satisfied with it. A month later I played them all to Graeme and he suggested we take these new recordings and add some professional vocalists to them, singing the parts we always wanted to sing but never could, and I agreed with him. So it's a project that may last my entire life. Every ten years we'll probably record a bunch of new parts, then live with that version for a while before deciding to alter things again. I think we're trying to perfect it and don't want to release it until it's perfect. I know that's stupid, but as long as it's still fun we'll keep pursuing it.

When I was filming the comedy specials in 2017 I listened to WORRY. by Jeff Rosenstock backstage to calm myself down between shows. I had wanted to film my stand-up shows for so long, but now I was in the middle of a falling out with my agent and was so stressed I was certain I was going to deliver a shitty performance and the end result would be disappointing. The final track on WORRY. is called 'Perfect Sound Whatever' and features the lyrics, 'Perfect always takes so long because it don't exist'. I had never realised those were the lyrics until that day. It's maybe the only example I have of song lyrics breaking through exactly when you need them. Not only was the message important for me in the context of the day but also in the context of the year – a year when I'd repeatedly dragged myself over every mistake I'd ever made and spent too much time wishing I'd got everything right.

WORRY. changed my life. So did Telefone. So did so many albums I can't even begin to list here. Before I started buying these albums my 'Greatest Albums of All Time' list was fairly short and easy to compile. Now it's a nightmare. I have to have a separate list of 2016 albums from the GOAT list because otherwise it looks insane. This is why I'd be lying if I said that any other year was the greatest year for music of all time – because so many albums released in 2016 had a profound effect on me. And, yes, this is mainly because I actively went looking for them, but so what? You might think that anyone could do this with any year in music but you'd be wrong. Before the internet there simply weren't as many albums being released, so you'd do well to find 366 albums you liked from one year in the 70s. But you absolutely *can* do this with years after 2000. And if you chose a post-2000 year and did the sort of deep dive I did with 2016, you would probably also find hundreds of albums you liked and some of those albums would end up changing your life and becoming your favourite albums of all time. Whatever year you find yourself in now, know that your favourite album will be, or already has been, released this year but you haven't found it because you haven't looked yet. When you've finished reading this book, search 'best albums of' whatever year you're in, or even the previous year like I did, read the lists that come up and listen to the ones you like the sound of. Within minutes you'll have found an album you genuinely love. I promise.

2016 is the greatest year for music of all time because it's *my* greatest year for music of all time – I'm not really trying to convince *you* it's the best year, I'm trying to convince you to find your own best year. And just know that whatever year you find to be the greatest year for music of all time because you have a personal connection to it is absolutely, well and truly, a big pile of bullshit unless it's 2016 because, guess what – it's not even subjective, 2016 is officially the greatest year for music of all time, taste doesn't even enter into it, there has never been a better year before or since, and if you disagree then bring me 366 albums you love from a different year and we'll talk. But until then – 2016 was the greatest, the best and the most awesome, and that is a solid gold fact. In. Your. Face.

I'm doing much better these days, by the way.

Rock the Fuck On Forever

I feel that before we properly put an end to this book I should be honest with you and let you know that I am actually still purchasing music from 2016. It's currently 2019 as I write this and I've not kicked the habit yet. My purchasing has slowed down significantly, but every now and then I'll have a little browse online and find another chunk of gold. Within the last month I've discovered *CONARIUM*, an orchestral electronic album by Latvian multi-instrumentalist **Elizabete Balčus** based on a series of disconnected dreams she had and then musically interpreted upon waking (the flute work is worth your money alone). I've unearthed **The Sooper Swag Project**'s mind-melting math-rap odyssey *Badd Timing*, an album that I urge you to seek out immediately – even if only to view the worst album cover of all time. I won't describe it here because I want you to experience it first hand, but, please know, the music is as exhilarating as the cover is hilariously ugly. Just last week, I watched a YouTube video called *Best Post-Goth & Dark Avant-Garde Music 2016* (uploaded by a channel named GothicBop: Batwave & Guilty Pleasures) and it introduced me to *Heartless* by **Bestial Mouths**. The album features bleak, dissonant synths, wailing lead vocals and endless tom fills – what more could I honestly ask for? Three more 2016 projects that I can't stop listening to and want to tell everyone about. Best year for music of all time. No question. The latest album count is 562. I currently own 562 albums from 2016. Five hundred and sixty-two.

With this 2016 project I've managed to reconnect with modern music in general: I buy way more new releases these days than ever before and my life is honestly all the better for it. But while I've bought plenty of music from 2017, 2018 and 2019, I've always remained open to a 2016 release I've not heard before as it's probably the only subject in the entire universe that I can claim to be the leading expert on, and the thought of missing a cracker or two still doesn't sit well with me. Also, something about discovering yet another tremendous album from the same year makes me a more optimistic person in general, maybe because my faith is being rewarded in some way. You can take the boy out of church but you can't take the endless desire for purpose and meaning out of the boy.

Thanks for reading this book and I hope you found some albums you like along the way. That's the main point of it, really. That and the fact that writing a book about all the albums I bought makes them tax deductible.

366 Projects from 2016!

These are in no particular order, but here's a stunner a day for you to listen to throughout the next leap year:

JANUARY

monday	tuesday	wednesday	thursday	friday	saturday	sunday
				1 Noname *Telefone*	2 Jeff Rosenstock *WORRY.*	3 Danny Brown *Atrocity Exhibition*
4 Jon Bap *What Now?*	5 Pixvae *Pixvae*	6 Zeal & Ardor *Devil Is Fine*	7 Katie Dey *Flood Network*	8 Surface To Air Missive *AV*	9 Laura Mvula *The Dreaming Room*	10 Katie Kim *Salt*
11 uKanDanZ *Awo*	12 40 Watt Sun *Wider Than the Sky*	13 The Tuts *Update Your Brain*	14 Law Holt *City*	15 Mike Cooper *New Guitar Old Hat Knew Blues*	16 Buttering Trio *Threesome*	17 Youngster Jiji *Sui // Rap*
18 Anarchist Republic of Bzzz *United Diktatürs of Europe*	19 David Thomas Broughton *Crippling Lack*	20 Rats On Rafts & De Kift *Rats On Rafts / De Kift*	21 Public Speaking *Caress, Redact*	22 Car Seat Headrest *Teens Of Denial*	23 Claire Cronin *Came Down a Storm*	24 Ben Sollee feat. Jordan Ellis *Infowars*
25 Arabrot *The Gospel*	26 Cave Story *West*	27 Joana Gomila *Folk Souvenir*	28 Ensemble Dal Niente *Balter/Saunier*	29 TRIM *1-800 Dinosaur Presents...*	30 Market *Not Good At Spending Time Alone a.k.a. Cleanliness*	31 Mal Devisa *Kiid*

FEBRUARY

monday	tuesday	wednesday	thursday	friday	saturday	sunday
1 **Falling** *Out of Sight*	2 **Marissa Nadler** *Strangers*	3 **Andy Shauf** *The Party*	4 **Kal Marks** *Life Is Alright, Everybody Dies*	5 **Islet** *Liquid Half Moon*	6 **Rob Crow's Gloomy Place** *You're Doomed. Be Nice.*	7 **J Thoubbs** *Unreleasable Material*
8 **Foonyap** *Palimpsest*	9 **Death Grips** *Bottomless Pit*	10 **Christian Fitness** *This Taco is Not Correct*	11 **Fog** *For Good*	12 **Martin Creed** *Thoughts Lined Up*	13 **Wei Zhongle** *Nice Mask over an Ugly Face*	14 **Crying** *Beyond the Fleeting Gales*
15 **TW Walsh** *Fruitless Research*	16 **Sélébéyone** *Sélébéyone*	17 **Un Blonde** *Will Come to You*	18 **Doomsday Student** *A Self-Help Tragedy*	19 **Cloud Becomes Your Hand** *Rest in Fleas*	20 **Karima Walker** *Hands in Our Names*	21 **Wes Borland** *Crystal Machete*
22 **Bologna Violenta** *Discordia*	23 **Cate le Bon** *Crab Day*	24 **Run The Jewels** *RTJ3*	25 **Metá Metá** *MM3*	26 **Kendrick Lamar** *untitled unmastered.*	27 **Nick Cave & The Bad Seeds** *Skeleton Tree*	28 **Aesop Rock** *The Impossible Kid*
29 **Fauxe** *Half Of My Love*						

MARCH

monday	tuesday	wednesday	thursday	friday	saturday	sunday
	1 The Drones *Feelin Kinda Free*	2 The Sooper Swag Project *Badd Timing*	3 LITHICS *Borrowed Floors*	4 Flanch *Flanch*	5 Eric Bachmann *Eric Bachmann*	6 Rocks & Waves Song Circle *Songs I-V*
7 Frank Ocean *Blonde*	8 Beyoncé *Lemonade*	9 David Bowie *Blackstar*	10 Weaves *Weaves*	11 Esperanza Spalding *Emily's D+ Evolution*	12 Lord Rao + Cupp Cave + Hermutt Lobby *Woof*	13 Ichiko Aoba *Mahoroboshiya*
14 Xenia Rubinos *Black Terry Cat*	15 Adam Torres *Pearls to Swine*	16 Blood Orange *Freetown Sound*	17 Tancred *Out Of The Garden*	18 Open Mike Eagle + Paul White *Hella Personal Film Festival*	19 Jamila Woods *HEAVN*	20 Hypnopazūzu *Create Christ, Sailor Boy*
21 clipping. *Splendor & Misery*	22 A Tribe Called Quest *We Got It From Here... Thank You 4 Your Service*	23 Solange *A Seat at the Table*	24 Jesu & Sun Kil Moon *Jesu/Sun Kil Moon*	25 Gregory Alan Isakov *With the Colorado Symphony*	26 The Colorist & Emiliana Torrini *The Colorist & Emiliana Torrini*	27 Veda Hille *Love Waves*
28 Johnnie Frierson *Have You Been Good To Yourself*	29 Sad13 *Slugger*	30 Montaigne *Glorious Heights*	31 Frankie Cosmos *'Next Thing*			

APRIL

monday	tuesday	wednesday	thursday	friday	saturday	sunday
				1 serpentwithfeet *blisters*	2 Kanye West *The Life of Pablo*	3 Larry Wish & His Guys *Not from My Come From*
4 Jenny Hval *Blood Bitch*	5 Big Thief *Masterpiece*	6 The I.L.Y's *Scum With Boundaries*	7 Kojey Radical *23Winters*	8 Leonard Cohen *You Want it Darker*	9 Bon Iver *22, a Million*	10 Japanese Breakfast *Psychopomp*
11 Babyfather *'BBF' hosted by DJ Escrow*	12 Nico Muhly & Teitur *Confessions*	13 Cult Of Luna & Julie Christmas *Mariner*	14 PUP *The Dream is Over*	15 NOISIA *The Outer Edges*	16 Macmananaman *New Wave Of British BASEBALL Heavy Metal*	17 John Cale *M:FANS*
18 The Body *No One Deserves Happiness*	19 Marching Church *Telling It Like It Is*	20 Reginald Omas Mamode IV *Reginald Omas Mamode IV*	21 Kilo Kish *Reflections in Real Time*	22 Olga Bell *Tempo*	23 They Are Gutting A Body Of Water *They Are Gutting a Body of Water*	24 Mitski *Puberty 2*
25 Anderson .Paak *Malibu*	26 Krano *Requiescat In Plavem*	27 Ryley Walker *Golden Sings That Have been Sung*	28 Sleigh Bells *Jessica Rabbit*	29 The Wedding Present *Going, Going...*	30 Yeah You *Id Vendor*	

MAY

monday	tuesday	wednesday	thursday	friday	saturday	sunday
						1 **Angel Du$t** *Rock the Fuck on Forever*
2 **Vaudou Game** *Kidayu*	3 **Frank Ocean** *Endless*	4 **Will Butler** *Friday Night*	5 **NAILS** *You Will Never be One of Us*	6 **Moken** *Chapters of My Life*	7 **Will Wood & The Tapeworms** *Self-ish*	8 **Every Time I Die** *Low Teens*
9 **Half Japanese** *Perfect*	10 **Exit Verse** *Grant No Glory*	11 **RM Hubbert** *Telling the Trees*	12 **YUNGMORPHEUS** *44 Laws of Mentalizm*	13 **Lucy Dacus** *No Burden*	14 **Ali Beletic** *Legends of These Lands Left to Live*	15 **Moor Mother** *Fetish Bones*
16 **Dinosaur Jr.** *Give a Glimpse of What Yer Not*	17 **A Bunch Of Dead People** *Your Eternal Reward*	18 **PJ Harvey** *The Hope Six Demolition Project*	19 **James Ferraro** *Human Story 3*	20 **The Lennon Claypool Delirium** *Monolith of Phobos*	21 **Dillinger Escape Plan** *Dissociation*	22 **TEEN** *Love Yes*
23 **My Vitriol** *The Secret Sessions*	24 **Angel Olsen** *MY WOMAN*	25 **Listening Woman** *Getting Mystic*	26 **LVL UP** *Return to Love*	27 **Róisín Murphy** *Take Her Up to Monto*	28 **True Love** *Heaven's Too Good for Us*	29 **Animal Collective** *Painting With*
30 **Lisa/Liza** *Deserts of Youth*	31 **Yoni & Geti** *Testarossa*					

JUNE

monday	tuesday	wednesday	thursday	friday	saturday	sunday
		1 Ty Segall *Emotional Mugger*	2 Rafter *XYZ*	3 Princess Nokia *1992*	4 Car Bomb *Meta*	5 King Gizzard & The Lizard Wizard *Nonagon Infinity*
6 Salami Rose Joe Louis *Son Of A Sauce!*	7 Wreck & Reference *Indifferent Rivers Romance End*	8 Conor Oberst *Ruminations*	9 Eleanor Friedberger *New View*	10 Deerhoof *The Magic*	11 Gaika *SECURITY*	12 Jank *Versace Summer*
13 KA *Honor Killed the Samurai*	14 Uni Ika Ai *Keeping A Golden Bullseye In The Corner Of My Mind*	15 Willis Earl Beal *Through The Dark*	16 Childish Gambino *'Awaken, My Love!'*	17 KAYTRANADA *99.9%*	18 Trust Fund *We Have Always Lived in the Harolds*	19 Shooter Jennings *Countach (for Giorgio)*
20 Roy Montgomery *R: Tropic of Anodyne*	21 Tord Gustavsen *What was Said*	22 Calo Wood *Diving Shadows*	23 Head Wound City *A New Wave of Violence*	24 San Cha *Me Demandó— DEMOS*	25 Hannah Epperson *Upsweep*	26 IAN SWEET *Shapeshifter*
27 ZOMBIE-CHANG *Zombie-Change*	28 Santa Marta Golden *Resilience*	29 MIKE *Longest Day, Shortest Night*	30 NǽnoćÿbbĊErǧ VbërrĦólökäävsF *Solar 2 / Lunar 2*			

JULY

monday	tuesday	wednesday	thursday	friday	saturday	sunday
				1 **The Hotelier** *Goodness*	2 **Seekersinternational** *The Ragga Preservation Society*	3 **KING** *We are KING*
4 **Melt Yourself Down** *Last Evenings on Earth*	5 **Motion Graphics** *Motion Graphics*	6 **Pinegrove** *Cardinal*	7 **Hakan** *II*	8 **Show Me The Body** *Body War*	9 **Above Top Secret** *Above Top Secret*	10 **Mo Troper** *Beloved*
11 **Oddisee** *Alwasta*	12 **Yohuna** *Patientness*	13 **Adam Betts** *Colossal Squid*	14 **NOFX** *First Ditch Effort*	15 **Matmos** *Ultimate Care II*	16 **Azna de L'Ader** *Zabaya*	17 **Young Thug** *JEFFERY*
18 **It's Not Night: It's Space** *Our Birth is But a Sleep and a Forgetting*	19 **Kelsey Lu** *Church*	20 **Sammus** *Pieces in Space*	21 **Zelooperz** *Bothic*	22 **Dieterich & Barnes** *The Coral Casino*	23 **Weezer** *The White Album*	24 **Iggy Pop** *Post Pop Depression*
25 **BCUC** *Our Truth*	26 **Lambchop** *FLOTUS*	27 **Modern Baseball** *Holy Ghost*	28 **Sony Smith** *Sees All Knows All*	29 **Rihanna** *ANTI*	30 **Weyes Blood** *Front Row Seat to Earth*	31 **Nicholas Allbrook** *Pure Gardiya*

AUGUST

monday	tuesday	wednesday	thursday	friday	saturday	sunday
1 **Homeboy Sandman** *Kindness for Weakness*	2 **Jon Phonics** *Letters to Home*	3 **C.C.T.V.** *Practice Tape 3.6.16*	4 **Bestial Mouths** *Heartless*	5 **James Tillman** *Silk Noise Reflex*	6 **Chairlift** *Moth*	7 **Fly Anakin** *The Grand Scheme of Things*
8 **Touché Amoré** *Stage Four*	9 **Chance the Rapper** *Coloring Book*	10 **Various Artists** *Southern Family*	11 **Shugo Tokumaru** *TOSS*	12 **Drugdealer** *The End of Comedy*	13 **Forests** *Sun Eat Moon Grave Party*	14 **JPEGMAFIA** *Black Ben Carson*
15 **Wati Watia Zorey Band** *Zanz in lanfèr*	16 **Radiohead** *A Moon Shaped Pool*	17 **P Money** *Live + Direct*	18 **Big Baby Driver Trio** *We Were Trying Not To Disturb You*	19 **Duchess Says** *Sciences Nouvelles*	20 **Wora Wora Washington** *Mirror*	21 **M.A.K.U. Soundsystem** *Mezcla*
22 **Lee Fields & The Expressions** *Special Night*	23 **G.L.O.S.S.** *Trans Day of Revenge*	24 **Stuck In November** *First Slice of Cake*	25 **Katie Gately** *Color*	26 **Mood Tattooed** *Hush Tarantula*	27 **Omar Rodriguez-Lopez** *A Lovejoy*	28 **Kaitlyn Aurelia Smith** *EARS*
29 **Melanie De Biasio** *Blackened Cities*	30 **Sturgill Simpson** *A Sailor's Guide to Earth*	31 **Noura Mint Seymali** *Arbina*				

SEPTEMBER

monday	tuesday	wednesday	thursday	friday	saturday	sunday
			1 Lido Pimienta *La Papessa*	2 Gensu Dean & Denmark Vessey *Whole Food*	3 Kamiyada+ *Static Depression*	4 Meilyr Jones *2013*
5 Kacy & Clayton *Strange Country*	6 Oathbreaker *Rheia*	7 Deakin *Sleep Cycle*	8 SUBROSA *For This We Fought The Battle of Ages*	9 Död Mark *Drabbad Av Sjukdom*	10 Xiu Xiu *Plays The Music of Twin Peaks*	11 Scallops Hotel *Too Much of Life is Mood*
12 WOMPS *Our Fertile Forever*	13 WIDT *WIDT*	14 Uranium Club *All of Them Naturals*	15 Elizabeta Läce *Songs About D*	16 Church Fire *Pussy Blood*	17 Kevin Abstract *American Boyfriend: A Suburban Love Story*	18 Kefaya *Radio International*
19 Respire *Gravity & Grace*	20 Elizabete Balčus *CONARIUM*	21 James Blake *The Colour in Anything*	22 Saul Williams *MartyrLoserKing*	23 ROAR *Impossible Animals*	24 Evasive Backflip *Turbo Chili Children*	25 ICHI *Maru*
26 KHOMPA *The Shape of Drums to Come*	27 SUPERTEEN *Isn't a Person*	28 Nina Ryser *I Hope All Of Your Dreams Come True*	29 Be *One*	30 Raging Speedhorn *Lost Ritual*		

OCTOBER

monday	tuesday	wednesday	thursday	friday	saturday	sunday
					1 **Comfort Food** *Waffle Frolic*	2 **Omni** *Deluxe*
3 **ABRA** *Princess*	4 **Ela & PomPom** *My New Music*	5 **ANOHNI** *Hopelessness*	6 **Tyrannamen** *Tyrannamen*	7 **Chris Cohen** *As If Apart*	8 **Big Ups** *Before a Million Universes*	9 **ScHoolboy Q** *Blank Face LP*
10 **Aragehonzi** *Hanatsuoto*	11 **Emily Jane White** *They Moved In Shadow All Together*	12 **Swans** *The Glowing Man*	13 **Tessa Dillon** *11:11*	14 **Guerilla Toss** *Eraser Stargazer*	15 **Gonjasufi** *Callus*	16 **L'Orange & Mr. Lif** *The Life & Death Of Scenery*
17 **BEHAVIOR** *3715 Images of Angels*	18 **Homebody** *Better Use of Leisure Time*	19 **Unloved** *Guilty of Love*	20 **Swet Shop Boys** *Cashmere*	21 **Rapsody** *Crown*	22 **Street Sects** *End Position*	23 **Mothers** *When You Walk a Long Distance You Are Tired*
24 **Michael Kiwanuka** *Love & Hate*	25 **case/lang/veirs** *case/lang/veirs*	26 **Body Meat** *Several Heads*	27 **Susso** *Keira*	28 **Kinit Her** *The Blooming World*	29 **NV** *Binasu*	30 **Slowly Rolling Camera** *All Things*
31 **The Avalanches** *Wildflower*						

NOVEMBER

monday	tuesday	wednesday	thursday	friday	saturday	sunday
	1 Anna Meredith *Varmints*	2 Brigid Mae Power *Brigid Mae Power*	3 Yussef Kamaal *Black Focus*	4 Kamaiyah *A Good Night in the Ghetto*	5 Kadhja Bonet *The Visitor*	6 SAWA *SAWA*
7 Greys *Outer Heaven*	8 Burnt Palms *Back on My Wall*	9 100 Gecs *100 Gecs*	10 David Coulter & Seb Rochford *Good Friday*	11 Isaiah Rashad *The Sun's Tirade*	12 Alfio Antico *Antico*	13 Parquet Courts *Human Performance*
14 Saqqara Mastabas *Libras*	15 POLYSICS *What's This???*	16 Xylouris White *Black Peak*	17 zeroh *Tinnitus*	18 Alex Anwandter *Amiga*	19 Harleighblu & Starkiller *Amorine*	20 Preoccupations *Preoccupations*
21 Thy Catafalque *Meta*	22 Charles Bradley *Changes*	23 Wren Kitz *For Evelyn*	24 Kero Kero Bonito *Bonito Generation*	25 Trái Bơ *Adulthood In The Context Of Total Noise*	26 Guts *Eternal*	27 Kate Jackson *British Road Movies*
28 Skepta *Konnichiwa*	29 Ian William Craig *Centres*	30 Throws *Throws*				

DECEMBER

monday	tuesday	wednesday	thursday	friday	saturday	sunday
			1 **Soft Hair** *Soft Hair*	2 **Zach Schimpf** *Who Speaks To You?*	3 **Siddiq & Vektroid** *Midnight Run*	4 **Cleft** *Wrong*
5 **Vulfpeck** *The Beautiful Game*	6 **Father** *I'm A Piece Of Shit*	7 **YG** *Still Brazy*	8 **KNOWER** *LIFE*	9 **ZHU** *Generationwhy*	10 **Paul Simon** *Stranger To Stranger*	11 **Mourn** *Ha, Ha, He.*
12 **Flock Of Dimes** *If You See Me, Say Yes*	13 **Ndagga Rhythm Force** *Yermande*	14 **Milly Mango & Jeremiah Jae** *Rango*	15 **The Lonely Island** *Popstar: Never Stop Never Stopping OST*	16 **Various Artists** *Biscuits For Your Outside Man*	17 **Nevermen** *Nevermen*	18 **Nicolas Jaar** *Sirens*
19 **Minyo Crusaders** *It Don't MinYo A Thing (If It Ain't Got That Bu-shi)*	20 **Blank Banshee** *MEGA*	21 **BADBAD-NOTGOOD** *IV*	22 **Injury Reserve** *Floss*	23 **Calo Wood** *Driving Shadows*	24 **Bully Fae** *Defy A Thing to Be*	25 **Salt People** *Deep Swim*
26 **clipping.** *Wriggle*	27 **Little Annie** *Trace*	28 **AJ Cornell & Tim Darcy** *Too Significant To Ignore*	29 **Lizzo** *Coconut Oil*	30 **Nine Inch Nails** *Not The Actual Events*	31 **Lycus** *Chasms*	

Appendix

There are so, so, so many albums that I was unable to include in the main body of the book – often they just didn't fit in with the main narrative – so here's a few more 2016 corkers I'd like to shine a light on, if you'd permit me.

●

One of the best feel-good power pop records of 2016 was *Out of the Garden* by **Tancred**. Tancred is the solo project of Jess Abbott, and *Out of the Garden* sounds like it could've been a 90s classic. Loud, angsty and charged with the spirit of unstoppable youth, this album saw a significant change in Abbot's attitudes towards herself and anything that oppresses her. She had recently taken up self-defence lessons due to never feeling safe when walking home late at night from the liquor store she worked at. The way she was treated during that time was aggressive in a way she'd not experienced before. She had always looked young and been treated like a girl, but that had recently changed – people were treating her like a woman now and she was having to deal with a whole new raft of shitty interactions with men. The self-defence lessons quickly helped her confidence – she'd always struggled with nerves when playing live, but with this new batch of songs she didn't feel that way for the first time and appeared way more comfortable in front of a crowd. When singing about relationships on *Out of the Garden*, Abbott deliberately kept things genderfluid because journalists had made presumptions about her sexuality in the past based on certain songs. It's not something the listener would particularly notice, but it's another example of Jess taking back control of her own narrative, this time in the media, and not letting others write it for her.

•

Portland based art rock outfit L I T H I C S produce avant-garde indie songs that adopt a minimalistic approach. The guitars resist strumming along to the song wherever possible, so jab and prod at you instead, always teasing the possibility of a melody but then opting to keep things erratic, repetitive and rhythmically focused. Their 2016 album *Borrowed Floors* was named after a misheard Nico lyric. In the 1967 song 'Wrap Your Troubles in Dreams', Nico sings 'bullies kick and kill young loves down on bar room floors'. It's a title that oddly suits the overall tone of the band – some misheard poetry that doesn't quite make sense. Plus, lead singer Aubrey Horner's vocals aren't too dissimilar to Nico's; if you were only half listening to a Lithics song you might assume Nico had taken it upon herself to form an art punk band, so a half-heard Nico lyric befits them nicely.

•

Lindsay Olsen is from a family of scientists. Her parents emigrated to the US from the Czech Republic, began working in labs upon their arrival and wanted the same for their children. So Lindsay went along with her parents' wishes and studied Earth and Planetary Sciences, focusing on Marine Biology and Ocean Chemistry. In 2015, Lindsay was working in a lab sorting tiny squid into groups and removing their ear bones. She'd committed to science but had recently fallen in love with music and was making an album, recording in her tiny bedroom using just a keyboard, a microphone and a drum machine. Around the same time, Lindsay had been making a sauce and taking it to friend's parties, proving quite the hit. The sauce was full of nuts and bell peppers, spices, garlic and olive oil and was meant to be used as a dip for bread. She was considering starting her own sauce company and naming it Son of a Sauce! after an inside joke she had with her sister. She knew she needed to promote the sauce company, so decided that she would name the album she was working on *Son of a Sauce!* as a way of getting the brand out there. Lindsay released *Son of a Sauce!* in March 2016 under the name **Salami Rose Joe Louis**. The sauce company sadly never came to fruition, but she still occasionally works in labs and is still releasing music.

•

Mo Troper was born in Los Angeles and spent most of his time there listening to music with his father, who collected records and Beatles memorabilia. But his parents had a pretty combustible relationship, which led to a divorce; his mother quickly married another man, and Mo was hustled out of LA to Portland. In Portland, the dynamic he shared with his birth father was torn apart, and that side of him was forcibly suppressed. For this reason, Portland and its residents don't come out looking too good on Mo's debut solo album.

Mo viewed the culture in Portland as passive aggressive, so a Portland rock record this direct held an enduring appeal to him. He wrote and recorded these songs while drinking heavily and at the height of his local popularity, but by the time it was released, he already felt socially lapped. People he knew thought the songs were about them and ignored him at shows. There are songs from this album that Mo gets uncomfortable listening to now and never wants to perform again. It's uncommon for a relatively obscure artist to come out of the gate with an album this bitter and personal. Mo feels that took some courage, although he was so drunk and unselfconscious when writing it that he didn't realise this at the time. *Beloved* was released in April 2016.

•

Early in 2005, Geoff Farina was in a cabin in the Dolomites with his wife, it was late at night and the mountains were silent, but he could hear a constant ringing that he eventually figured out was coming from inside his own head. Over the following months the ringing became louder until he'd even be able to hear it while listening to loud music. After he saw a couple of different audiologists, it was confirmed that he had tinnitus and permanent hearing damage from too many years of playing and attending loud shows. At the time he played guitar and sang in jazz-rock group Karate and tried to protect his ears with earplugs, but couldn't perform with them, so ended up cancelling part of a European tour and left the band that summer. For five years he only played acoustically, but when he moved to Chicago in 2010 he discovered a new range of in-ear monitors and earplugs and was finally able to play live again.

Geoff quickly formed a band with the intention of playing

loud music while drawing from 70s groups like Big Star and The Faces. The band was called **Exit Verse** and in 2016 they released their second album, *Grant No Glory*, one of Geoff's favourites out of all the records he's ever made. He wanted to make rock music that had the same kind of urgent energy Karate did, but that was also dignified and reflected his middle-aged identity. On *Grant No Glory* you hear the same guy from Karate with the same ear for melody and command of his instrument, but now he knows who he is and doesn't need to prove himself to anyone any more.

•

Felix Skinner and Ignat Frege are **Wreck & Reference** and in July 2016 they released *Indifferent Rivers Romance End*. Awash with synths and robotic drums, with vocals that flit between downbeat half-spoken passages and raw-throated screams, there's a blissful and irresistible sulkiness to every song. The production takes a quieter approach than most metal albums, though, allowing the songwriting to breathe more, while still keeping the heavier moments blunt and gruesome. *IRRE* was about the changes Ignat needed to make in his life in order to stop feeling miserable, especially the elements of that misery which were self-inflicted. He was getting out of the sort of relationship where both parties constantly punished each other, and instead of learning from this he'd just kept making the same mistakes over and over. This meant Ignat had accepted this permanent feeling of dissatisfaction, and become predisposed to viewing everything through a filter of negativity. The album's title is a reference to the Greek philosopher Heraclitus, who said 'no man ever steps in the same river twice', regarding the complicated relationship between discrete objects and change.

With this record, Felix and Ignat wanted to show what happens when you take this concept and mix it with booze, nihilism and being a shitty person.

•

Every time **James Tillman** turned on the radio in 2015 he felt like he was being beat over the head with super-loud vocals, super compression, super everything. Every song seemed to be screaming at him, telling him that he needed to like it. He wanted to hear the opposite of this, so he set about writing *Silk Noise Reflex*. The title is a statement of intent, the antithesis of what was dominating the mainstream in 2015. Lyrically the album is about his first few years living in New York and feeling isolated while being surrounded by millions of people every day. The sounds of New York are scattered throughout *Silk Noise* – Tillman would make field recordings using binaural headphones as he walked through Brooklyn, Union Square, Central Park, all the places he routinely encountered each and every week. True to the album's ethos the field recordings aren't at the forefront of anything, they're disguised so they contribute to the overall sound, and the background noises of his day-to-day become the background noises of his album. *Silk Noise Reflex* was released in August 2016.

•

Peter Solo of **Vaudou Game**, was born and raised in Lome, the capital of Togo, where voodoo was born. Voodoo is his way of living, he was born into voodoo and his mother performs voodoo ceremonies every day. Every voodoo ceremony involves singing and percussion – you cannot have voodoo without music, and the most important things about voodoo music

are the rhythm and the words. They sing about the energy of
the land and the force of the four elements (air, water, earth
and fire), they preach about how nature can feed you, how it
can heal you, how beautiful nature is and how spiritual. Every
time Peter has a drink of water he throws some on the ground,
giving it to divinity, and every time he eats food he puts some
aside for the energy we cannot see. The first thing he does
in the morning and the last thing he does before he goes to
sleep is to say 'Thank you, Nature'. In September 2016 Vaudou
Game released their second album, *Kidayu* – meaning 'Share'.
On *Kidayu*, Solo wanted to dismiss the Hollywood version of
voodoo that everyone has in their heads, of dolls and curses.
He wanted to get across the true meaning of voodoo: celebration and gratitude, togetherness and wonder, human beings'
relationships with each other and human beings' relationship
with Nature and how those two relationships are actually the
same thing.

•

While working on the group's second album, *Getting Mystic*,
Listening Woman bandleader Katie McShane was studying pri-
vately with, and participating in a large group run by, avant-garde
jazz pianist Anthony Coleman. These experiences deeply changed
her as a musician. She explored her craft in new ways, learnt
about the sorts of sounds she was drawn to, and as a bandleader
she learnt how to shape the sound of a live group of improvisors.
She would put herself in a situation where she could provide a
jumping-off point for a song, and the players around her could
fill in the blanks with things she wasn't anticipating; then Katie
would mould the whole group in real time as a sort of conductor.
Even though Katie fell into the position of bandleader, the music

Listening Woman were making became a collective statement of absurdity providing a small window into their group operations. In alphabetical order Listening Woman are: Evan Allen, Adrienne Arditti, Jeff Balter, Andrew Clinkman, Matt Delligatti, Wendy Eisenberg, Leo Hardman-Hill, Jesse Heasly, Nick Neuberg, Billy McShane and Katie McShane. *Getting Mystic* was released in September 2016.

•

As a teenager **Reginald Omas Mamode IV** smoked a lot of weed, and although he hasn't touched it since, he feels he still maintains a stoner vibe across the board. This attitude extends to his personal life; he knows he's trying his best to get things right, so when he does make a mistake he goes easy on himself. He knows it's a genuine mistake and not a sign he doesn't care or is a bad person. By the same token, he's not ashamed of the so-called 'mistakes' and imperfections in his music. Each individual song on Reginald's self-titled 2016 album (a mixture of neo soul, staggered hip hop beats and horizontal funk) was written and recorded within half an hour, each part was recorded in one take and the 'mistakes' were kept in. He played most instruments on the album but while recording he'd never look at the screen to make sure he was in perfect time with the parts he'd already laid down, it was all done by ear and recorded on OD 9 Logic (essentially like using a really old iMac). Nothing stressed him out during the process, nothing was hard and anything that might potentially become a problem he was happy to leave to chance and not fret about. *Reginald Omas Mamode IV* was released in October 2016.

•

Ruben Acosta moved to New York in 2006 and quickly joined an experimental jazz group named Afuche. Every member poured a lot into the band over the years, eventually securing a record deal with a label in 2011. But shortly after the release of their debut album, their saxophonist passed away. It was unexpected and ultimately devastating for the group. Ruben stopped performing music all together for a year; he would sometimes write alone but he couldn't sit down with an instrument the way he used to. He'd sit on trains and listen to the conversations around him, picking up on their natural rhythms and jotting them down during his journey. He also started pulling a lot from popular culture, making notes of trivia, philosophies or mantras that struck a chord with him. Lines from a Bill Withers documentary, the backstory to a Bachman Turner Overdrive song, a memorable phrase from *The Big Lebowski* – they all got noted down and interpreted musically somehow.

After a few years of steadily accumulating these disjointed ideas, and after many occasions when he nearly abandoned the project completely, an album was eventually recorded with a band under the name **A Bunch of Dead People**. But once the recording was done Ruben sat down, listened to a rough mix of the album and hated it. The vocal production especially sounded too perfect and not what the music was meant to be about. So one morning he grabbed the mic and delay pedal that he used on stage and put them through a guitar amp, micing the amp up like a guitar and singing into that. All the effects on his voice came from the amp and the pedal, they didn't use any plug-ins and those were the vocal takes that made it onto the record. *Your Eternal Reward* was released in October 2016.

•

By his early twenties, Adam Werven had become a firm fixture on the weirdo music scene in Minneapolis, performing under the name Larry Wish, and in 2016 released *Not from My Come From* with a backing band of local musicians collectively known as **Larry Wish & His Guys**. With this album Adam set out to tell stories, both real and made up, focusing on a mismatched cast of eccentric characters. One song was inspired by an elderly woman Adam would see waiting for the bus every day: she would talk to herself, push a wheelchair and carry a bag full of multi-coloured markers. She owned a house painted all sorts of colours, and locals who didn't know her would unimaginatively call her Crazy Mary. The track 'Indrid Cold' was named after a mysterious figure in *The Mothman Prophecies* by John Keel. In the book, which is presented as a factual report of paranormal goings on in 1966 West Virginia, townspeople describe seeing Indrid, a multidimensional being, walk down from a UFO before appearing at citizens' homes in the middle of the night and eerily knowing everything about the residents. 'The Quing of Engwin' is about a fictional character Werven created, a regal figure who gets tired of her life and status, longing to be free of the stresses and expectations of royalty, assuming that ordinary people have it easier than the royals. In all of these songs people are making assumptions about strangers, an idea Werven turns on himself during the final track, 'Mary Has a Wheelchair', criticising himself for singing about someone he knows nothing about and painting her in certain ways just to suit his own message. Checkmating himself like this right at the end of the album is a wonderful move, while wagging a finger at the judgemental attitudes of others he gets himself tangled up in the fine line between empathy and projection and in doing so only highlights the complexities within all of us. *Not from My Come From* was released in November 2016.

•

Kal Marks are made up of singer/guitarist Carl Shane, bassist Michael Geacone and drummer Alex Audette. Their raucous indie rock songs are full of dark humour, tight grooves and cranky vocals, and in 2016 they released *Life is Alright, Everybody Dies* – a record that on the surface is deeply dark, harsh and brash, but underneath lie very gentle, vulnerable compositions with thoughtful lyrics that encourage compassion. They wanted listeners to come out of this record feeling like they've been through the wringer, jerked all around, beaten to the ground, then yanked back up again. They wanted people to feel like dancing and crying at the same time because, for them, creating tension is what music is all about. The record came out in February but shortly after its release Alex hit a sort of rock bottom. They were about to embark on a four-and-a-half-week tour down to SXSW, something that should've felt like an extremely triumphant moment, but Alex was having breakdowns almost daily. He started missing rehearsals and cancelling shows, and ended up spending two weeks in a partial programme at a hospital just trying to get balanced enough to get through the tour without causing the whole thing to fall apart. Once he was out he made it two months before realising that he wasn't getting better and had to leave the band if he was going to get himself anywhere close to 'normal'. He felt like he'd let his bandmates down completely, and it was months before he could bring himself to talk to them. Alex rejoined the group in 2017 and in 2018 they released a brand-new record, entitled *Universal Care*.

•

Mariah Fortune, aka **Woven In**, wrote *Highs and Ultra Lows* while living in Philadelphia for the second time. She'd fallen on hard times and had to live with her dad to get on her feet again. She had previously been living in Atlanta but things didn't turn out as she expected and she'd been taken advantage of. Now back in Philadelphia, she was working an overnight job at Whole Foods stocking the shelves and felt like she had no life and no friends. The only people she knew besides her family were from when she was a kid in middle school. She felt like a failure, like she had worked so hard and got nowhere. She recorded this album in the duplex above her dad's place. Philadelphia is noisy, so she had to time recording sessions around firetrucks, alley cat fights and ice-cream truck sirens. This album is the epitome of DIY bedroom music, the raw production placing us in the duplex with her, and yet Mariah still manages to get her personality across on each song, using the lo-fi aesthetics to her advantage, squeezing whatever she can out of everything she's got to work with. *Highs and Ultra Lows* was released in June 2016. It's an album about feeling like you're back where you started.

Acknowledgements

THANK YOU!

Mum and Dad for introducing me to music and supporting me through every stage of my life. Ruth, Stephen, David, Amy, Val, Billy, Charlie, Toby, Freddie, Oscar – the best of families. Nish, Crosby, Ed Gamble and everyone who recommended albums to me in 2016. Every musician and YouTuber who gave their time to be interviewed for this book – you were all so generous and I'll always appreciate it. Graeme Wicks and Chris Hamilton for doing music with me. Hannah Rose for encouraging, humouring and improving this project. Joe Steinhardt and Kate Foulds – the greatest flatmates of all time. Richard Roper for giving me the freedom to write what I want. Caroline Chignell and Daisy Skepelhorn for making my professional life immediately better and easier. Rob Coleman, Tyler Amato and Steve Smooke for showing me how things should be done. Paul Bertellotti for letting me endlessly play albums from 2016 in the car on tour. Rob Deering, Simon Fox, Quincey May Brown, Bee Church, and Will Collier for making an album especially for me! Jake Ashton, Ben Foot, Tom Fox, Martin Patrick, Joe Palmer, Luke Palmer and Will Thomas for letting me use your stuff. John Robins and Lloyd Langford for handling the press in New York. Scott Blanks for putting up with the tiredest version of me. Mark Kearns for casting me as Jiminy Jodphurs. Michael Burdett for the iPods. And Gabriel Ebulue, who I have almost convinced that 2016 is the greatest year for music of all time and will convince one day if it's the last thing I do.